# MARY ENGELBREIT

# Garden of Stitches

The authorised representative in the EEA is Simon and Schuster Netherlands BV,
Herculesplein 96 3584 AA Utrecht, Netherlands.
(info@simonandschuster.nl)

Andrews McMeel Publishing
a division of Andrews McMeel Universal
1130 Walnut Street, Kansas City, Missouri 64106

www.andrewsmcmeel.com

25 26 27 28 29 RLP 10 9 8 7 6 5 4 3 2 1

ISBN: 979-8-8816-0262-8

Library of Congress Control Number: 2025945824

Photography by Tarmine Guichette

Editor: Danys Mares
Art Director/Designer: Gina Martin
Production Editor: Julie Railsback
Production Manager: Chuck Harper

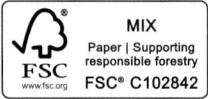

MIX
Paper | Supporting
responsible forestry
FSC® C102842
FSC
www.fsc.org

ATTENTION: SCHOOLS AND BUSINESSES
Andrews McMeel books are available at quantity discounts with bulk purchase for
educational, business, or sales promotional use. For information, please email the
Andrews McMeel Publishing Special Sales Department: sales@andrewsmcmeel.com.

# MARY ENGELBREIT

# Garden of Stitches

### 30 Floral Embroidery Patterns to Brighten Your Day

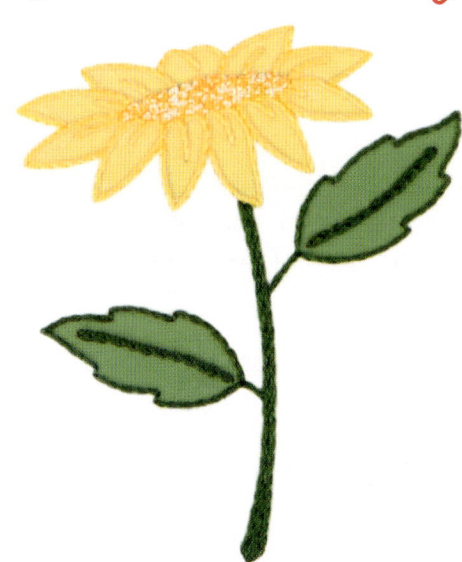

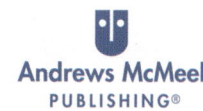

Andrews McMeel
PUBLISHING®

# Contents

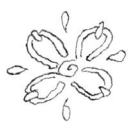

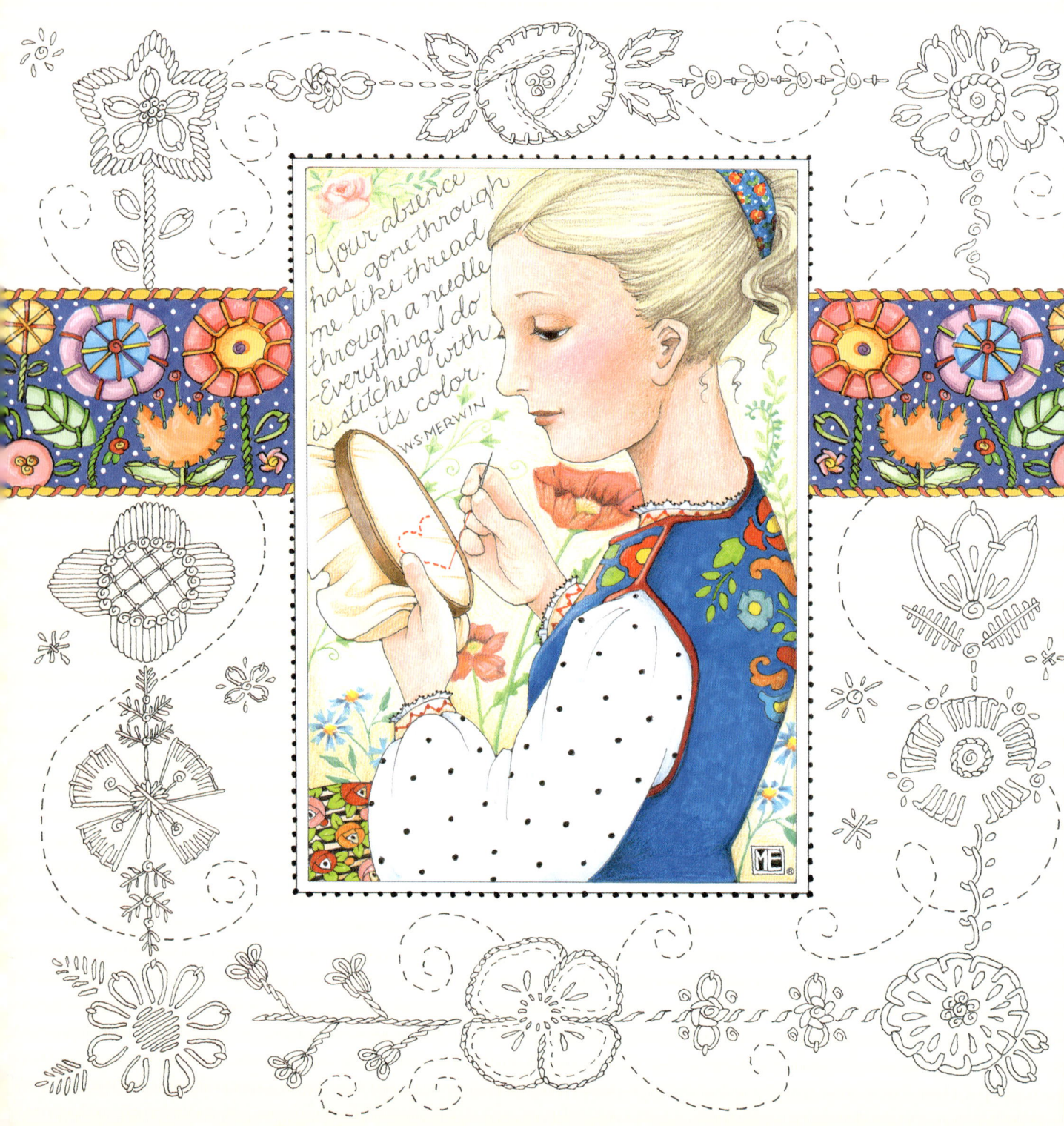

Your absence
has gone through
me like thread
through a needle.
Everything I do
is stitched with
its color.
—W.S. MERWIN

# A Note from Mary

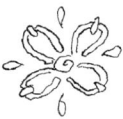

Welcome to *Garden of Stitches*!

This book is a celebration of creativity, patience, and the timeless charm of embroidery. For years, I've been sharing my drawings with you, but now I'm so happy to share a new way to experience my art—through needle and thread!

Embroidery is a lot like gardening, the difference being—at least in my case—at the end you'll have something to show for all your hard work! Embroidery requires care, attention, and a touch of imagination. Each stitch is like planting a seed, and with time, a beautiful design blooms. Whether you're an experienced needleworker or someone picking up a needle for the first time, this book invites you to join in the joy of creating something truly unique.

The designs in this collection are full of vibrant flowers, cheerful critters, and whimsical details. You'll find projects that range from simple, beginner-friendly patterns to more intricate pieces that will challenge even the most experienced stitcher. They're all patterns inspired by the many imaginary gardens I picture in my head, ensuring that your finished pieces bring a smile to your face.

In these pages, you'll discover clear, step-by-step instructions and helpful tips to guide you through every project. From small, portable motifs perfect for quick projects to larger, detailed designs ideal for home décor, there's something here for every skill level and interest.

Embroidery isn't just about the finished product—it's about the process. It's so calming, and as you stitch, you'll create not just art but memories. Perhaps you'll recall a loved one who stitched before you or find joy in learning a new skill. Whatever your story, each piece is sure to become a personal treasure.

*Mary Engelbreit*

# Introduction

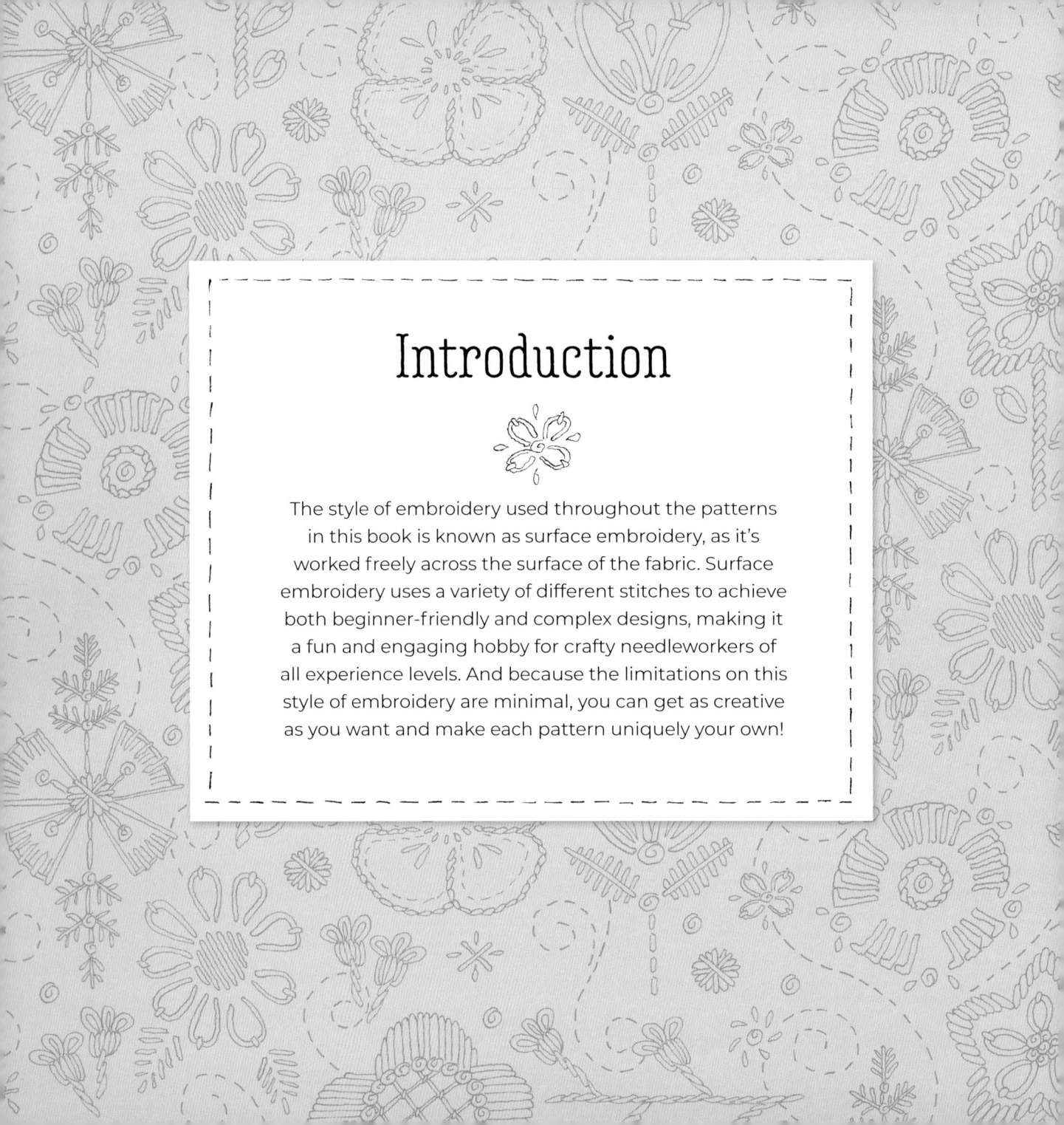

The style of embroidery used throughout the patterns in this book is known as surface embroidery, as it's worked freely across the surface of the fabric. Surface embroidery uses a variety of different stitches to achieve both beginner-friendly and complex designs, making it a fun and engaging hobby for crafty needleworkers of all experience levels. And because the limitations on this style of embroidery are minimal, you can get as creative as you want and make each pattern uniquely your own!

# Tools and Supplies

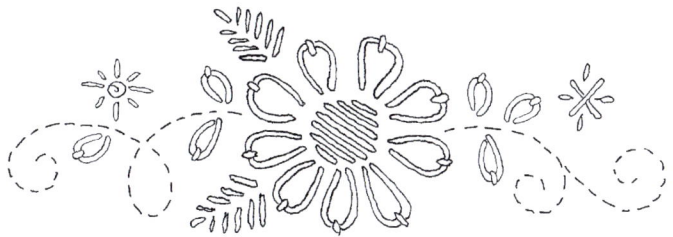

## NEEDLES

When starting a new embroidery project, choosing the right style and size of needle to work with is essential. For surface embroidery, the best styles of needle to use are embroidery and milliner.

• Embroidery needles have an oval eye that is wider than the shaft, making them easier to handle while pulling through the fabric. They come in a variety of different sizes and can vary from stitch to stitch.

• Milliner needles are longer and used for embroidering knots. The eye and shaft are the same width, so they pull easily through the wraps of thread that make up the knot. These also come in different sizes.

The projects in this book can all be done with size seven and nine needles. Use the size seven when you're stitching with three or more strands of thread and the nine for one and two strands. You'll use the milliner needle for French knots and embroidery needles for the rest of the stitches.

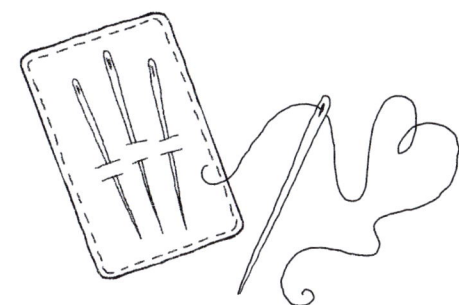

## THREAD

Stranded cotton embroidery thread, also called floss, is made up of six strands of floss twisted into one. Depending on what each pattern calls for, you can separate your thread into individual strands when stitching to achieve a desired level of thickness in your artwork. The following projects all use standard DMC floss, but there are many color conversion charts online if you prefer a different brand.

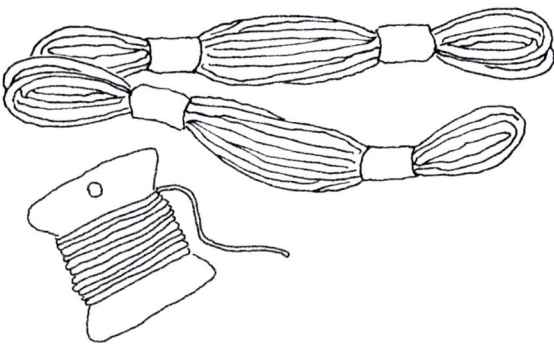

To get started, measure out and cut off about 18-inches (46 cm) of floss, or roughly the length from the tip of your middle finger to the point of your elbow. Once removed from the skein, count out the number of strands you need and slide your finger down the length of the floss to separate them.

## SCISSORS

A pair of specialty embroidery scissors works best—you can find them anywhere you would also purchase floss or hoops—but any scissors with thin, sharp edges will work as well to help keep your floss from fraying.

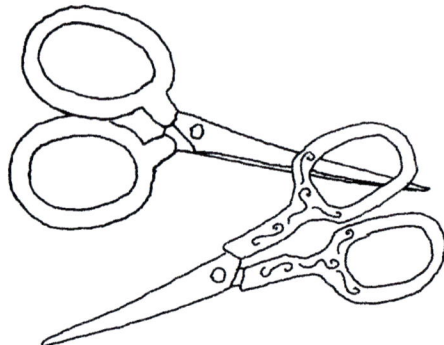

**TIP:** A seam ripper can come in handy for unpicking floss that has already been stitched to the fabric. Be sure to use a good-quality one that will slice cleanly through the stitching you wish to remove without damaging surrounding work.

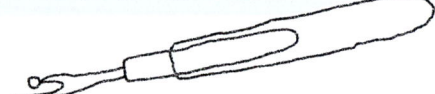

## HOOP

An embroidery hoop provides you with a steady and consistent surface for completing your patterns. The screw on each hoop allows you to adjust the tautness of the fabric to find what works best for you and helps to keep your embroidery from puckering. Most of the designs in this collection will fit into a standard 8-inch (20 cm) hoop, but if you find you're struggling to work the stitches comfortably, switch to a 4-inch (10 cm) or 5-inch (12.5 cm) hoop and move it around on your fabric as you go.

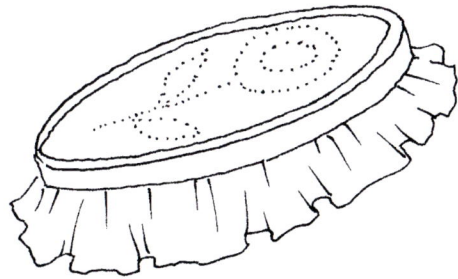

To use the hoop, loosen the screw and put the inner ring on a flat surface. Lay your fabric atop the inner ring and place the outer ring snug over it. Tighten the screw until the hoop is gripping the fabric firmly. Work your way around the hoop, easing your fabric through the rings until it's taut.

## THIMBLE

A thimble is a small, pitted cup used to protect your finger while embroidering. It is most often used on the middle finger or thumb and allows you to use that finger to push your needle through the fabric without hurting yourself. It is not a requirement but can be helpful if you're just getting started learning the rhythm of embroidery.

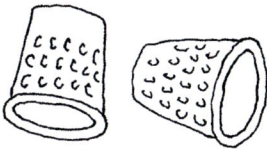

## FABRIC MARKERS

Fabric markers come in a variety of color options and can be used to trace or draw a design directly onto your chosen embroidery fabric. This is a great option because, depending on the brand, the ink can be removed with water, heat, or friction after the project is complete or if you make a mistake.

Fabric markers can also be used to add more color to your finished patterns. While you can fill in open spaces with colorful floss, fabric markers are an easy and versatile way to add texture and express creativity, helping you to make each new project its own unique piece of art.

# Choosing Fabric

## LAYERING FABRIC

Many experienced embroiderers will layer two pieces of fabric when working on surface embroidery patterns. Your ground fabric is the top, outward-facing layer that will be visible behind your embroidery. Your backing fabric is the layer underneath that is only visible on the back of your work.

> **TIP:** When working with patterns that call for the use of white or light-colored floss, choosing a colored ground fabric will help ensure all details of the final piece are visible.

## GROUND FABRIC

No matter what you're using, ask these questions when considering a ground fabric:

### What is it made of?

Fabrics made from natural fibers are the easiest to embroider on and hold up well in the hoop, making them well-suited to hand embroidery. They're also durable and wash well.

Look for cotton, linen, hemp, and blends of these for the best experience. Cotton and cotton blends are widely available at a range of prices but can differ vastly in quality. If you're unsure, go for quilting cotton. Linen and hemp have a luxurious feel to them and although a little pricier, may be worth it for a special project.

### Does it stretch?

The stretch factor of your fabric is another important quality to consider. When testing your options, hold the fabric in both hands and pull it in all directions to see how much it stretches. The less stretch, the easier it will be to embroider on.

### What is the weight like?
When it comes to the weight of the fabric, you want something substantial enough to handle a needle and thread being pulled through it over and over, but not so thick that you struggle to pull your needle through.

### How does it feel?
Run your hand over the surface of the fabric. The smoother it is, the easier it'll be to stitch precisely.

### How tightly woven is it?
Fabric with a tighter weave will hold your stitches in place better. This is particularly important for surface embroidery where your design sits atop the fabric.

### BACKING FABRIC
The backing fabric is an extra layer that helps to stabilize your stitching. Cotton voile is a great choice, as it's made from natural fibers and is both soft and lightweight, but any lightweight natural fabric will do.

Backing your ground fabric is optional, though, especially if the ground fabric is weighty enough to support your stitches on its own.

> **TIP:** Wash your ground and backing fabric before you trace on the design. If either is going to shrink, it's better this happens before you start embroidering on it.

After you've transferred the design to your ground fabric (see page 14, Transferring the Designs), you'll add a piece of backing fabric to the back. Stack the fabrics on a flat surface and smooth both layers out, then tack by hand, machine stitch, or serge the edges to hold them together and stop the fabrics from fraying as you embroider.

> **TIP:** You can also use Scotch, masking, or washi tape to bind the edges of your fabric.

# Transferring the Designs

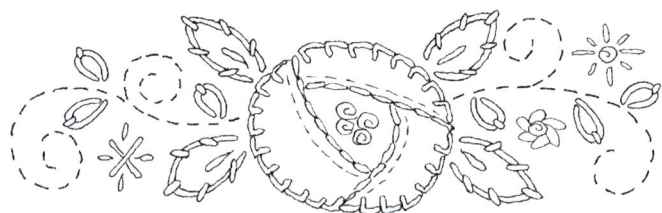

## TRACE

Tracing your chosen design directly onto fabric may be the most tried-and-true method for transferring a pattern, as it is fairly simple to accomplish, especially if you don't have a lot of embroidery supplies. You can use fabric markers, water-soluble pens, or chalk pencils—whatever you find that works best for you. Bear in mind that a finer line will be easier to cover with embroidery.

**TIP:** If you are working with white or light colored fabric, it can be placed directly over the pattern in the book for easy tracing. If your chosen fabric is darker, a better option would be to print the pattern and trace directly over a light source, like a lightbox, a lightbox app on your laptop or tablet, or window on a sunny day.

Steps for how to transfer a design using a light source to trace:

1. Photocopy or take a picture of the chosen design.

2. Print your design and tape it to your desired light source.

3. Tape your fabric over the printed design.

4. Trace the design directly onto your fabric.

5. Check that you've traced over all the lines before removing your fabric from the light source.

## IRON-ON TRANSFER

You can make your own transfer by using an iron-on transfer pen or pencil. Before getting started, be sure to flip your design backward so that it will appear in the correct orientation upon completion. Use a window, lightbox, or the flip function on your phone or tablet to redraw the printed lines on the back of the transfer.

Steps for how to transfer a design using an iron-on transfer:

1. Flip your design and trace the mirror image onto sturdy tracing paper using an iron-on transfer pen.

2. Place the design face down on your fabric—it should appear the correct orientation now—and run a **dry** iron over it. Take care not to shift the paper as you iron. It should only take a few seconds for the design to transfer.

3. Lift a corner to check that the design has transferred before lifting it completely off the fabric. If it has not, simply iron over it again.

## EMBROIDERY PAPER

Water-soluble embroidery stabilizer allows you to stick the design directly to your fabric, stitch through it, then wash it away when you're done. This is an easy way to get your design onto fabric if you struggle with tracing by hand.

Steps for how to transfer a design using embroidery paper:

1. Scan the design and print onto a sheet of embroidery paper. You can also trace it by hand directly from the page if you prefer or do not have access to a printer.

2. Cut out the design and peel off the backing paper.

3. Adhere it directly onto your fabric.

**TIP:** Iron your fabric before transferring the design, as it is easier to get an accurate transfer when working on smooth fabric.

# Starting and Ending

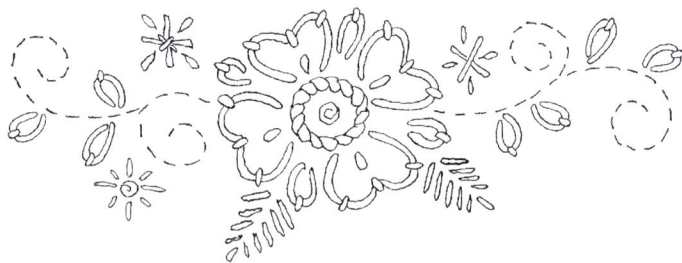

When you have gotten all of your tools, chosen your thread and fabric, and secured your hoop, you are ready to start creating your art!

First things first, learn to secure your thread at the start so that it doesn't come undone.

Here are some easy ways to do that:

### START WITH A DOUBLE STITCH

If you've backed your fabric, begin with a double stitch—either straight or back— through the backing fabric only, under the line or section you're preparing to embroider.

### START WITH A KNOT

Use a knot when the stitch on the back won't create a bump on the surface of your fabric.

Lastly, it's time to wrap things up! When you get to the end of your floss or need to switch colors, it's important to efficiently secure the tail before moving on to the next step.

### WEAVE AWAY TO END

Take your thread through to the back of the fabric and run your needle under the last few stitches to secure it. Do this in one direction or weave back and forth before cutting away the excess floss. Your needle should not pierce the fabric again.

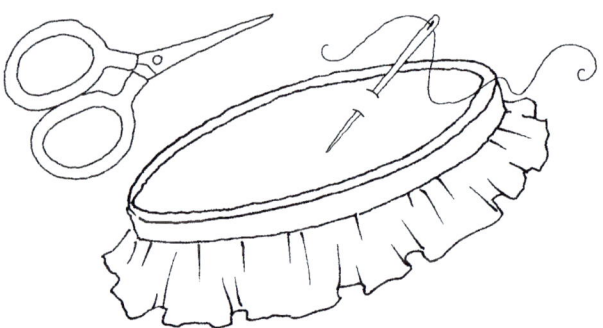

# How to Use the Patterns

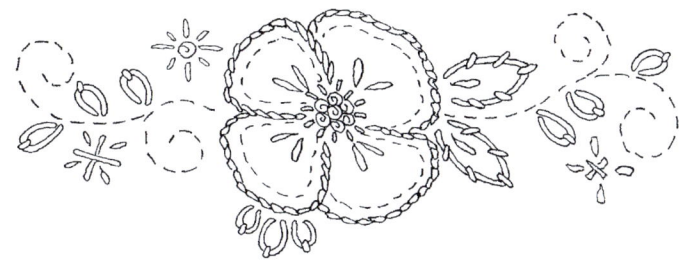

The design instructions are given to fit the recommended size. On a larger design, you may want to use more strands of thread so that the embroidery has more weight. Conversely, when you size down, using fewer threads can keep the lines looking delicate. Or get creative and make it your own!

Each of the designs doubles as the embroidery instructions for the project, telling you which stitch, color, and how many strands of floss to use for each section.

Here is an example for how to read the instructional shorthand:

**Stem 562 (3)**
Stem = embroidery stitch
562 = DMC thread color
(3) = number of strands

Refer to the embroidery stitch library starting on page 153 for instructions on how to create every stitch mentioned in this book.

**TIP:** Good light is essential when working on an embroidery project, the best being natural daylight. A well-lit workspace helps you to stitch with more accuracy, you won't be straining your eyes, and your embroidery will turn out cleaner.

# The
# Patterns

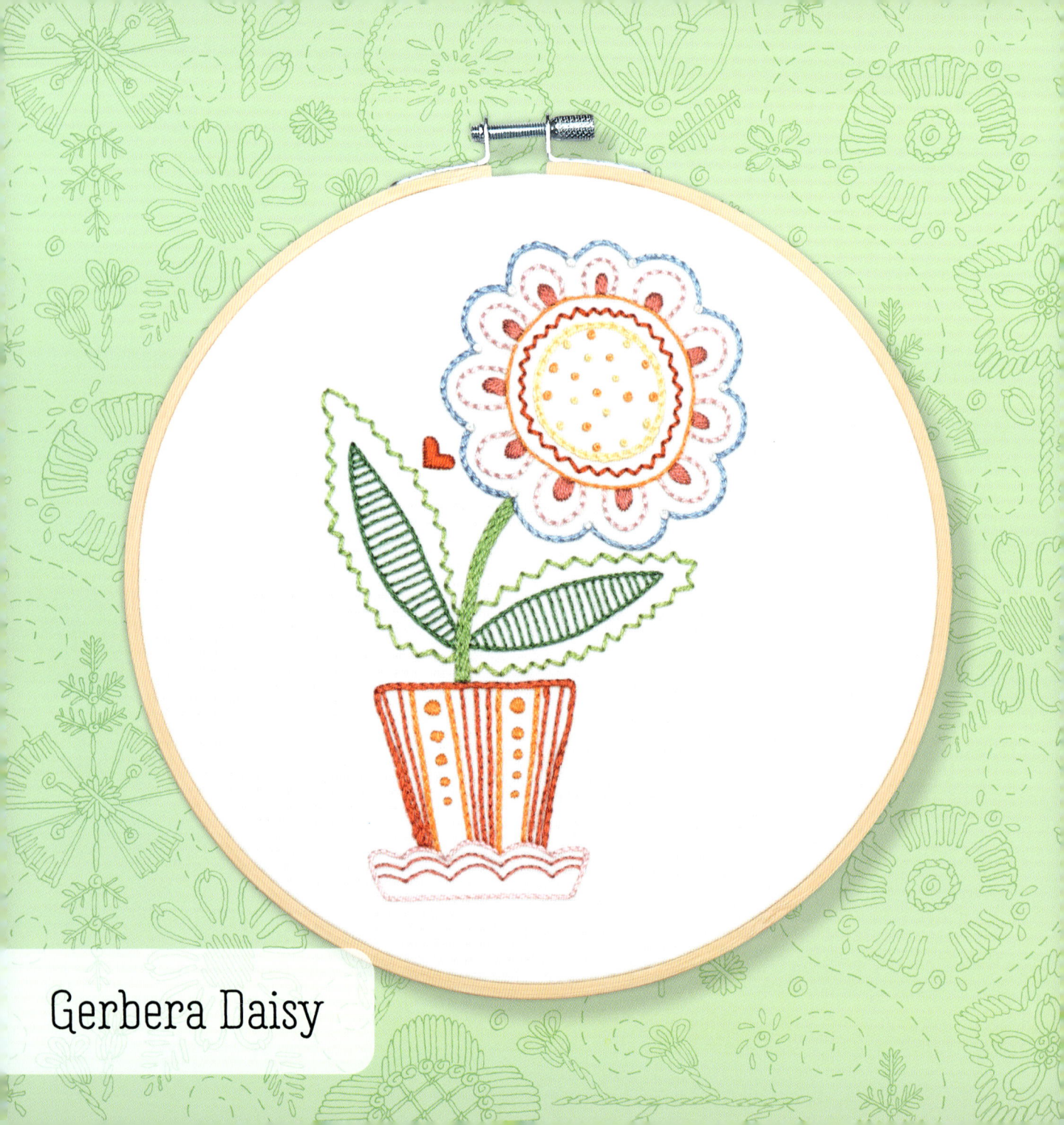

Gerbera Daisy

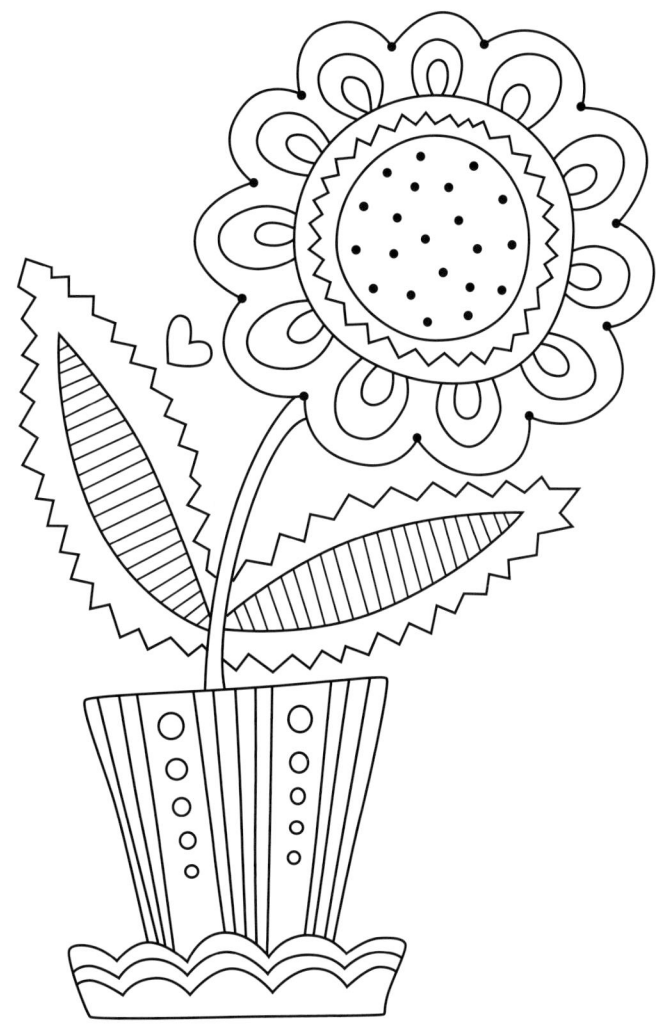

## SUPPLIES

**Fabric**

12 x 12 inch (30x30cm)
ground fabric
12 x 12 inch (30x30cm)
backing fabric (optional)

**DMC six-stranded floss**

| | | |
|---|---|---|
| ■ | 347 | Egyptian Red |
| ■ | 700 | Meadow Green |
| ■ | 703 | Metallic Spring Green |
| ■ | 704 | Lime |
| ■ | 727 | Primrose |
| ■ | 3687 | Berry Smoothie |
| ■ | 3689 | Pale Orchid |
| ■ | 3755 | Pastel Blue |
| ■ | 3831 | Wild Strawberry |
| ■ | 3853 | Copper |
| ■ | 3854 | Chai Spice |
| ☐ | B5200 | Pearlescent White Light |

**Needles**

Embroidery: size 7 and 9
Milliner: size 7 and 9

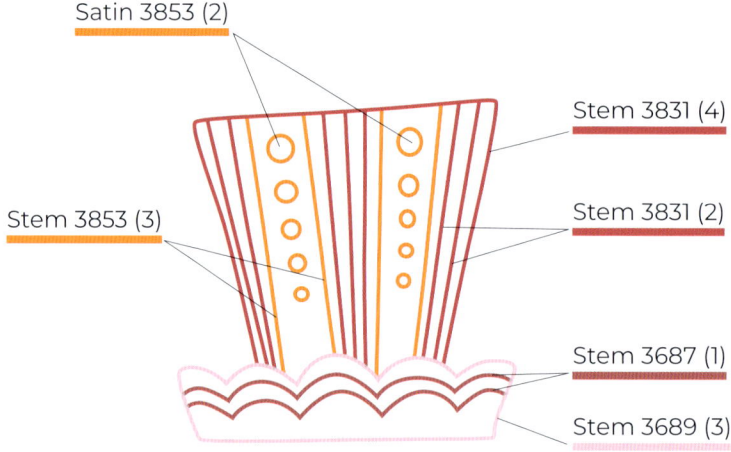

Satin 3853 (2)

Stem 3831 (4)

Stem 3853 (3)

Stem 3831 (2)

Stem 3687 (1)

Stem 3689 (3)

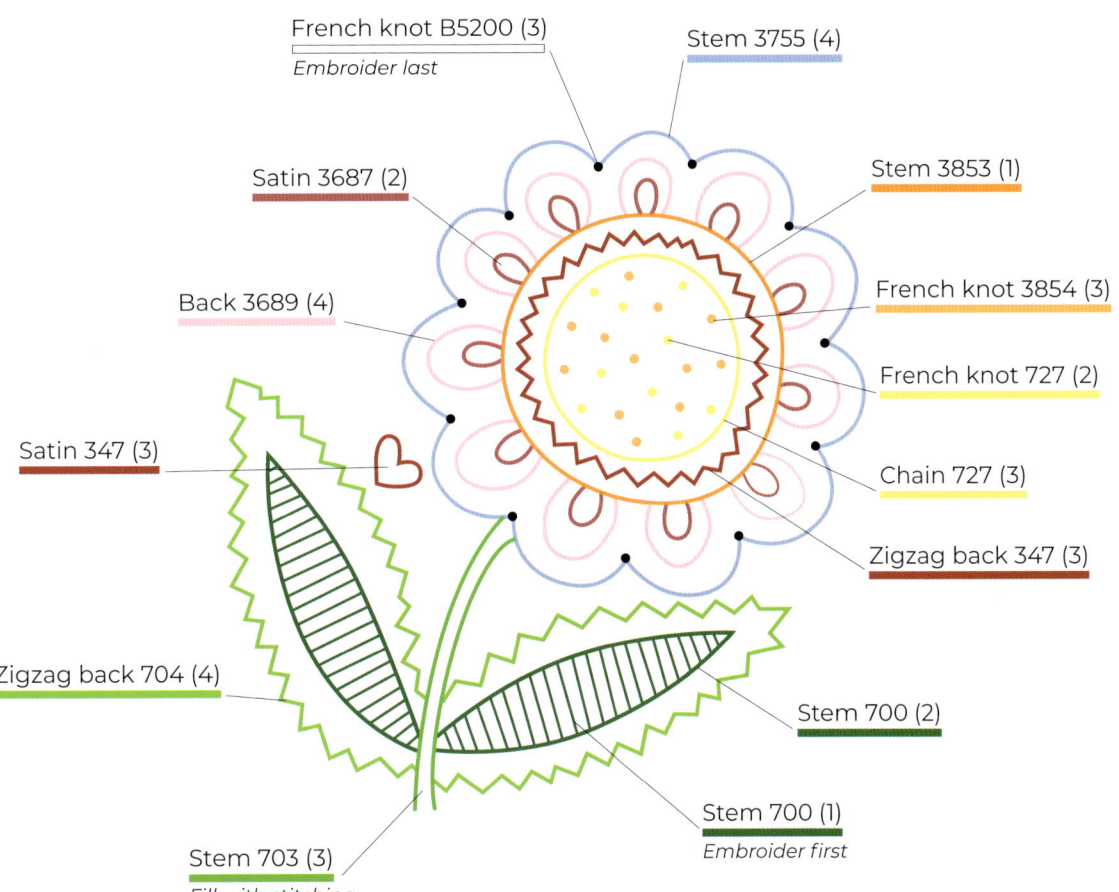

French knot B5200 (3)
*Embroider last*

Stem 3755 (4)

Satin 3687 (2)

Stem 3853 (1)

Back 3689 (4)

French knot 3854 (3)

French knot 727 (2)

Satin 347 (3)

Chain 727 (3)

Zigzag back 347 (3)

Zigzag back 704 (4)

Stem 700 (2)

Stem 700 (1)
*Embroider first*

Stem 703 (3)
*Fill with stitching*

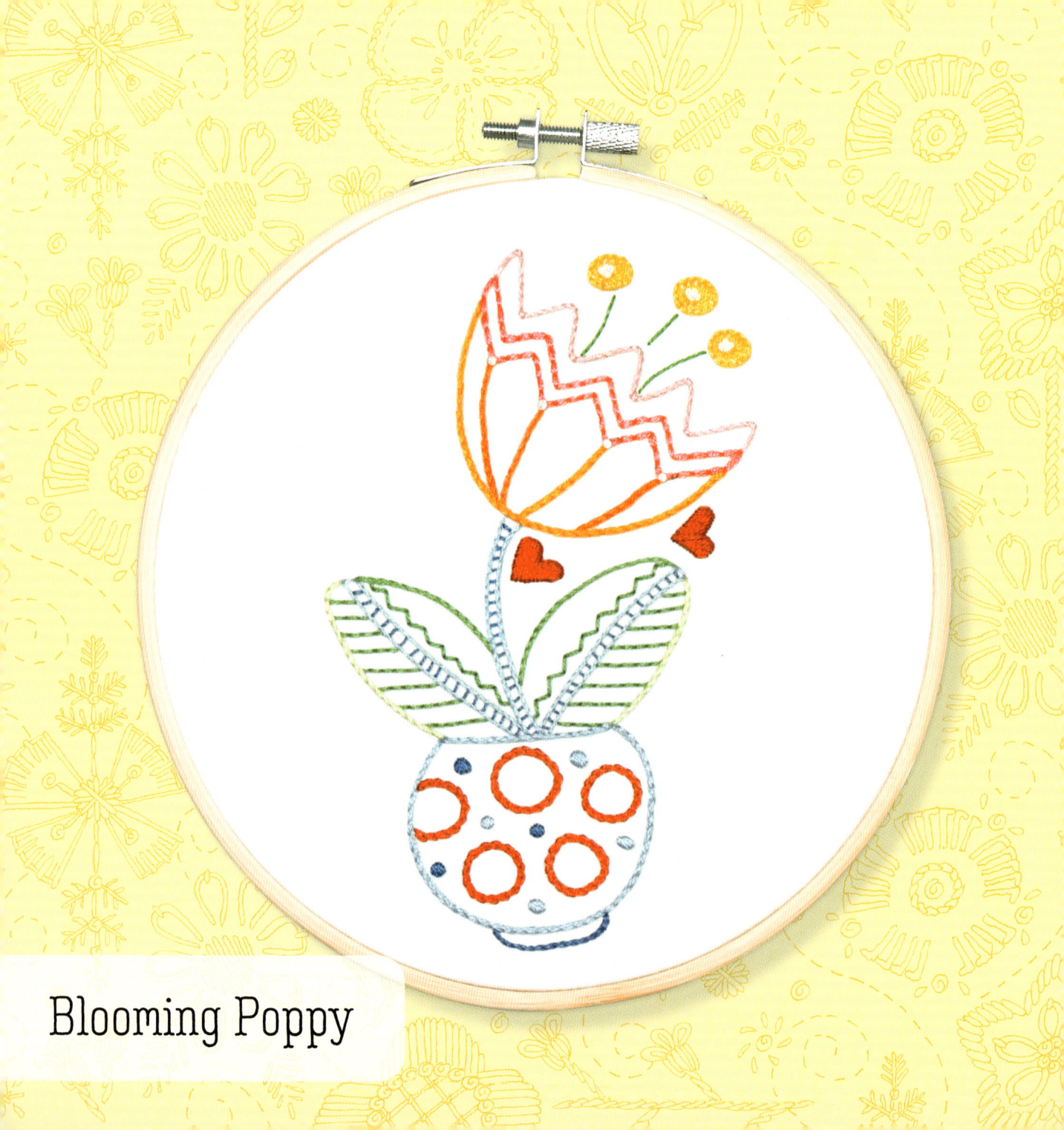

Blooming Poppy

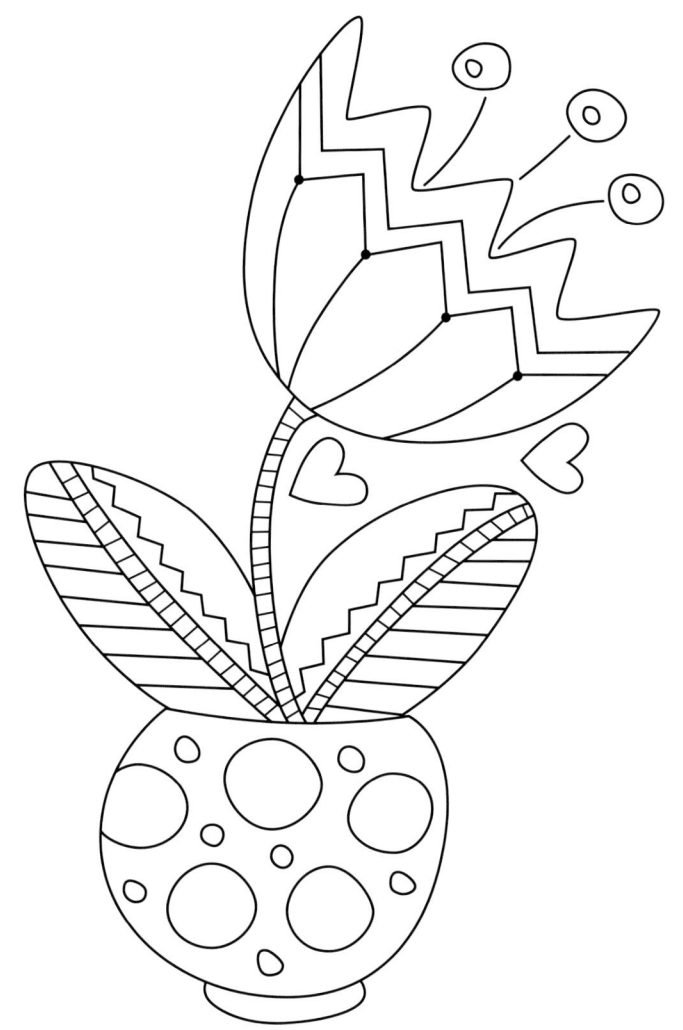

# SUPPLIES

## Fabric

12 x 12 inch (30x30cm)
ground fabric
12 x 12 inch (30x30cm)
backing fabric (optional)

## DMC six-stranded floss

| | | |
|---|---|---|
| 15 | Spring Onion |
| 321 | Metallic Carmine |
| 349 | Red Pepper |
| 517 | Nautical Blue |
| 519 | Bluish Spray |
| 701 | Grass |
| 702 | Spring Lawn |
| 741 | Mandarin |
| 743 | Banana |
| 946 | Fire |
| 956 | Hot Pink |
| 3716 | Peony |
| B5200 | Pearlescent White Light |

## Needles

Embroidery: size 7 and 9
Milliner: size 7 and 9

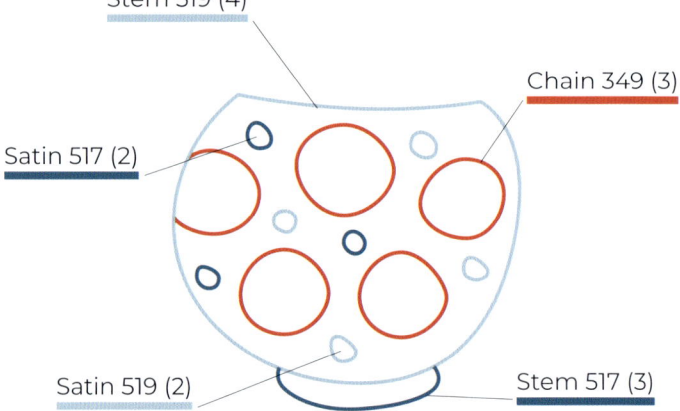

Stem 519 (4)

Chain 349 (3)

Satin 517 (2)

Satin 519 (2)

Stem 517 (3)

Stem 3716 (3)

French knot B5200 (2)

Back 956 (6)

Stem 702 (1)

French knot B5200 (3)
*Embroider last*

Open blanket
pinwheel 743 (3)
*Embroider first*

Stem 946 (4)

Stem 741 (4)

Straight 517 (2)
*Embroider first*

Stem 946 (4)

Stem 519 (2)

Satin 321 (3)

Zigzag back 701 (3)

Straight 517 (2)
*Embroider first*

Stem 702 (3)

Stem 519 (1)

Back 702 (3)
*Embroider first*

Stem 15 (3)

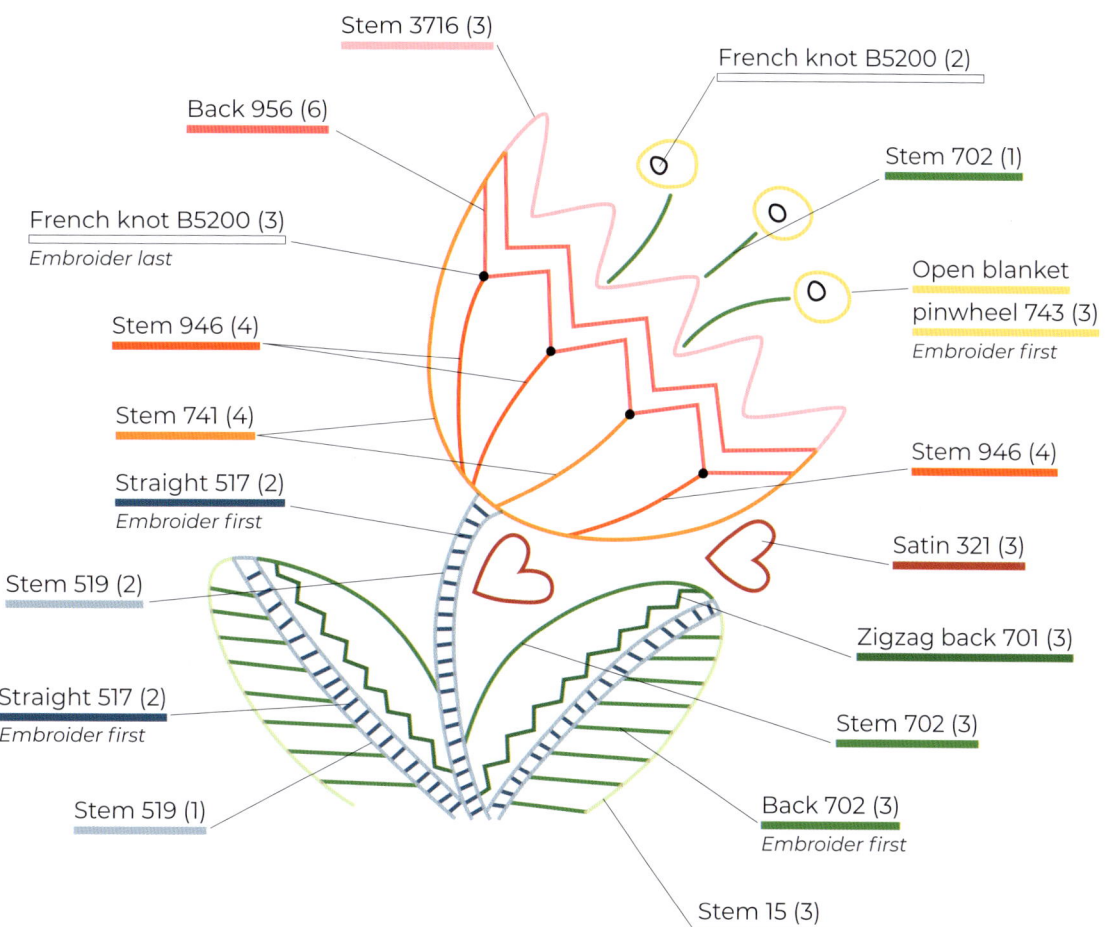

27

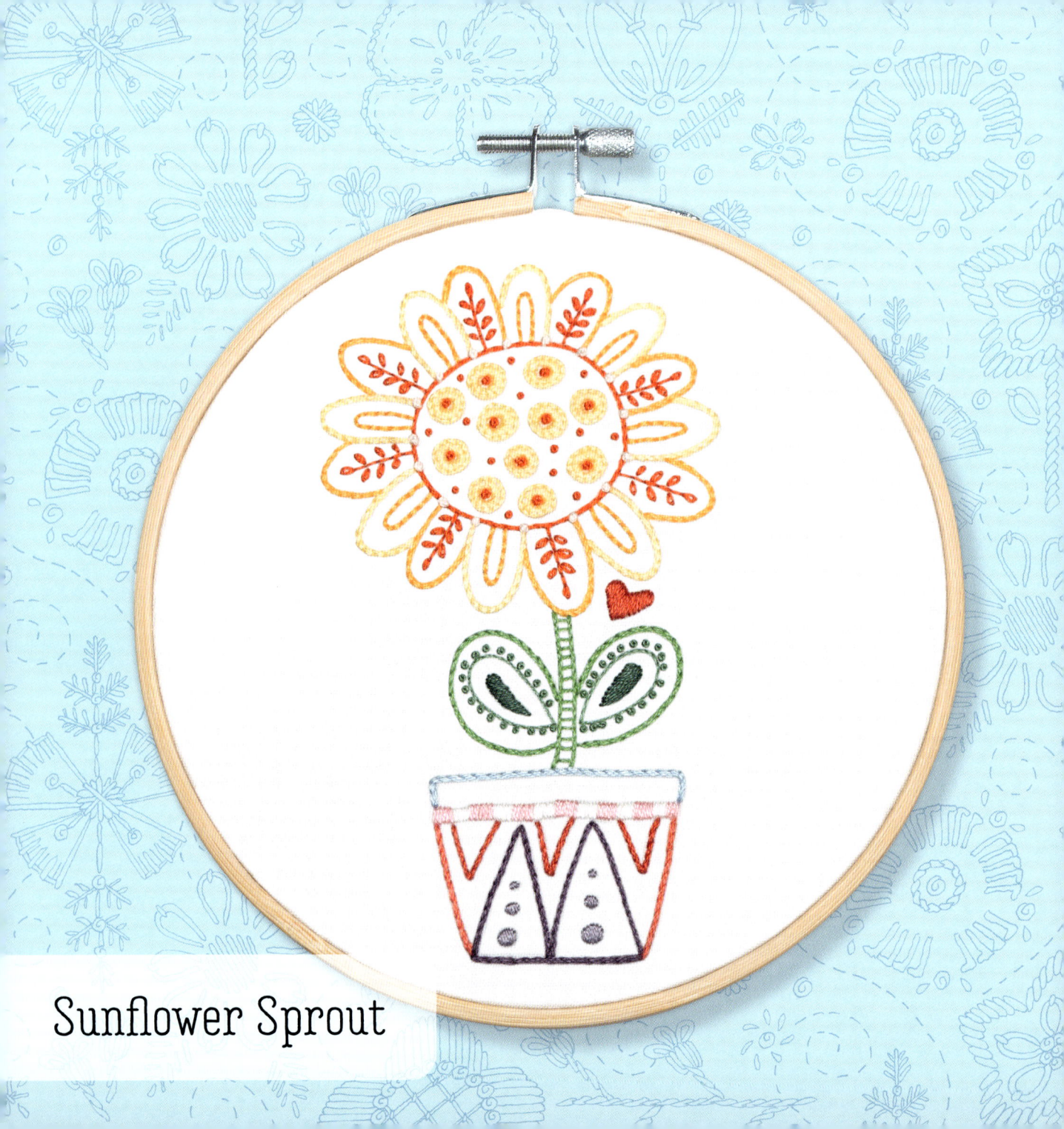

Sunflower Sprout

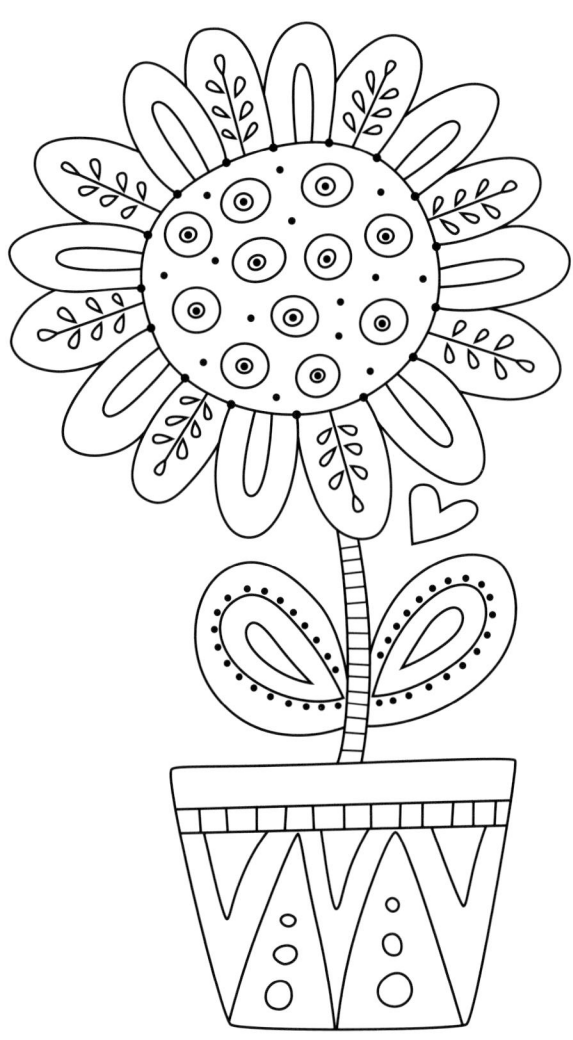

# SUPPLIES

## Fabric
12 x 12 inch (30x30cm)
ground fabric
12 x 12 inch (30x30cm)
backing fabric (optional)

## DMC six-stranded floss

| | | |
|---|---|---|
| ■ | 28 | Lavender Gray |
| ■ | 29 | Emperor Purple |
| ■ | 350 | Vermillion |
| ■ | 561 | Cypress Green |
| ■ | 562 | Malachite |
| ■ | 605 | Rosebud |
| ■ | 702 | Spring Lawn |
| ■ | 727 | Primrose |
| ■ | 742 | Clementine |
| ■ | 827 | Forget-Me-Knot |
| ■ | 3831 | Wild Strawberry |
| ■ | 3832 | Strawberry |
| □ | B5200 | Pearlescent White Light |

## Needles
Embroidery: size 7 and 9
Milliner: size 7 and 9

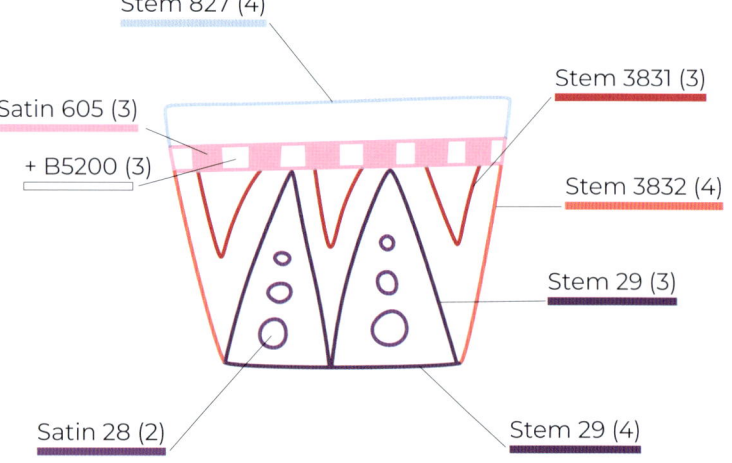

Stem 827 (4)

Stem 3831 (3)

Satin 605 (3)

Stem 3832 (4)

+ B5200 (3)

Stem 29 (3)

Satin 28 (2)

Stem 29 (4)

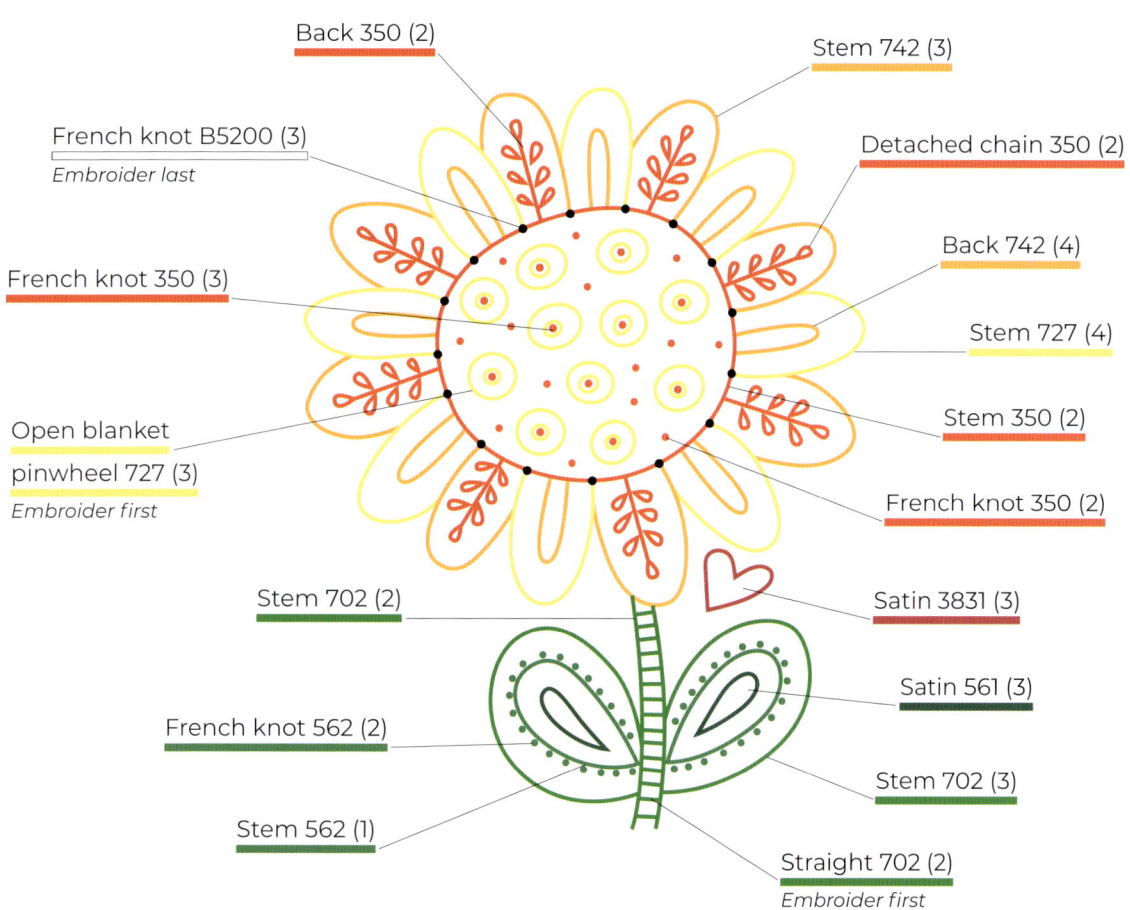

Back 350 (2)

Stem 742 (3)

French knot B5200 (3)
*Embroider last*

Detached chain 350 (2)

French knot 350 (3)

Back 742 (4)

Stem 727 (4)

Stem 350 (2)

Open blanket
pinwheel 727 (3)
*Embroider first*

French knot 350 (2)

Stem 702 (2)

Satin 3831 (3)

Satin 561 (3)

French knot 562 (2)

Stem 702 (3)

Stem 562 (1)

Straight 702 (2)
*Embroider first*

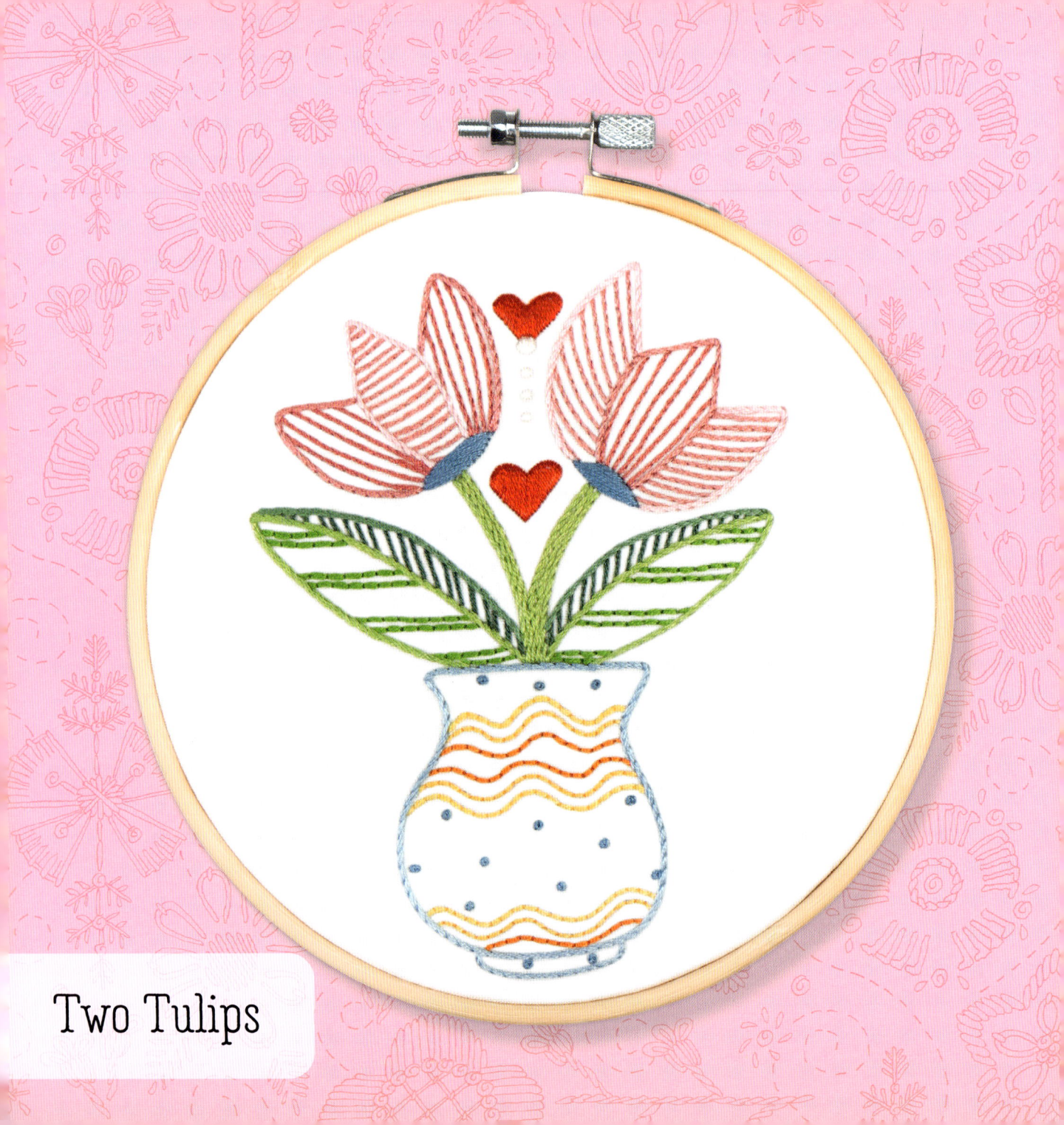

Two Tulips

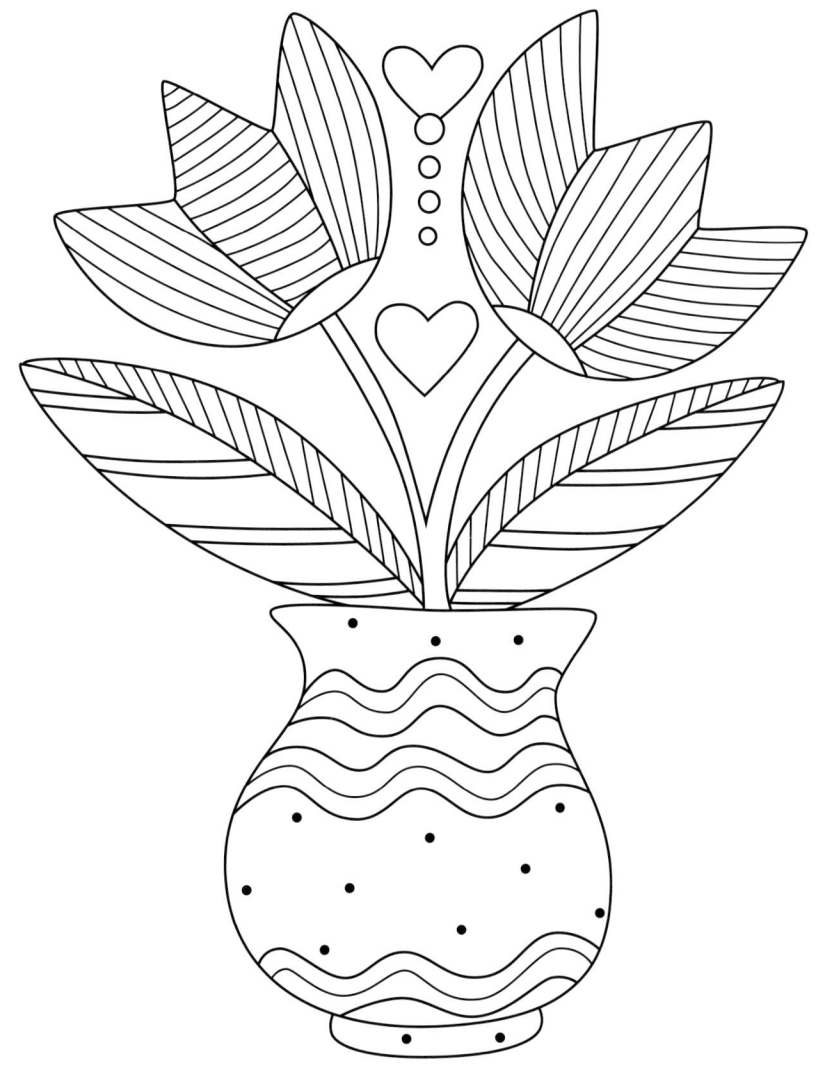

# SUPPLIES

## Fabric
12 x 12 inch (30x30cm)
ground fabric
12 x 12 inch (30x30cm)
backing fabric (optional)

## DMC six-stranded floss

| | | |
|---|---|---|
| ■ | 347 | Egyptian Red |
| ■ | 518 | Nattier Blue |
| ■ | 519 | Bluish Spray |
| ■ | 561 | Cypress Green |
| ■ | 562 | Malachite |
| ■ | 704 | Lime |
| ■ | 726 | Mimosa |
| ■ | 743 | Banana |
| ■ | 906 | Mistletoe |
| ■ | 3687 | Berry Smoothie |
| ■ | 3688 | Pink Lupine |
| ■ | 3689 | Pale Orchid |
| ■ | 3853 | Copper |
| □ | B5200 | Pearlescent White Light |

## Needles
Embroidery: size 7 and 9
Milliner: size 7

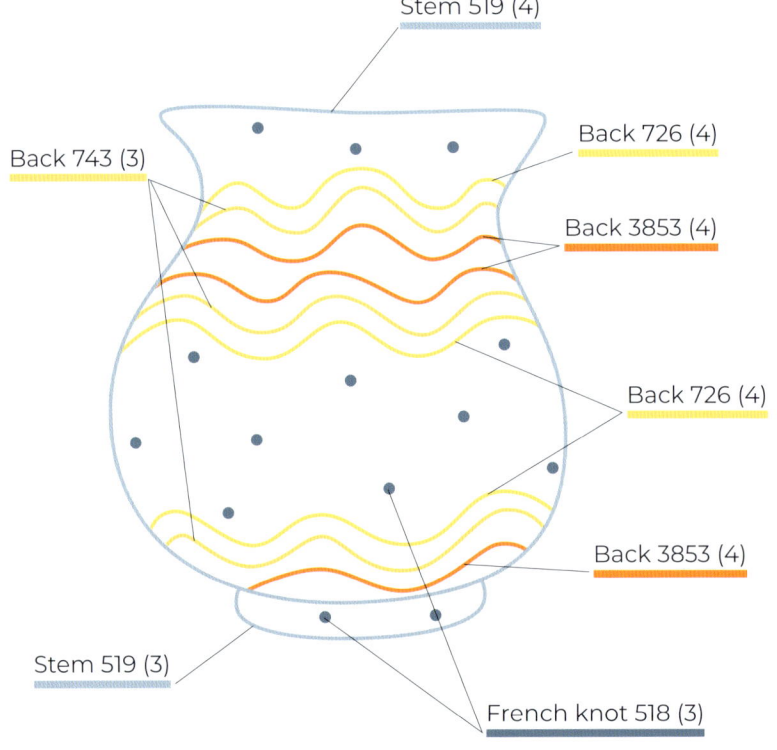

Stem 519 (4)

Back 726 (4)

Back 743 (3)

Back 3853 (4)

Back 726 (4)

Back 3853 (4)

Stem 519 (3)

French knot 518 (3)

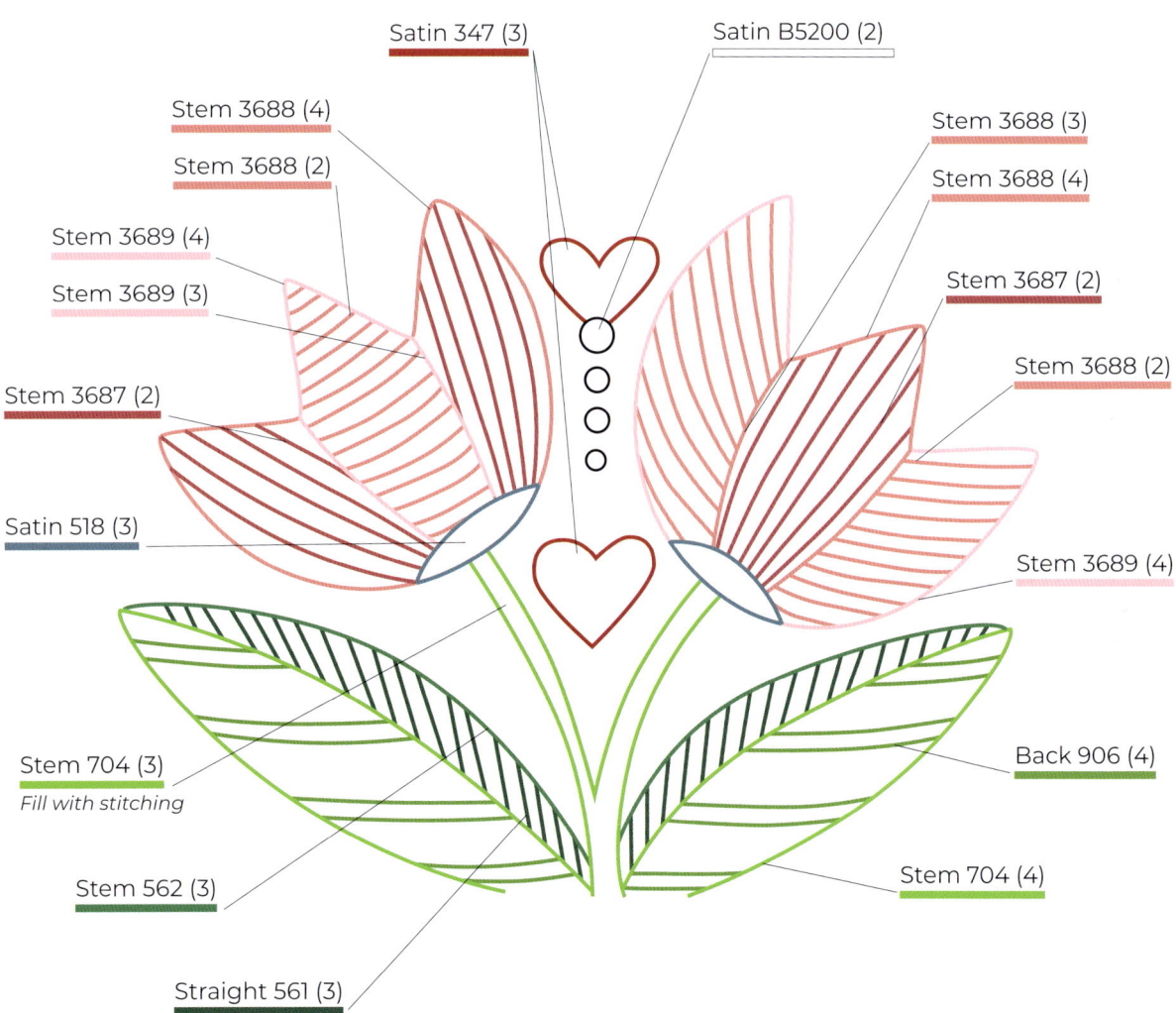

Satin 347 (3)

Satin B5200 (2)

Stem 3688 (4)

Stem 3688 (3)

Stem 3688 (2)

Stem 3688 (4)

Stem 3689 (4)

Stem 3687 (2)

Stem 3689 (3)

Stem 3688 (2)

Stem 3687 (2)

Satin 518 (3)

Stem 3689 (4)

Stem 704 (3)
*Fill with stitching*

Back 906 (4)

Stem 562 (3)

Stem 704 (4)

Straight 561 (3)

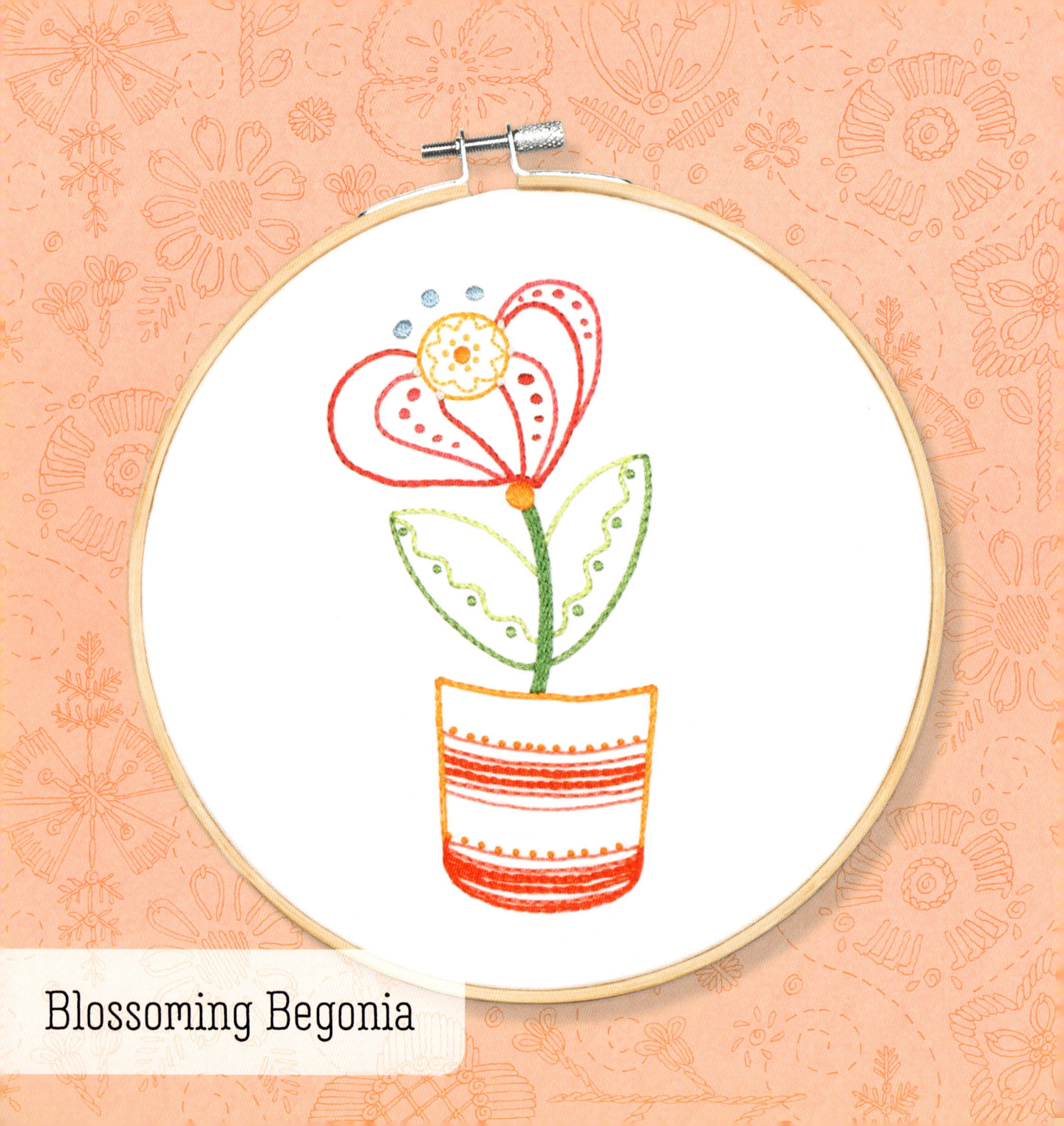

Blossoming Begonia

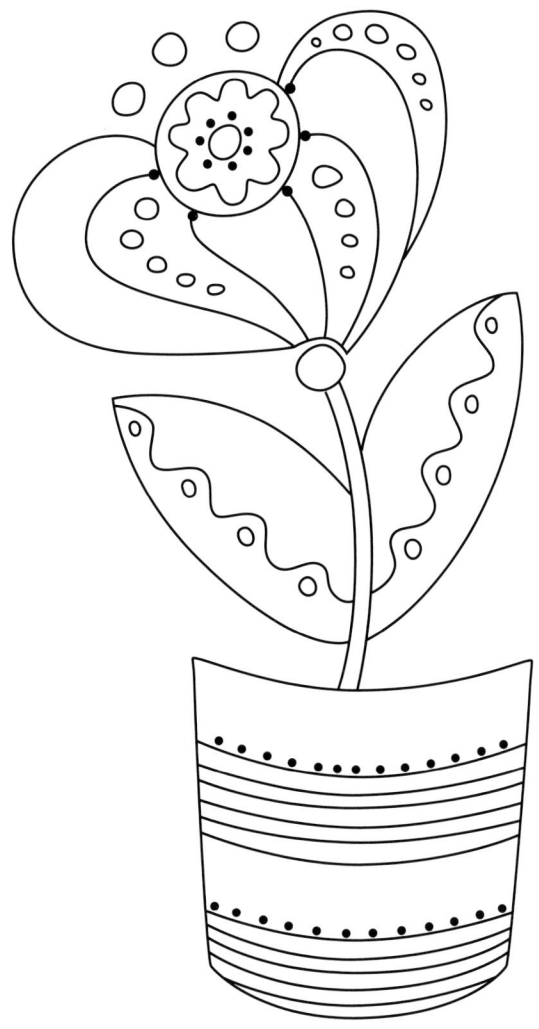

# SUPPLIES

## Fabric

12 x 12 inch (30x30cm)
ground fabric
12 x 12 inch (30x30cm) backing
fabric (optional)

## DMC six-stranded floss

| | | |
|---|---|---|
| 16 | Sprout |
| 519 | Bluish Spray |
| 601 | Impatiens |
| 602 | Pink Verbena |
| 702 | Spring Lawn |
| 703 | Metallic Spring Green |
| 726 | Mimosa |
| 741 | Mandarin |
| 893 | Dahlia |
| 972 | Curry |
| 3801 | Tulip Red |
| B5200 | Pearlescent White Light |

## Needles

Embroidery: size 7 and 9
Milliner: size 7 and 9

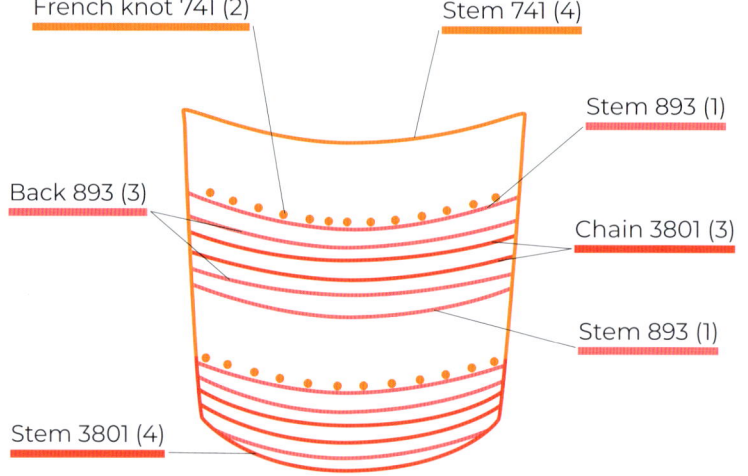

French knot 741 (2)

Stem 741 (4)

Stem 893 (1)

Back 893 (3)

Chain 3801 (3)

Stem 893 (1)

Stem 3801 (4)

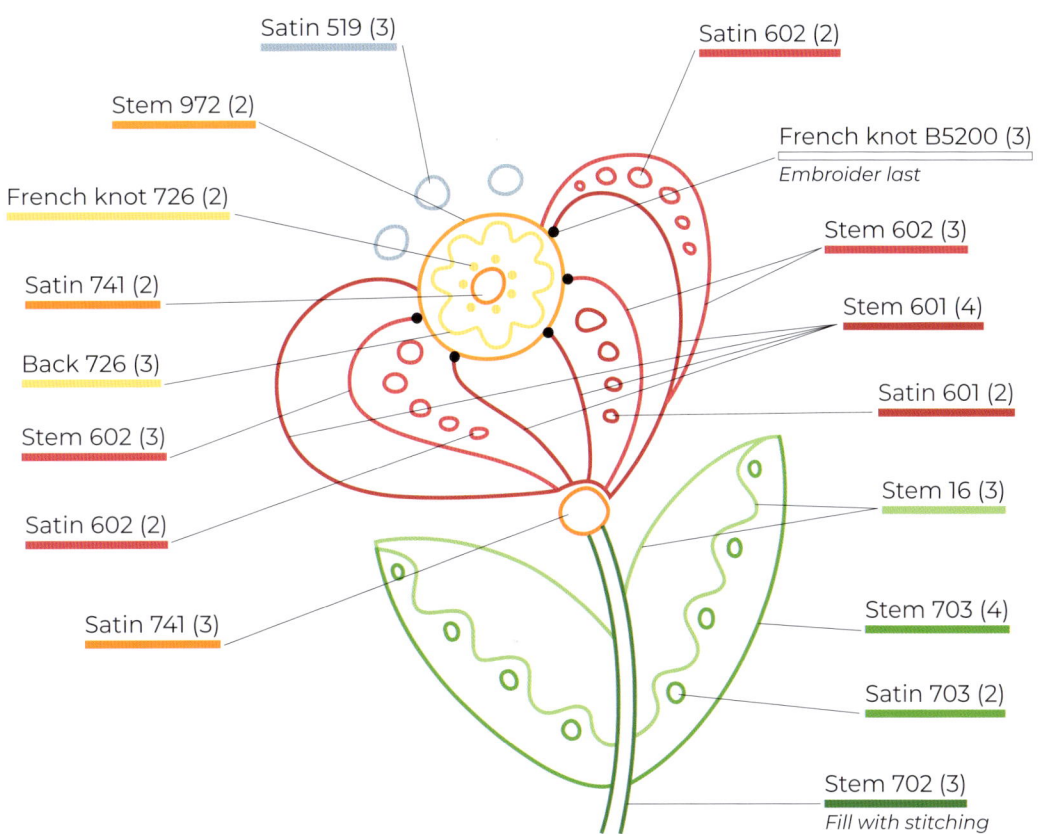

Satin 519 (3)

Satin 602 (2)

Stem 972 (2)

French knot B5200 (3)
*Embroider last*

French knot 726 (2)

Stem 602 (3)

Satin 741 (2)

Stem 601 (4)

Back 726 (3)

Satin 601 (2)

Stem 602 (3)

Stem 16 (3)

Satin 602 (2)

Stem 703 (4)

Satin 741 (3)

Satin 703 (2)

Stem 702 (3)
*Fill with stitching*

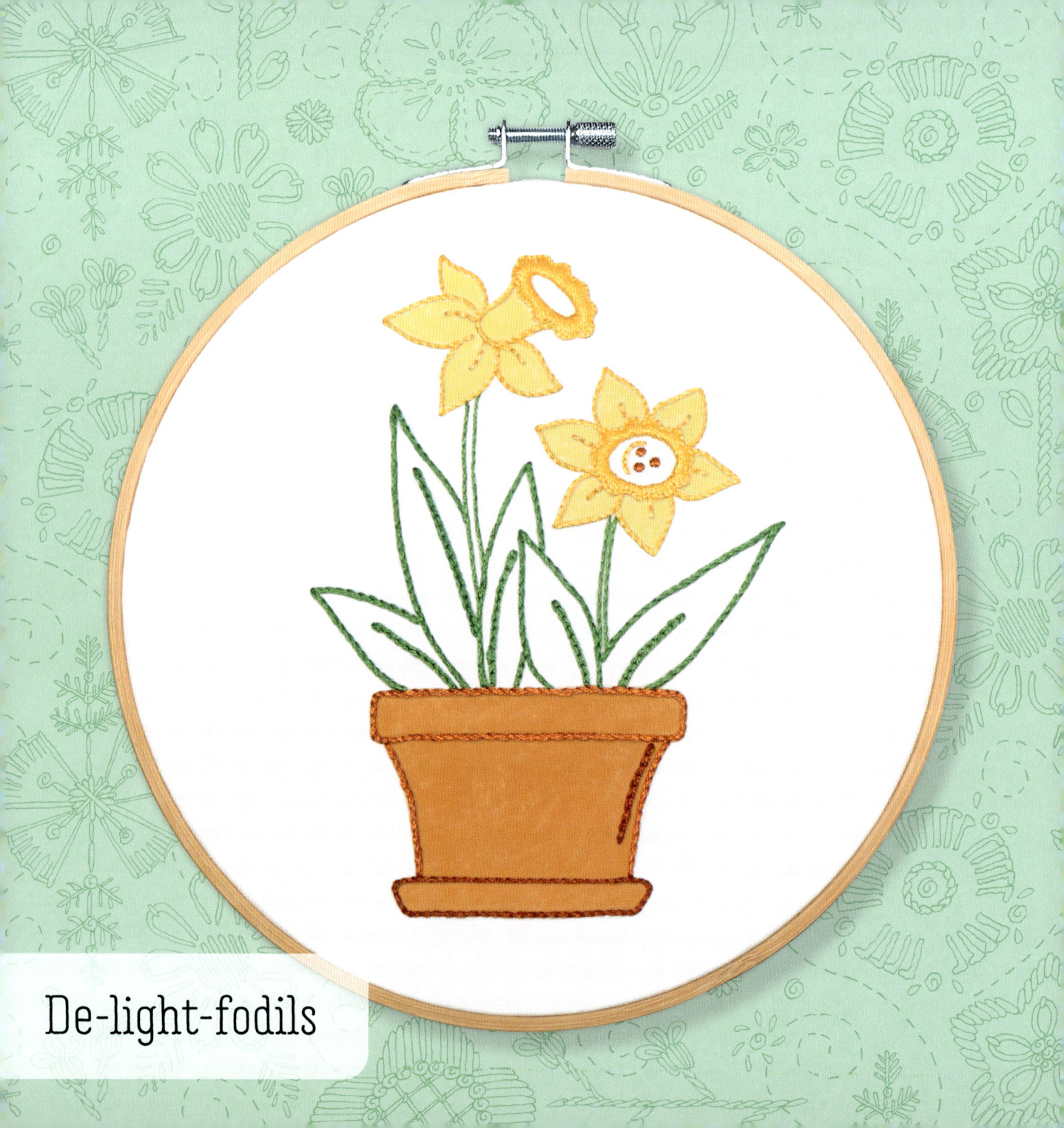

De-light-fodils

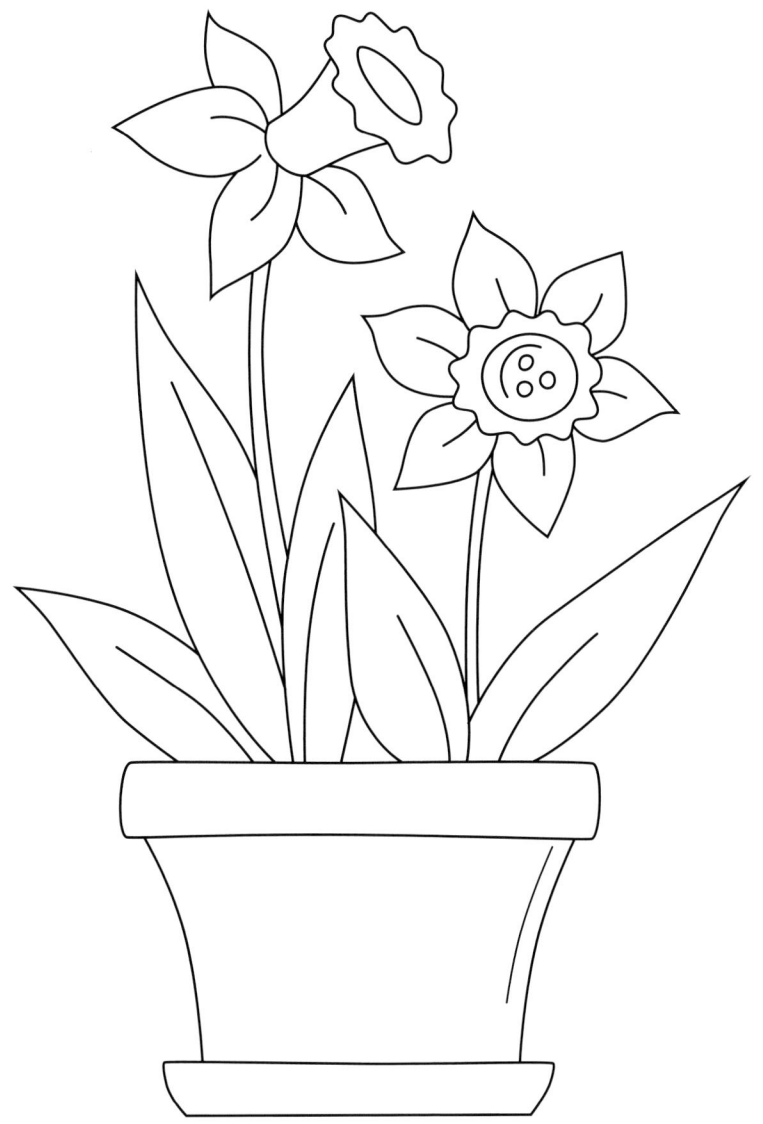

# SUPPLIES

## Fabric

12 x 12 inch (30x30cm)
ground fabric
12 x 12 inch (30x30cm)
backing fabric (optional)

## DMC six-stranded floss

- 301  Metallic Squirrel
- 400  Conker
- 701  Grass
- 702  Spring Lawn
- 725  Buttercup

## Needles

Embroidery: size 7 and 9

## Optional Fabric Marker Colors

Yellow and Brown
See page 40 for color placement.

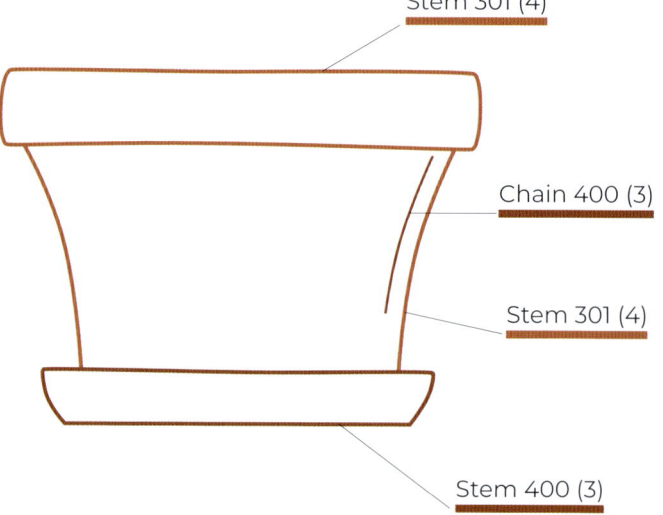

Stem 301 (4)

Chain 400 (3)

Stem 301 (4)

Stem 400 (3)

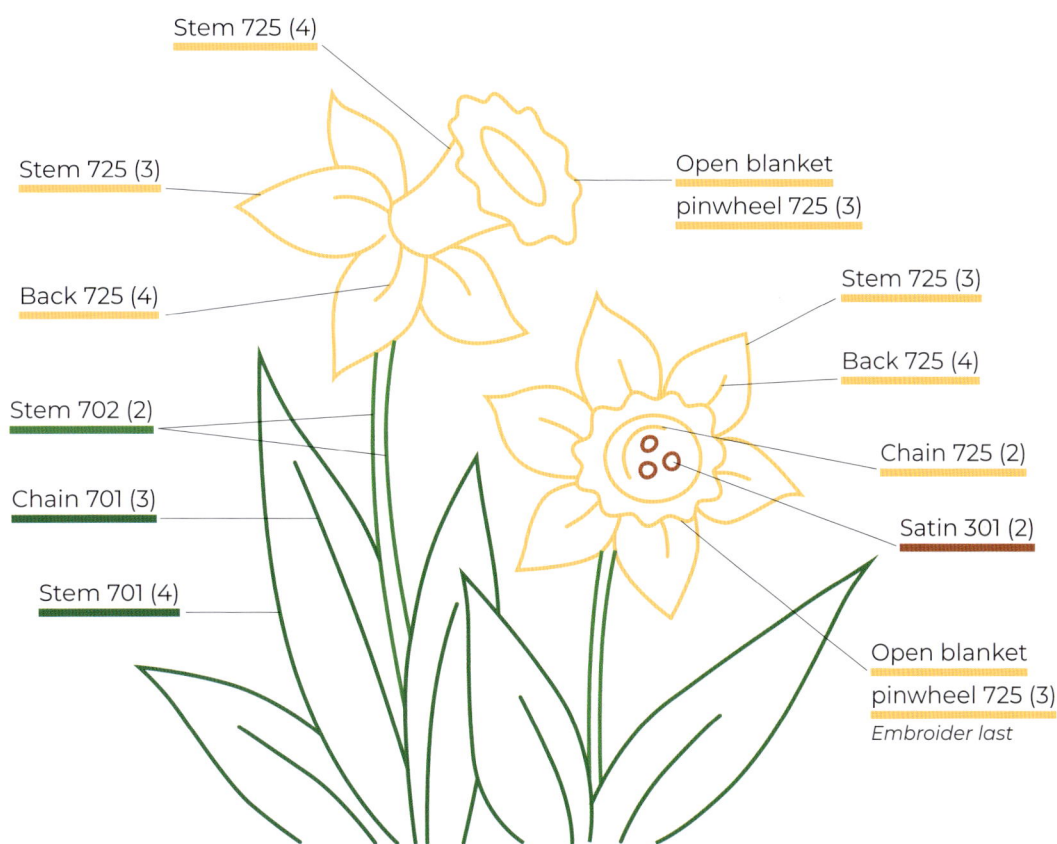

Stem 725 (4)

Stem 725 (3)

Back 725 (4)

Stem 702 (2)

Chain 701 (3)

Stem 701 (4)

Open blanket
pinwheel 725 (3)

Stem 725 (3)

Back 725 (4)

Chain 725 (2)

Satin 301 (2)

Open blanket
pinwheel 725 (3)
*Embroider last*

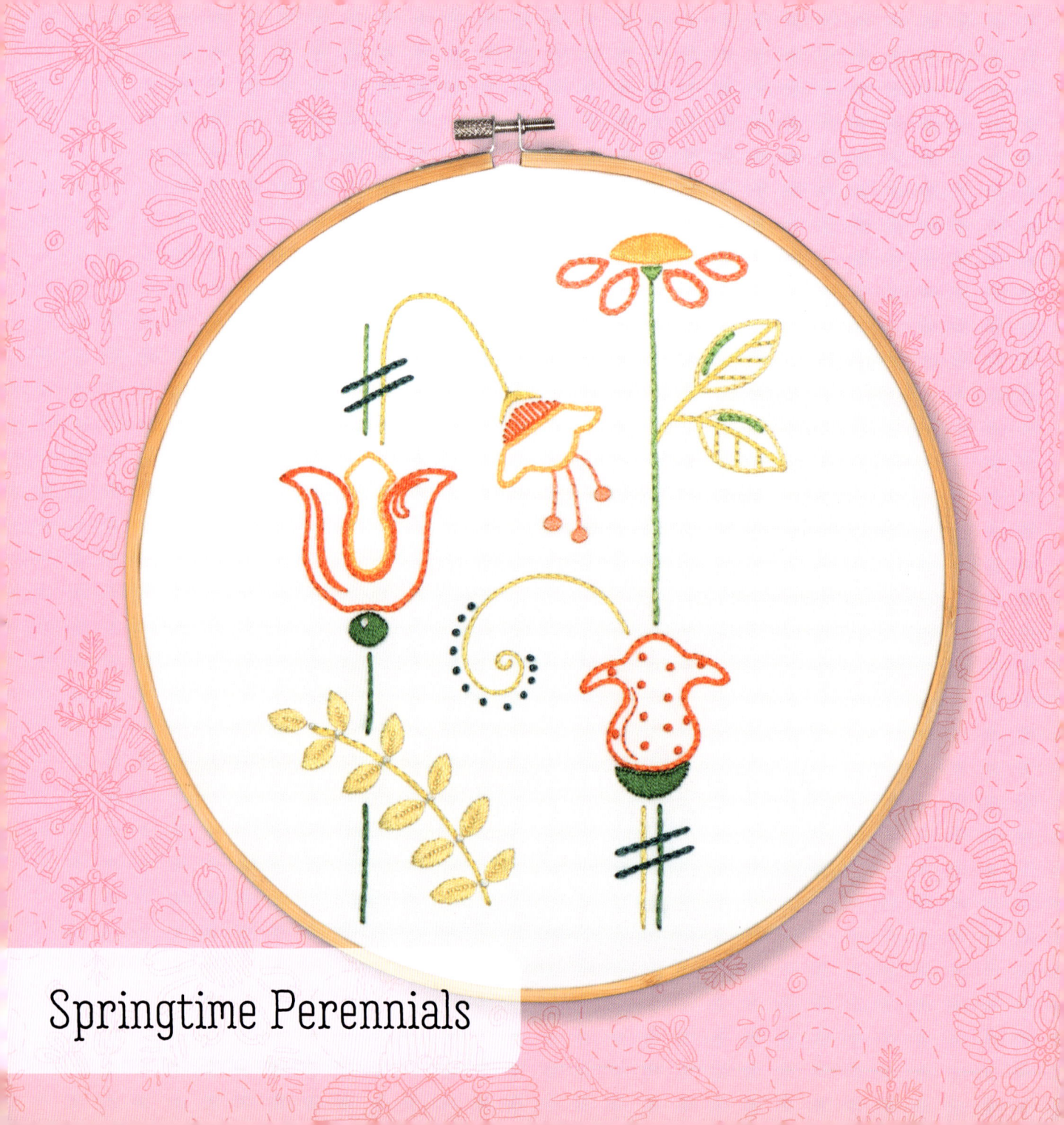

Springtime Perennials

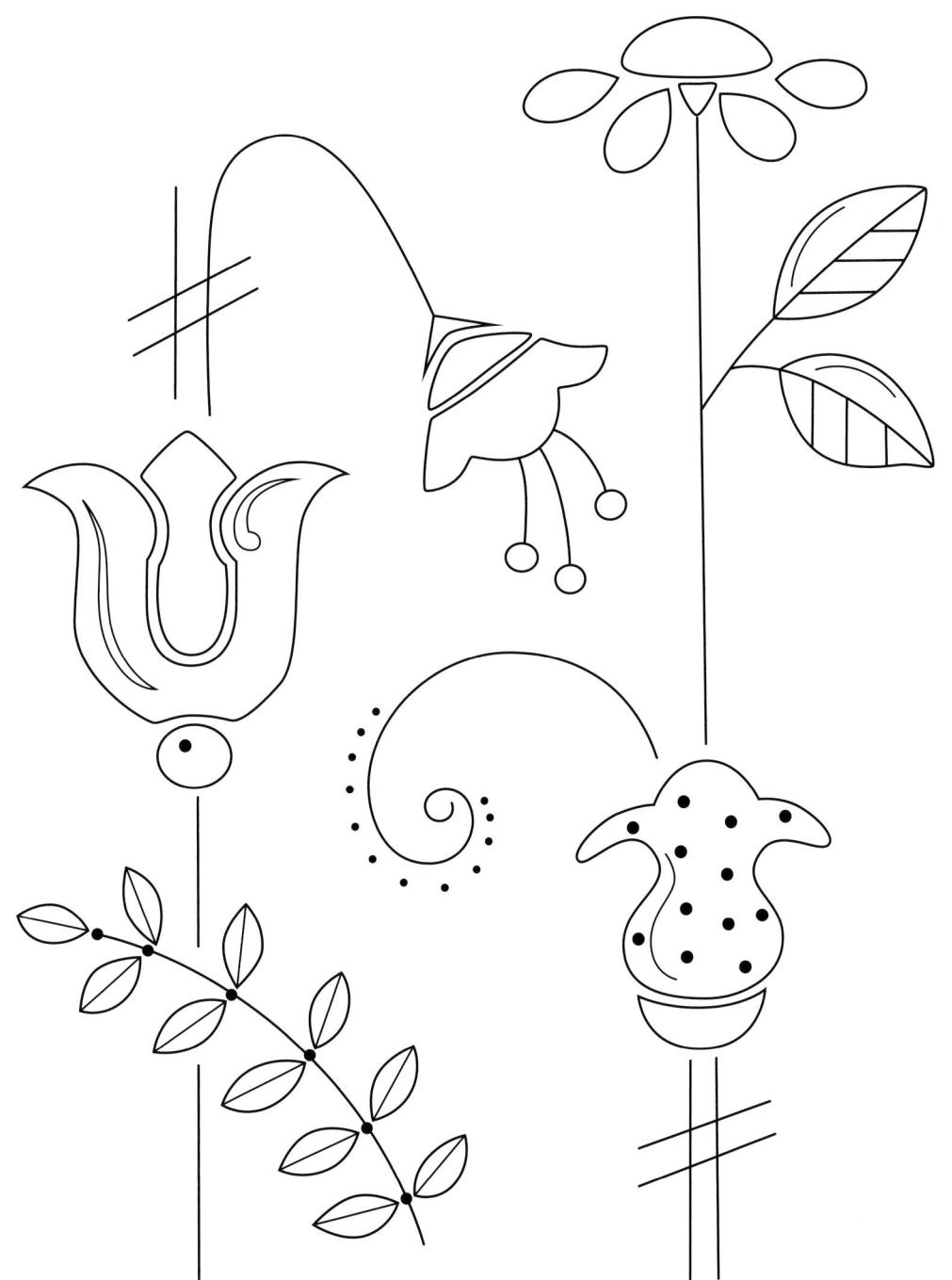

## SUPPLIES

### Fabric

12 x 12 inch (30x30cm)
ground fabric
12 x 12 inch (30x30cm)
backing fabric (optional)

### DMC six-stranded floss

| | | |
|---|---|---|
| 165 | Linden Green |
| 351 | Coral |
| 352 | Salmon |
| 701 | Grass |
| 703 | Metallic Spring Green |
| 743 | Banana |
| 991 | Frog |
| 3819 | Aurous Green |
| B5200 | Pearlescent White Light |

### Needles

Embroidery: size 7 and 9
Milliner: size 7

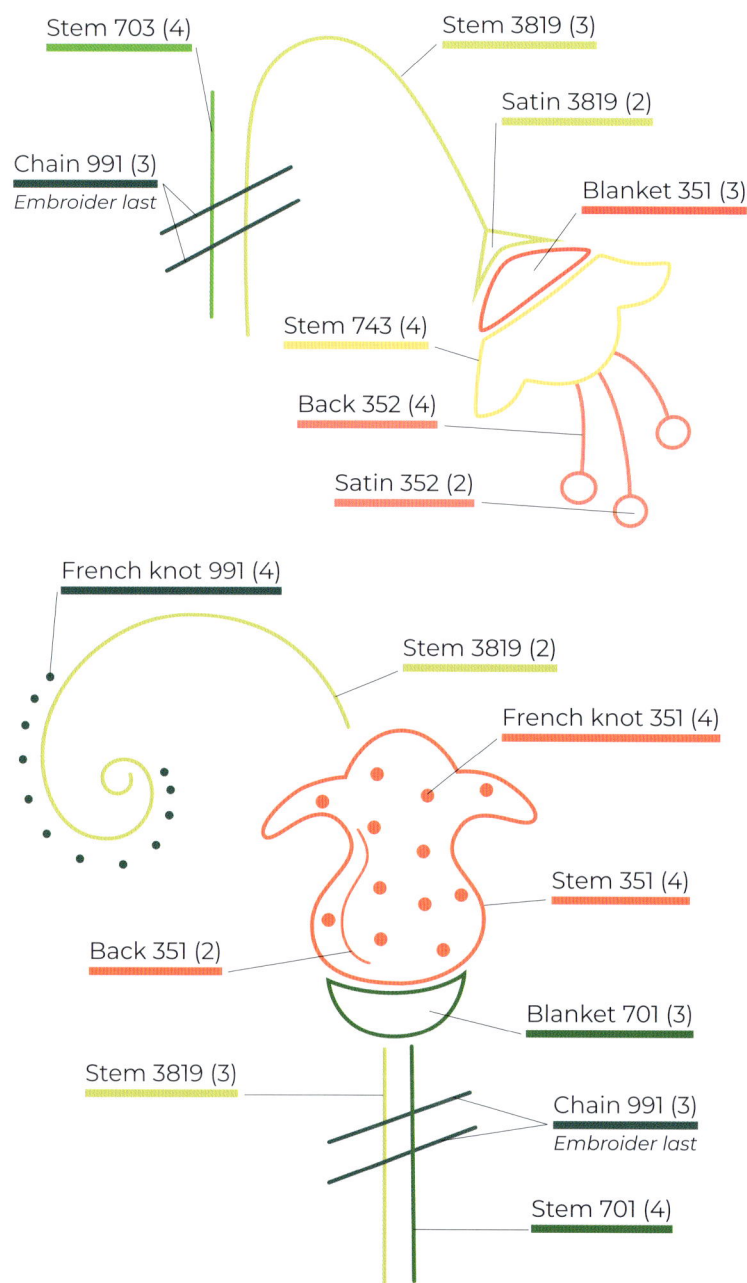

Stem 703 (4)

Stem 3819 (3)

Satin 3819 (2)

Chain 991 (3)
*Embroider last*

Blanket 351 (3)

Stem 743 (4)

Back 352 (4)

Satin 352 (2)

French knot 991 (4)

Stem 3819 (2)

French knot 351 (4)

Stem 351 (4)

Back 351 (2)

Blanket 701 (3)

Stem 3819 (3)

Chain 991 (3)
*Embroider last*

Stem 701 (4)

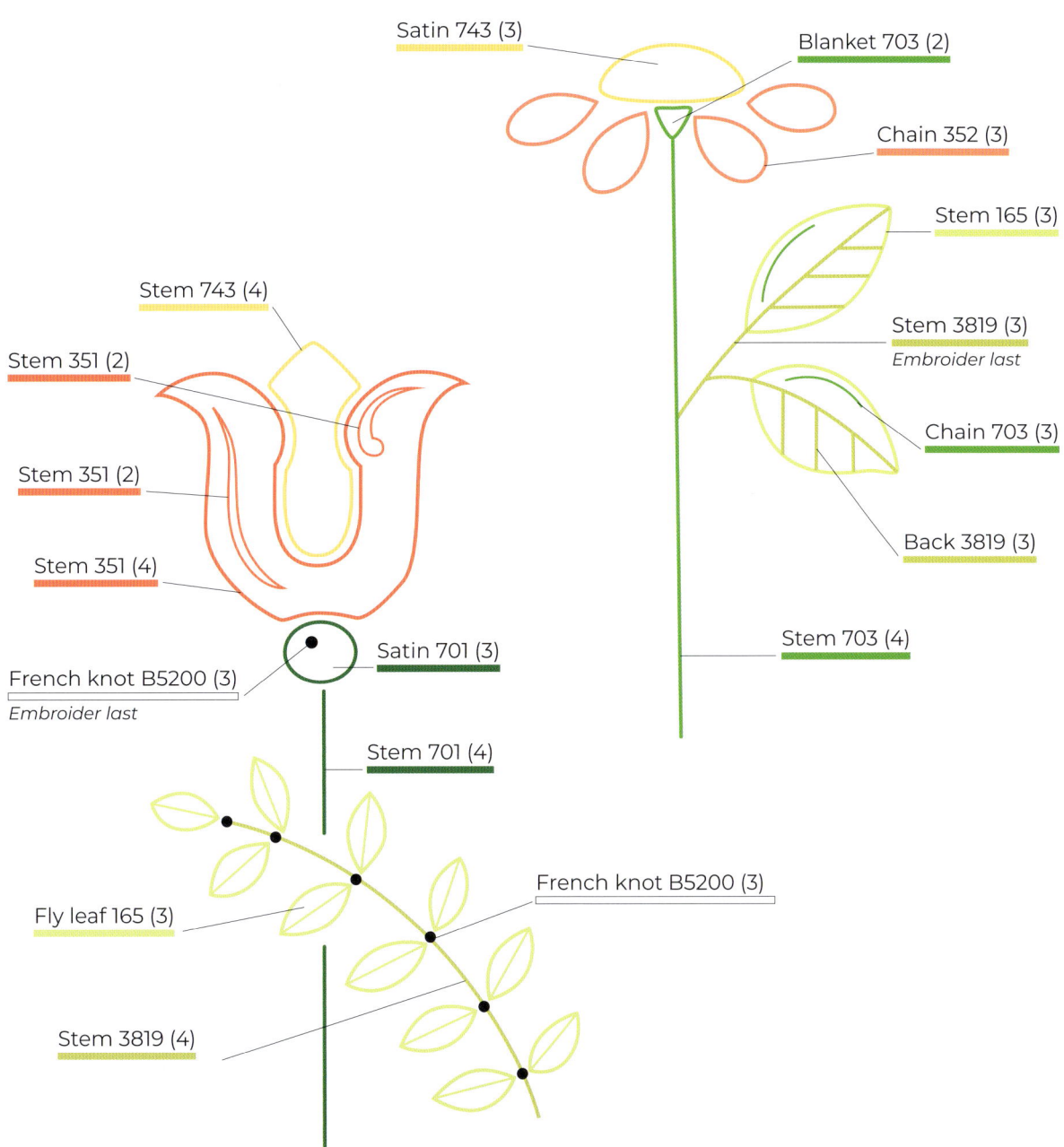

Satin 743 (3)

Blanket 703 (2)

Chain 352 (3)

Stem 165 (3)

Stem 3819 (3)
*Embroider last*

Chain 703 (3)

Back 3819 (3)

Stem 703 (4)

Stem 743 (4)

Stem 351 (2)

Stem 351 (2)

Stem 351 (4)

French knot B5200 (3)
*Embroider last*

Satin 701 (3)

Stem 701 (4)

French knot B5200 (3)

Fly leaf 165 (3)

Stem 3819 (4)

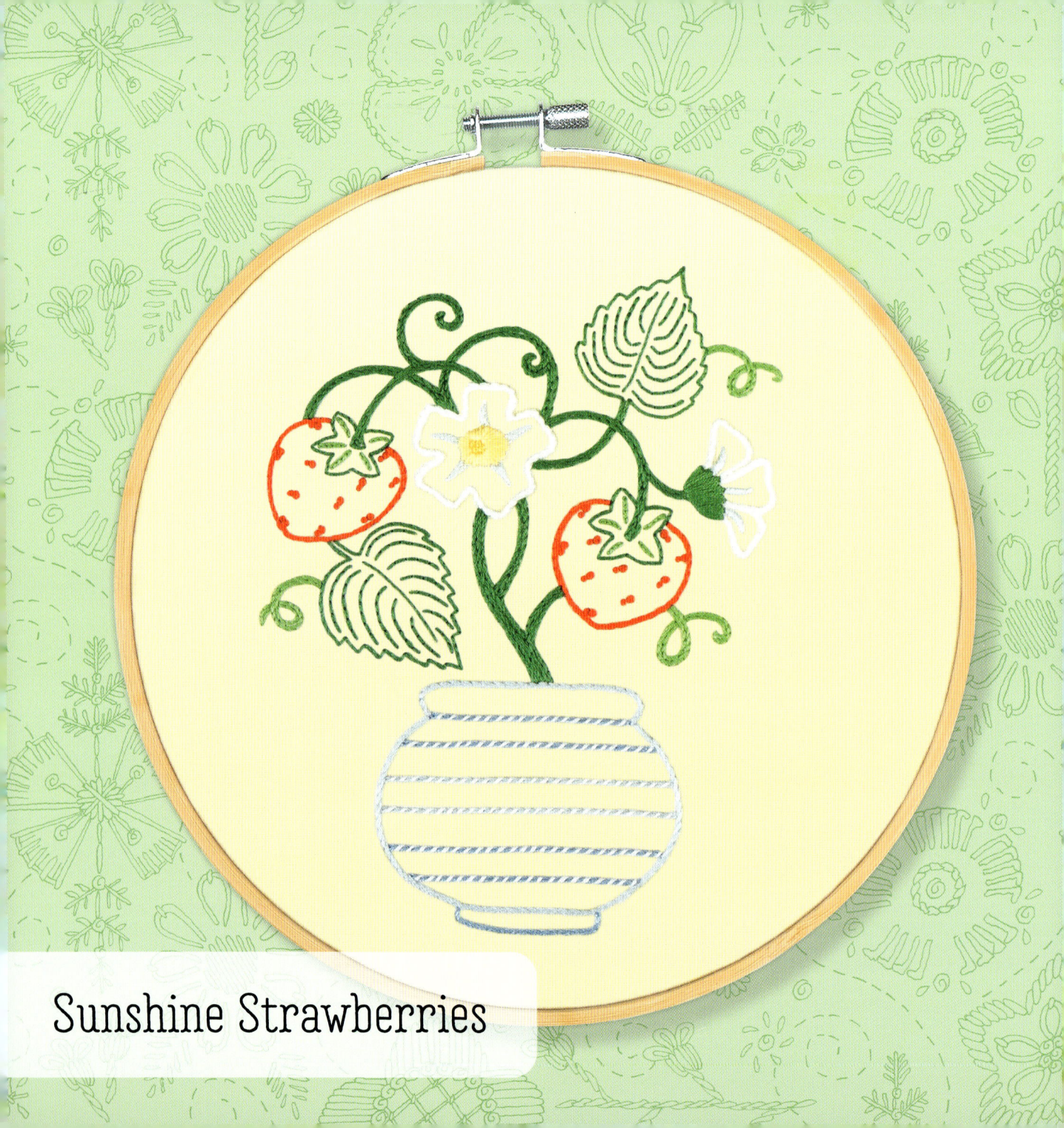

Sunshine Strawberries

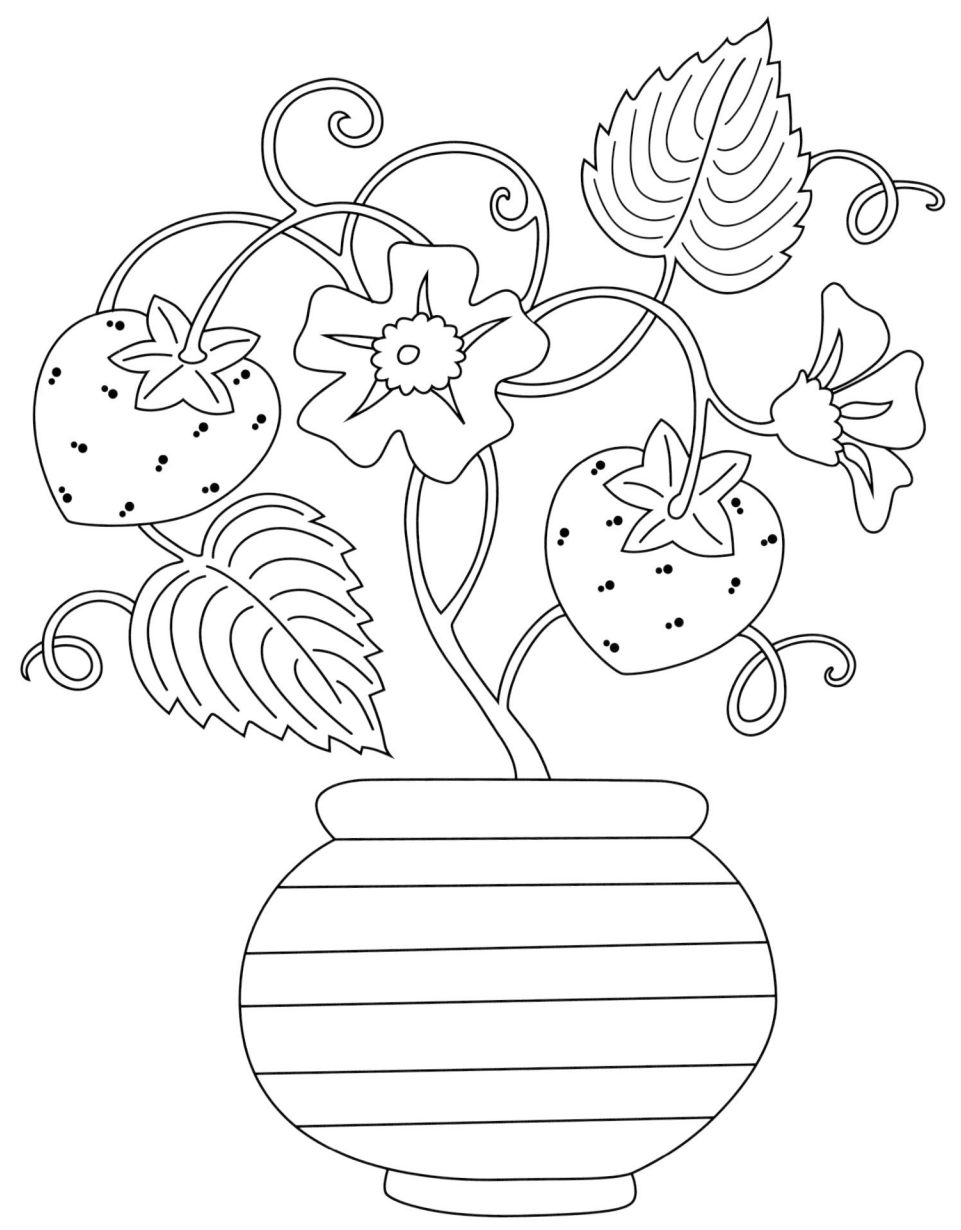

# SUPPLIES

## Fabric

12 x 12 inch (30x30cm)
ground fabric
12 x 12 inch (30x30cm)
backing fabric (optional)

## DMC six-stranded floss

| | | |
|---|---|---|
| 🟩 | 701 | Grass |
| 🟩 | 703 | Metallic Spring Green |
| 🟨 | 726 | Mimosa |
| 🟨 | 727 | Primrose |
| | 775 | Blue Summer Rain |
| 🟦 | 3755 | Pastel Blue |
| 🟧 | 3801 | Tulip Red |
| | 3841 | Igloo Blue |
| ⬜ | B5200 | Pearlescent White Light |

## Needles

Embroidery: size 7 and 9
Milliner: size 7 and 9

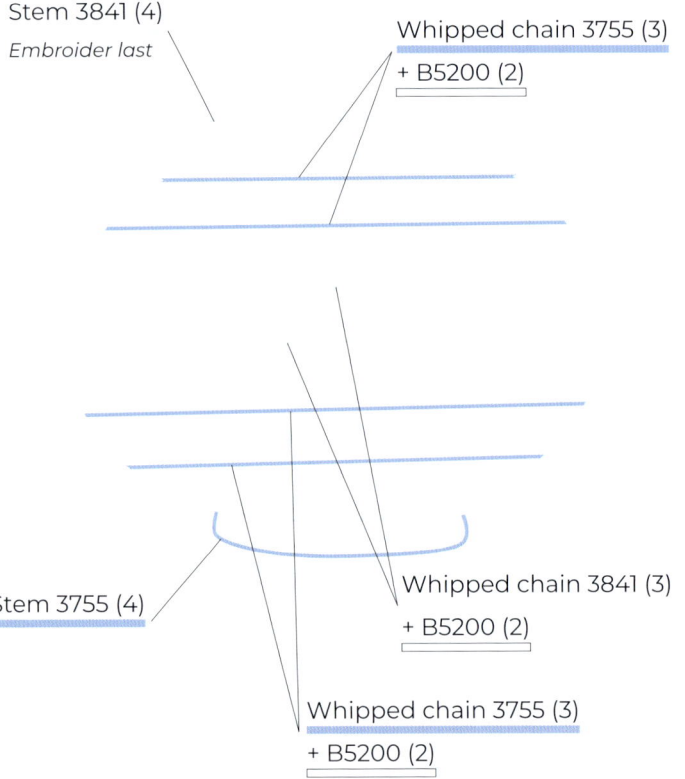

Stem 3841 (4)
*Embroider last*

Whipped chain 3755 (3)
+ B5200 (2)

Stem 3755 (4)

Whipped chain 3841 (3)
+ B5200 (2)

Whipped chain 3755 (3)
+ B5200 (2)

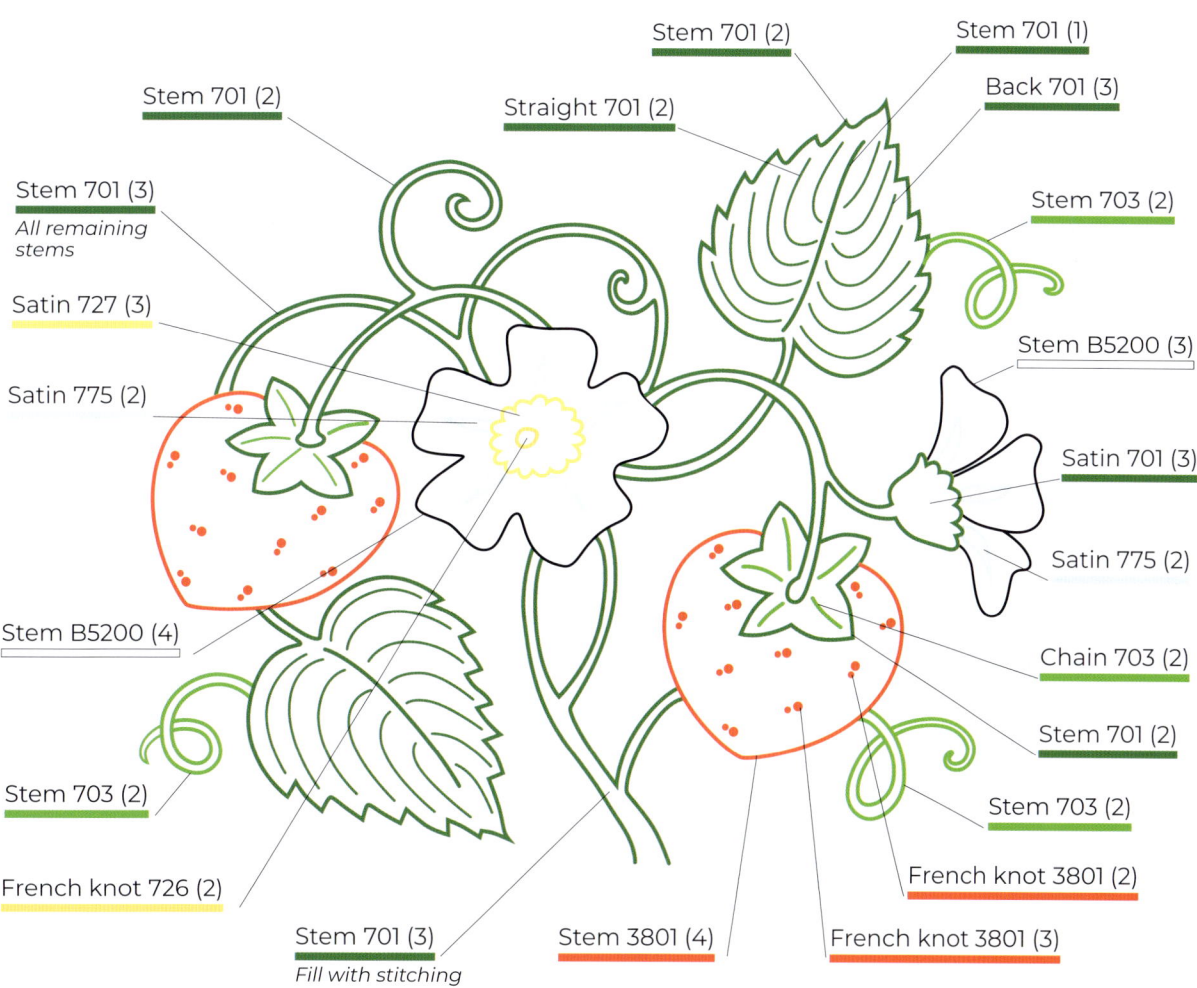

Stem 701 (2)

Stem 701 (1)

Back 701 (3)

Straight 701 (2)

Stem 701 (2)

Stem 703 (2)

Stem 701 (3)
*All remaining stems*

Satin 727 (3)

Satin 775 (2)

Stem B5200 (3)

Satin 701 (3)

Satin 775 (2)

Chain 703 (2)

Stem B5200 (4)

Stem 701 (2)

Stem 703 (2)

Stem 703 (2)

French knot 726 (2)

French knot 3801 (2)

Stem 701 (3)
*Fill with stitching*

Stem 3801 (4)

French knot 3801 (3)

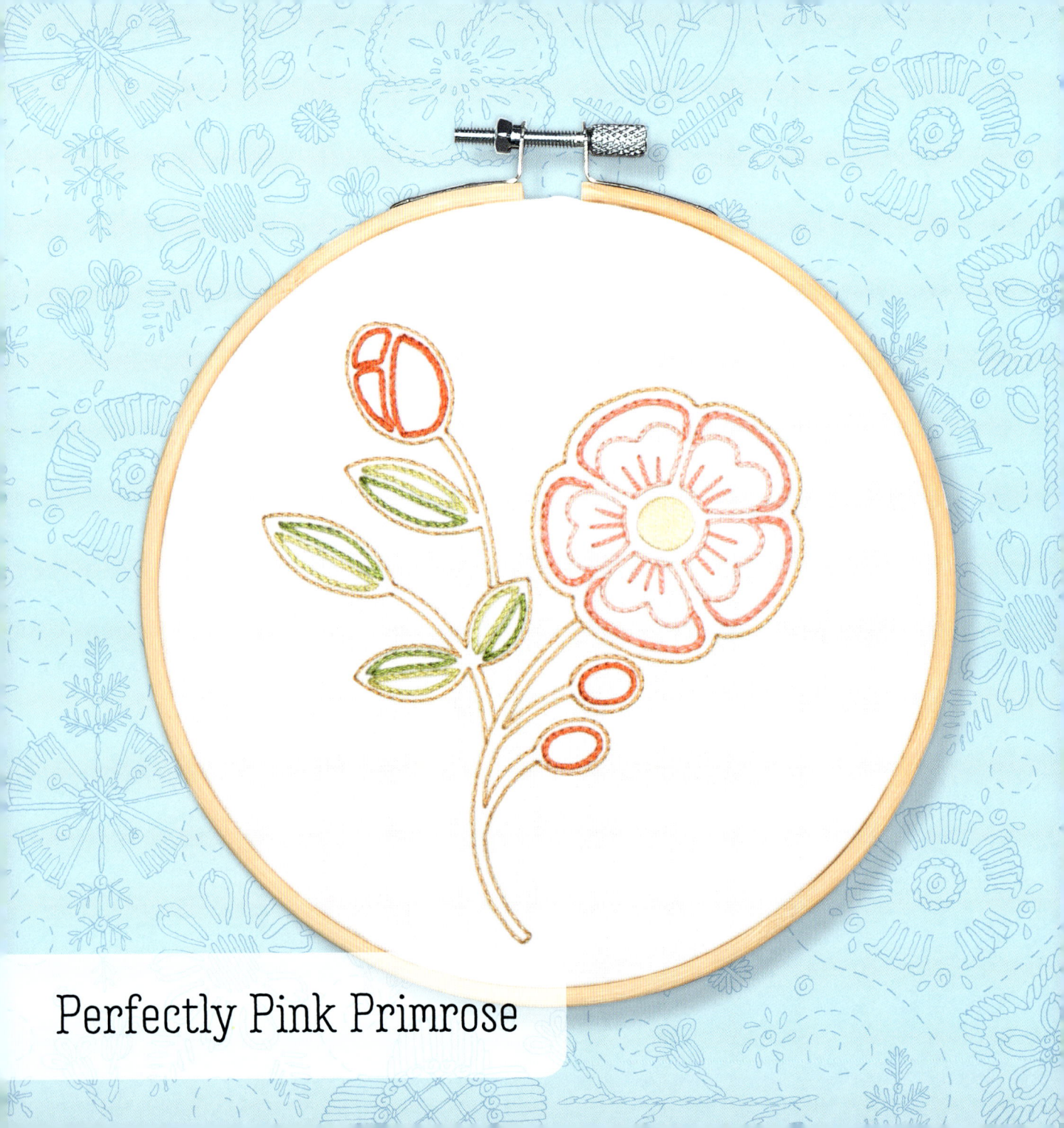

Perfectly Pink Primrose

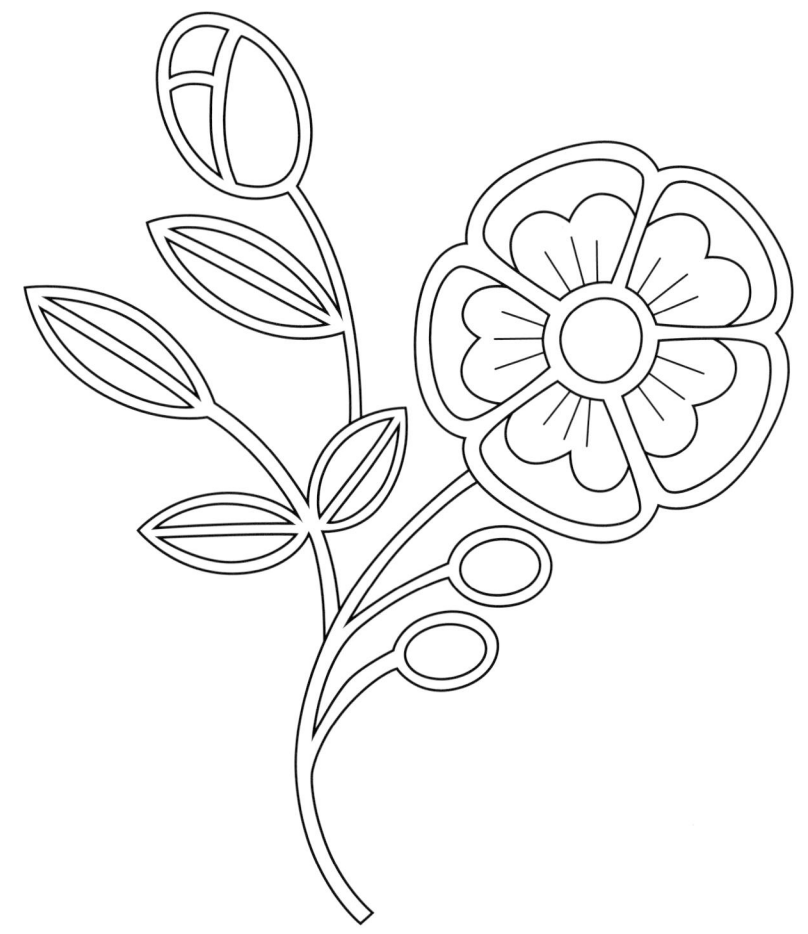

## SUPPLIES

**Fabric**

12 x 12 inch (30x30cm)
ground fabric
12 x 12 inch (30x30cm)
backing fabric (optional)

**DMC six-stranded floss**

| | | |
|---|---|---|
| | 422 | Light Oak |
| | 470 | Olive Green |
| | 472 | Green Bud |
| | 760 | Dusty Pink |
| | 761 | Rose Dawn |
| | 3078 | Buttermilk |
| | 3328 | Amaranth |

**Needles**

Embroidery: size 7 and 9

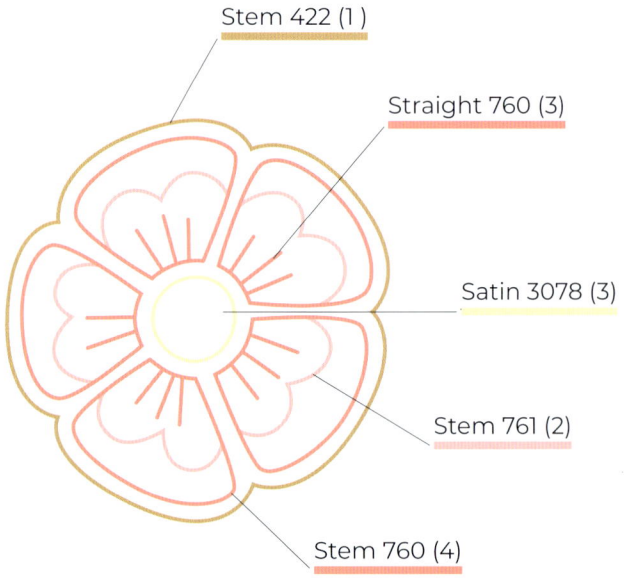

Stem 422 (1 )

Straight 760 (3)

Satin 3078 (3)

Stem 761 (2)

Stem 760 (4)

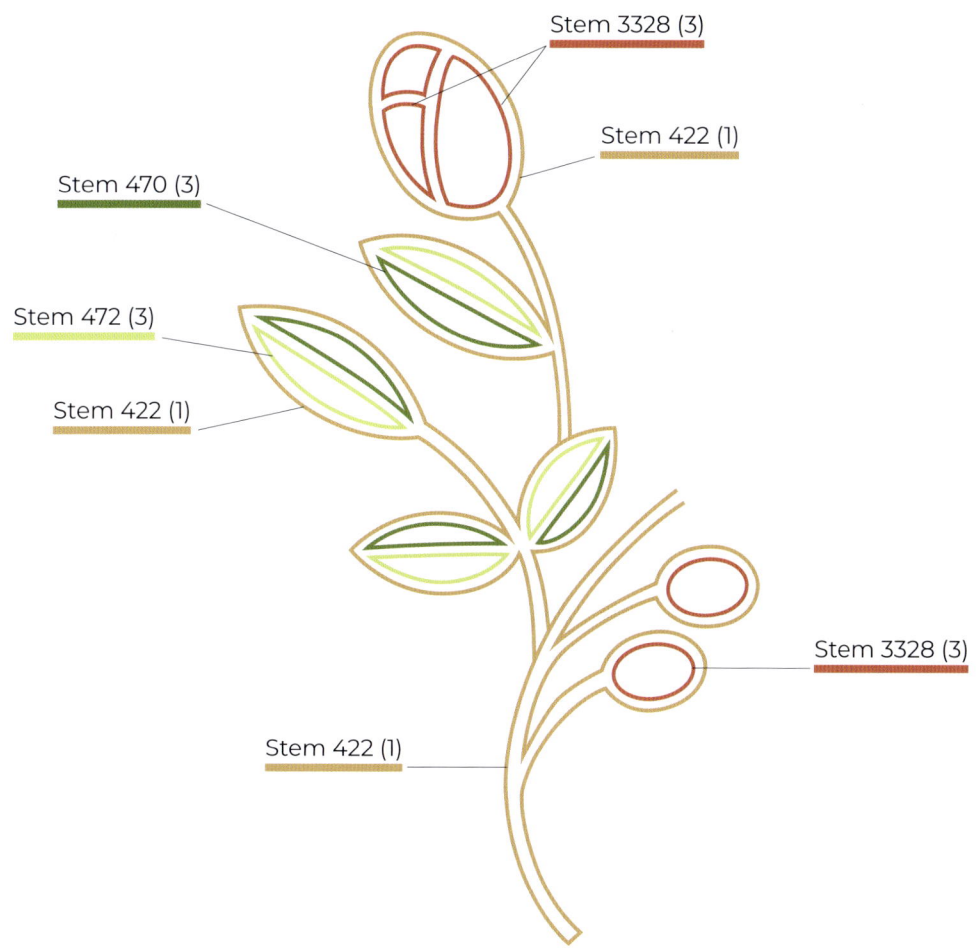

Stem 3328 (3)

Stem 422 (1)

Stem 470 (3)

Stem 472 (3)

Stem 422 (1)

Stem 3328 (3)

Stem 422 (1)

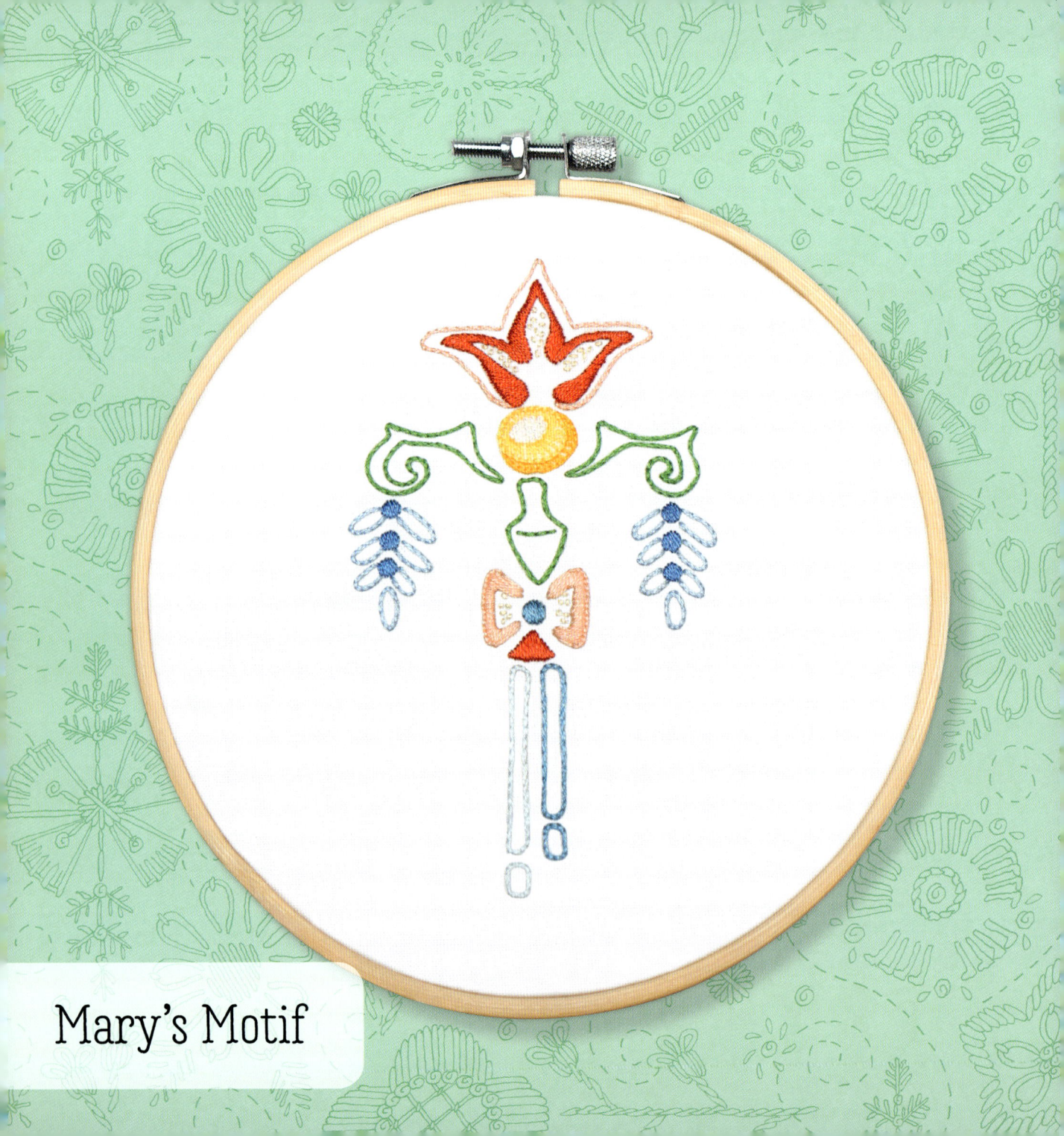

Mary's Motif

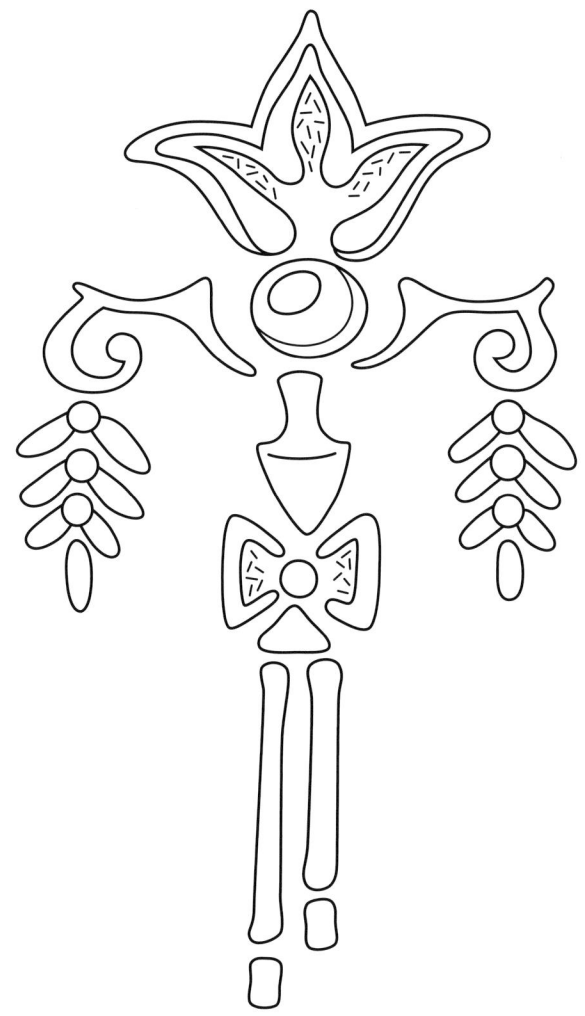

## SUPPLIES

### Fabric
12 x 12 inch (30x30cm)
ground fabric
12 x 12 inch (30x30cm)
backing fabric (optional)

### DMC six-stranded floss

| | | |
|---|---|---|
| 702 | Spring Lawn |
| 726 | Mimosa |
| 747 | Pearlescent Blue Sea Mist |
| 807 | Turquoise Tide |
| 826 | Tuareg Blue |
| 827 | Forget-Me-Knot |
| 972 | Curry |
| 3078 | Buttermilk |
| 3779 | Burnished Pink |
| 3831 | Wild Strawberry |
| B5200 | Pearlescent White Light |

### Needles
Embroidery: size 7 and 9
Milliner: size 9

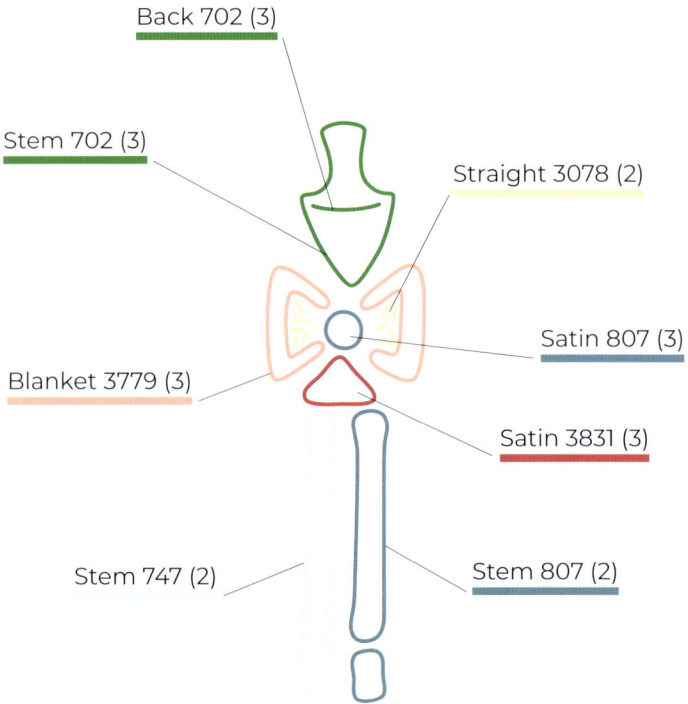

Back 702 (3)

Stem 702 (3)

Straight 3078 (2)

Satin 807 (3)

Blanket 3779 (3)

Satin 3831 (3)

Stem 747 (2)

Stem 807 (2)

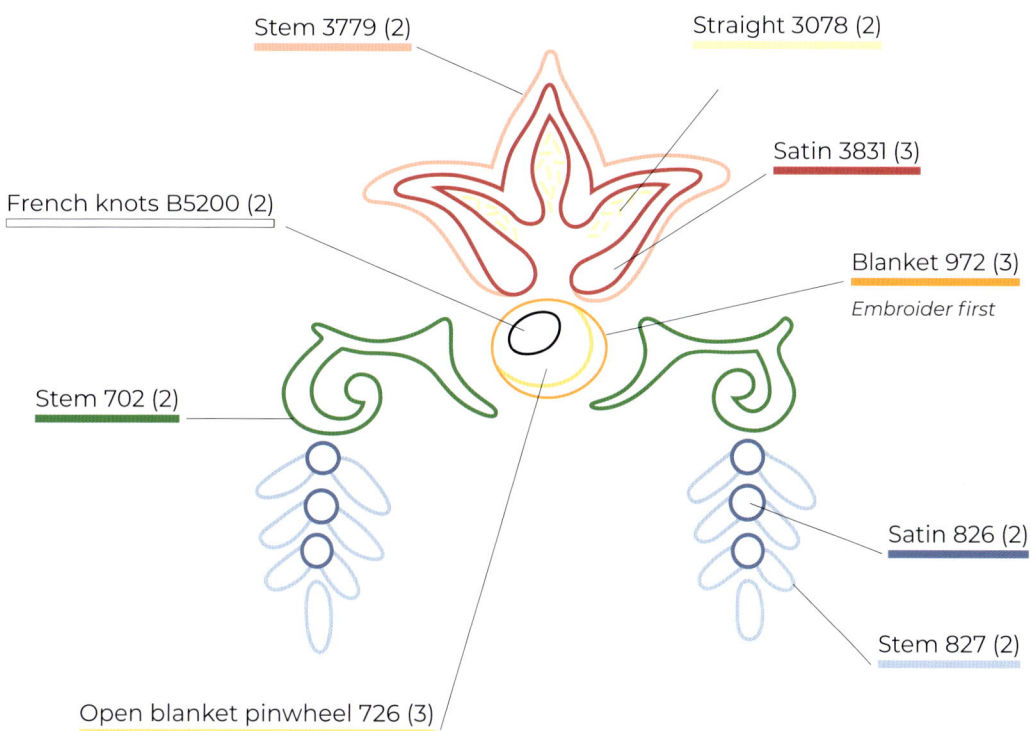

Stem 3779 (2)

Straight 3078 (2)

Satin 3831 (3)

French knots B5200 (2)

Blanket 972 (3)

*Embroider first*

Stem 702 (2)

Satin 826 (2)

Stem 827 (2)

Open blanket pinwheel 726 (3)

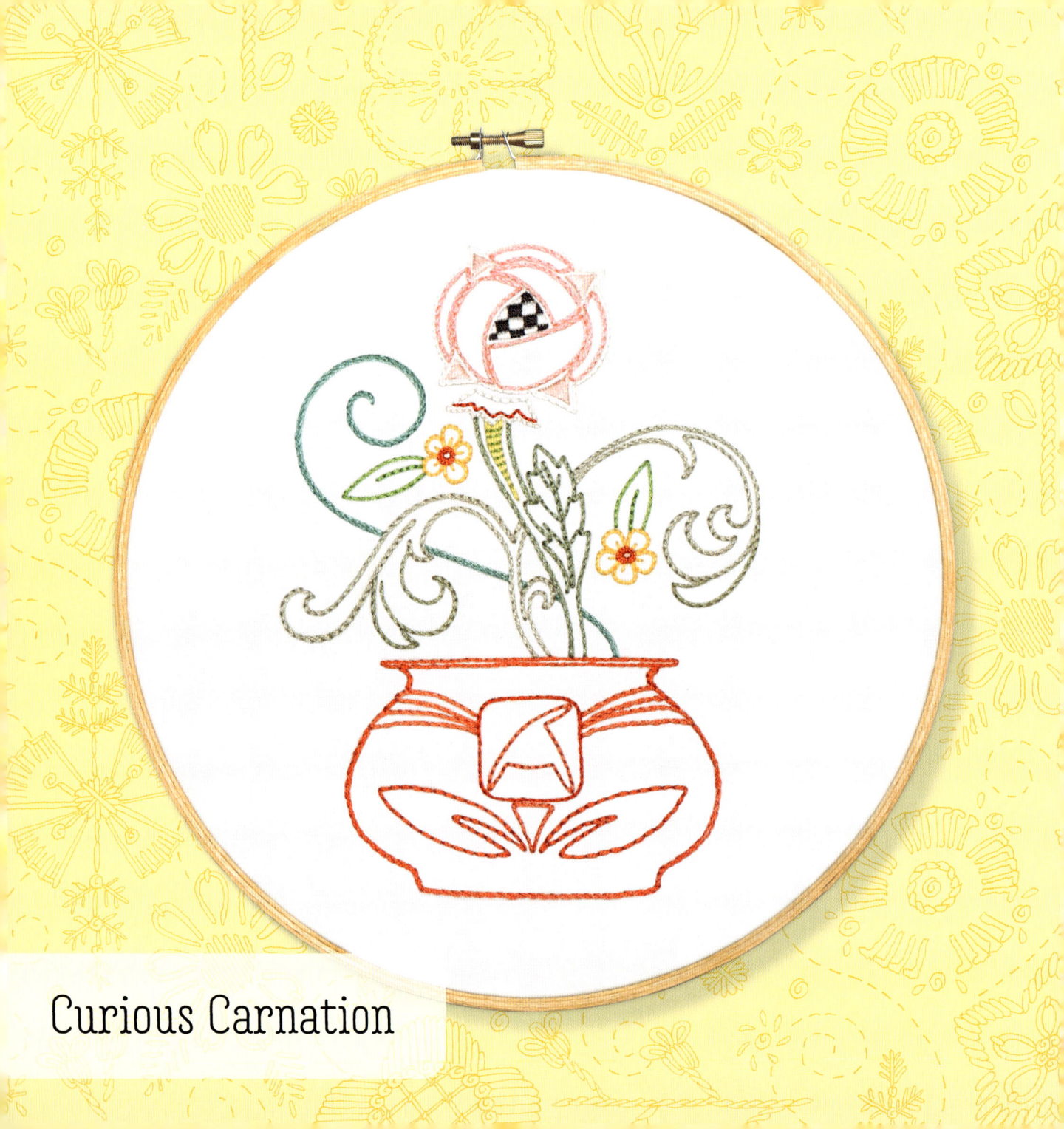

Curious Carnation

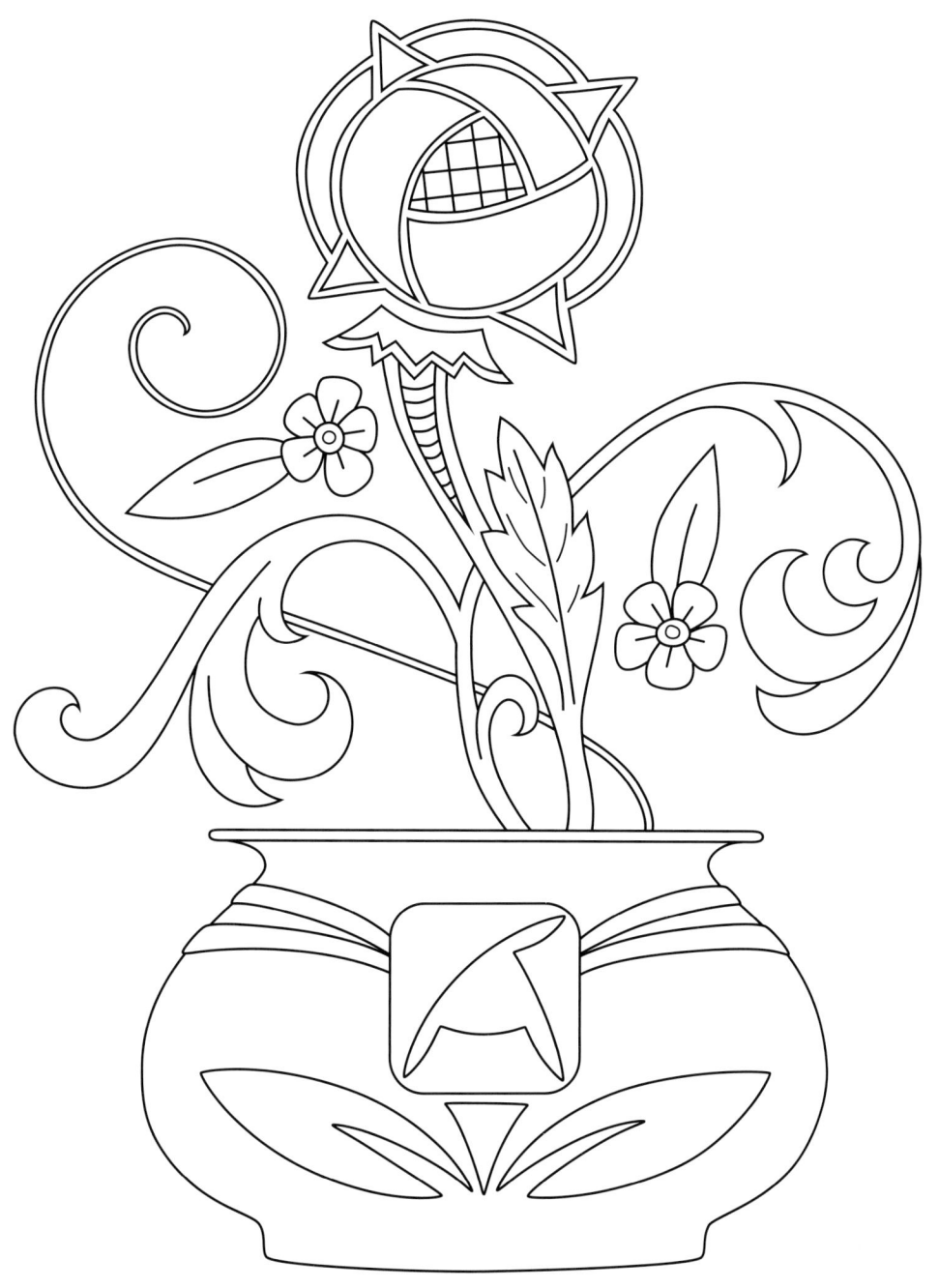

## SUPPLIES

### Fabric

12 x 12 inch (30x30cm)
ground fabric
12 x 12 inch (30x30cm)
backing fabric (optional)

### DMC six-stranded floss

| | | |
|---|---|---|
| 12 | Citrus Yellow |
| 347 | Egyptian Red |
| 522 | Lattice Green |
| 523 | Green Ash |
| 524 | Pebble Green |
| 703 | Metallic Spring Green |
| 726 | Mimosa |
| 992 | Mint |
| 993 | Peppermint |
| 3326 | Wild Rose |
| 3328 | Amaranth |
| 3712 | Blush |
| 3713 | Rose Quartz |
| 3799 | Anthracite |
| B5200 | Pearlescent White Light |

### Needles

Embroidery: size 7 and 9

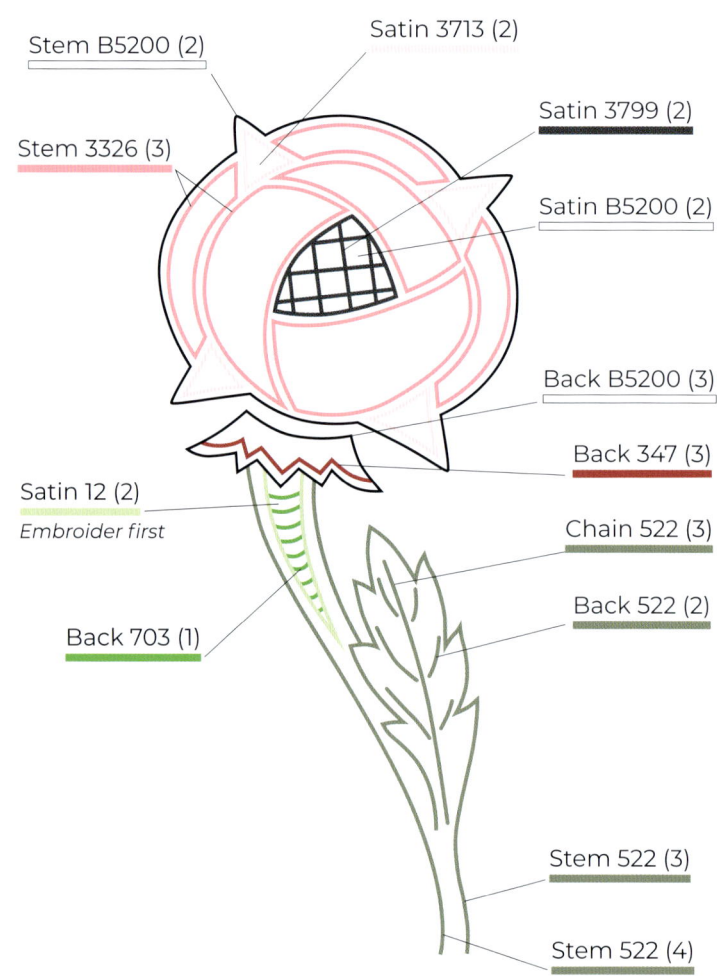

Stem B5200 (2)

Stem 3326 (3)

Satin 3713 (2)

Satin 3799 (2)

Satin B5200 (2)

Back B5200 (3)

Back 347 (3)

Chain 522 (3)

Back 522 (2)

Satin 12 (2)
*Embroider first*

Back 703 (1)

Stem 522 (3)

Stem 522 (4)

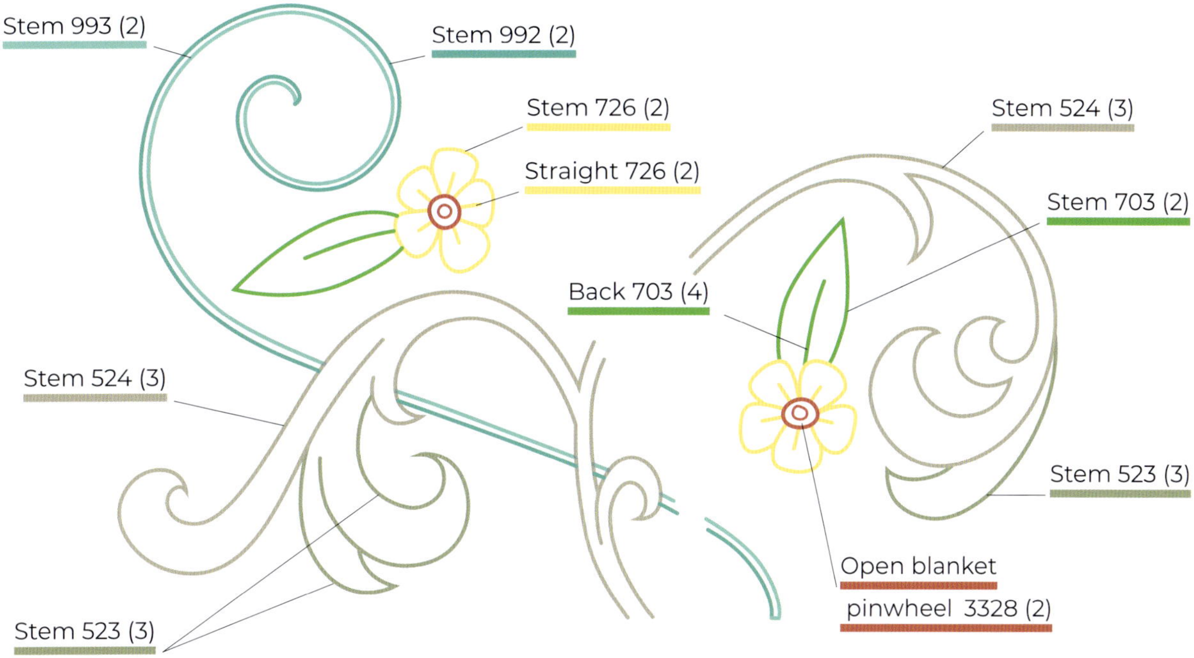

Stem 993 (2)

Stem 992 (2)

Stem 726 (2)

Straight 726 (2)

Stem 524 (3)

Stem 703 (2)

Back 703 (4)

Stem 524 (3)

Stem 523 (3)

Stem 523 (3)

Open blanket
pinwheel 3328 (2)

Stem 3328 (2)

Stem 3712 (3)

Back 3712 (4)

Stem 347 (2)

Back 3328 (4)

Stem 3712 (3)

Stem 3328 (4)

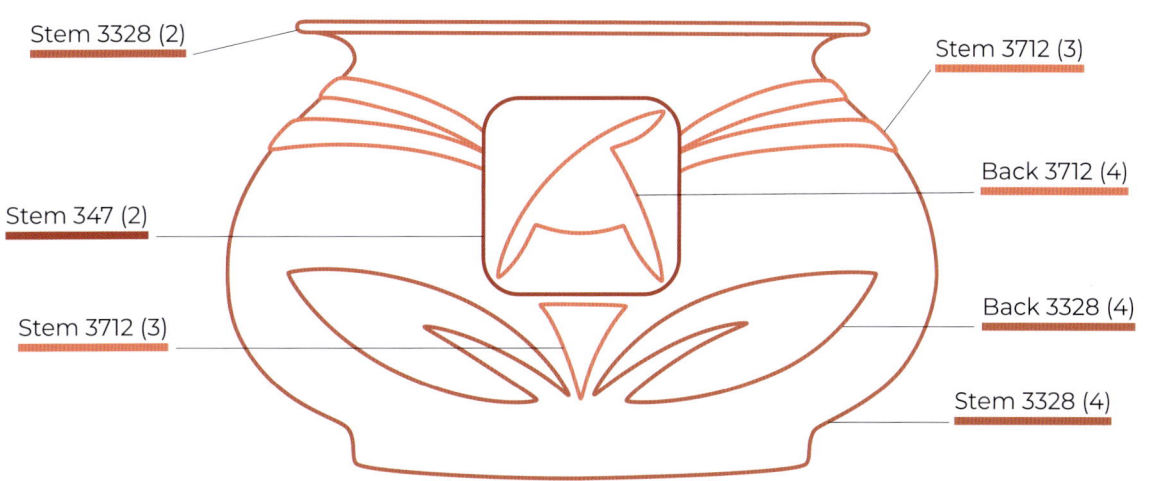

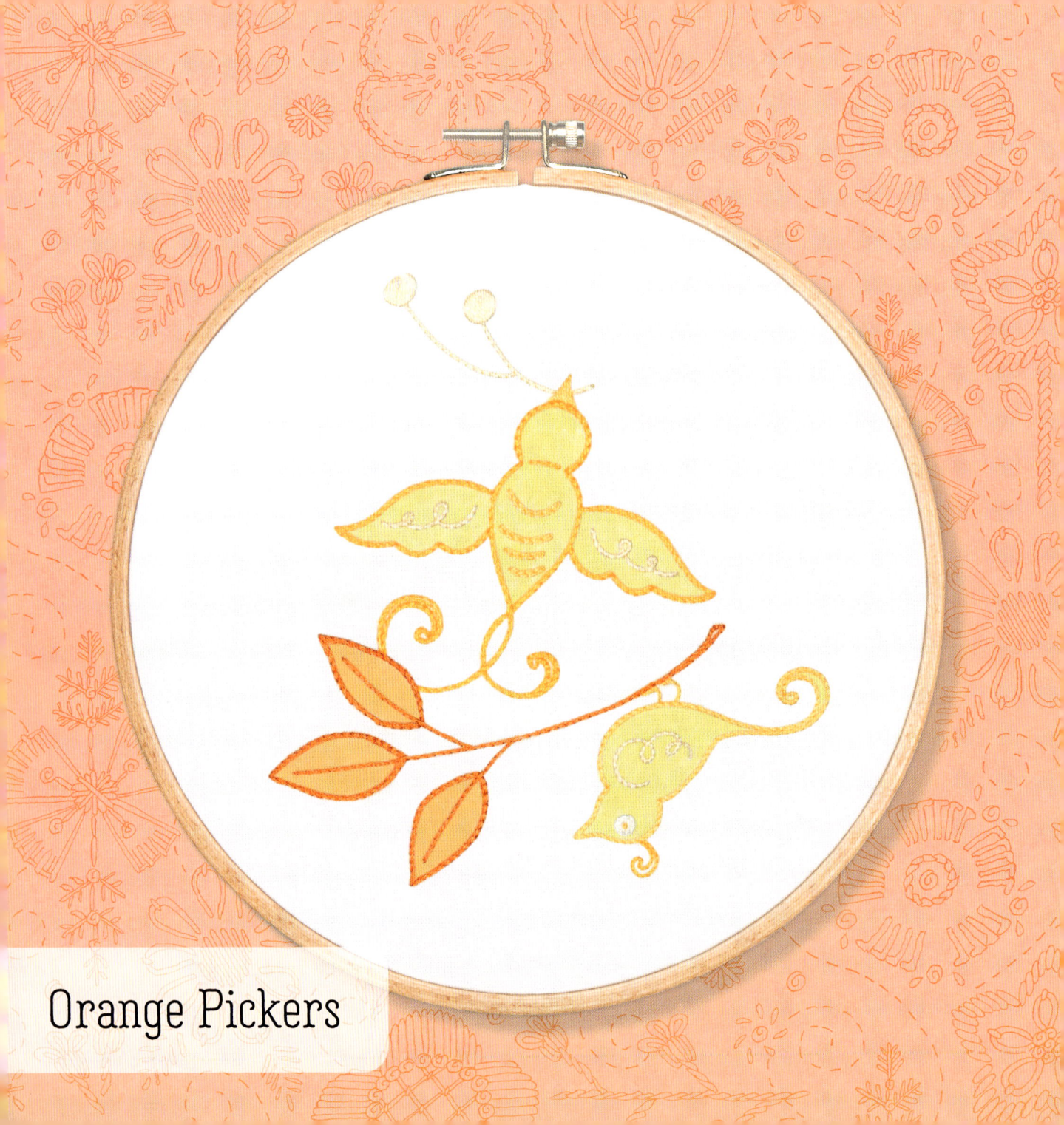

Orange Pickers

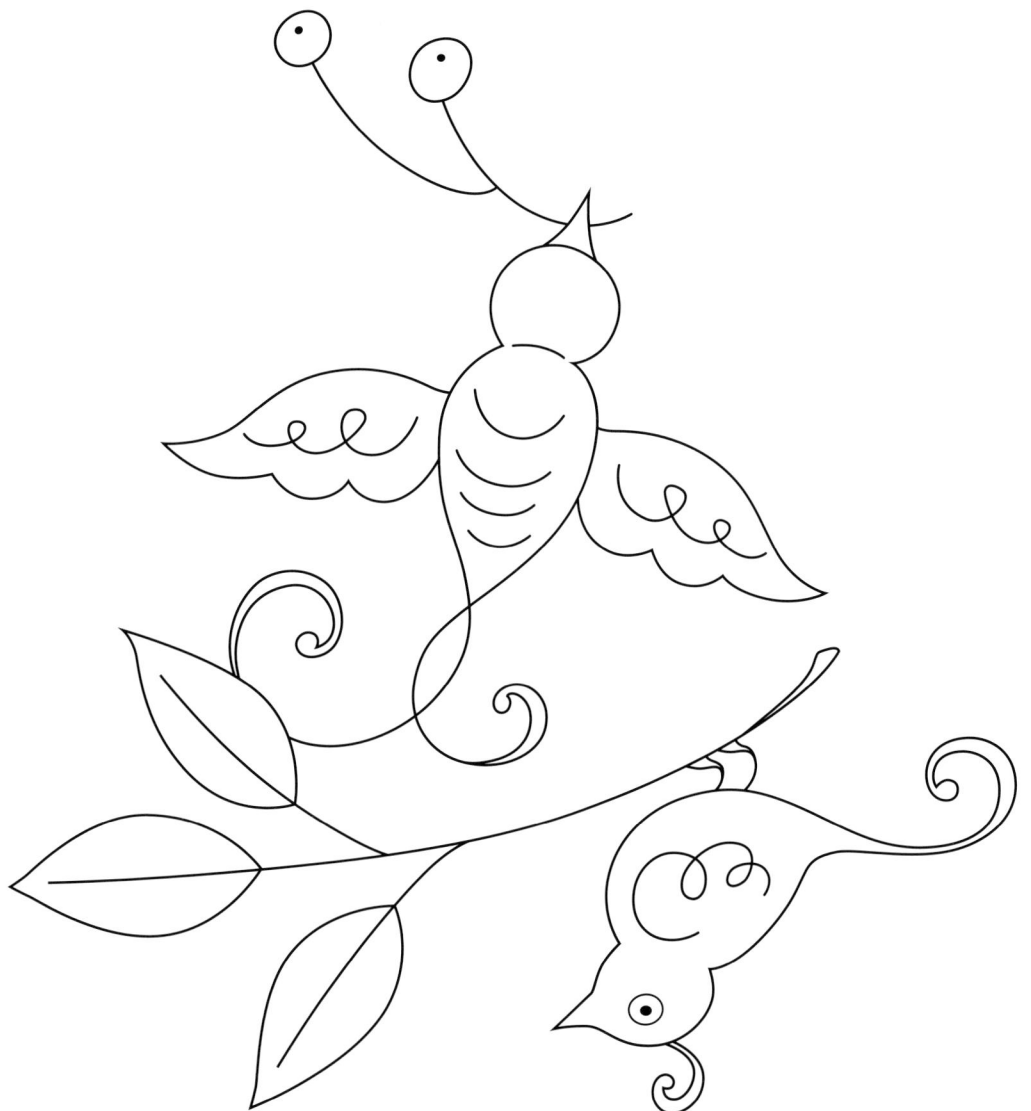

# SUPPLIES

## Fabric
12 x 12 inch (30x30cm)
ground fabric
12 x 12 inch (30x30cm)
backing fabric (optional)

## DMC six-stranded floss
| | | |
|---|---|---|
| ▦ | 677 | Metallic Sand |
| ▦ | 725 | Buttercup |
| ▦ | 742 | Clementine |
| ▦ | 921 | Tuscan Ochre |
| ☐ | B5200 | Pearlescent White Light |

## Needles
Embroidery: size 7 and 9
Milliner: size 9

## Optional Fabric Marker Colors
Yellow and Orange
See page 64 for color placement.

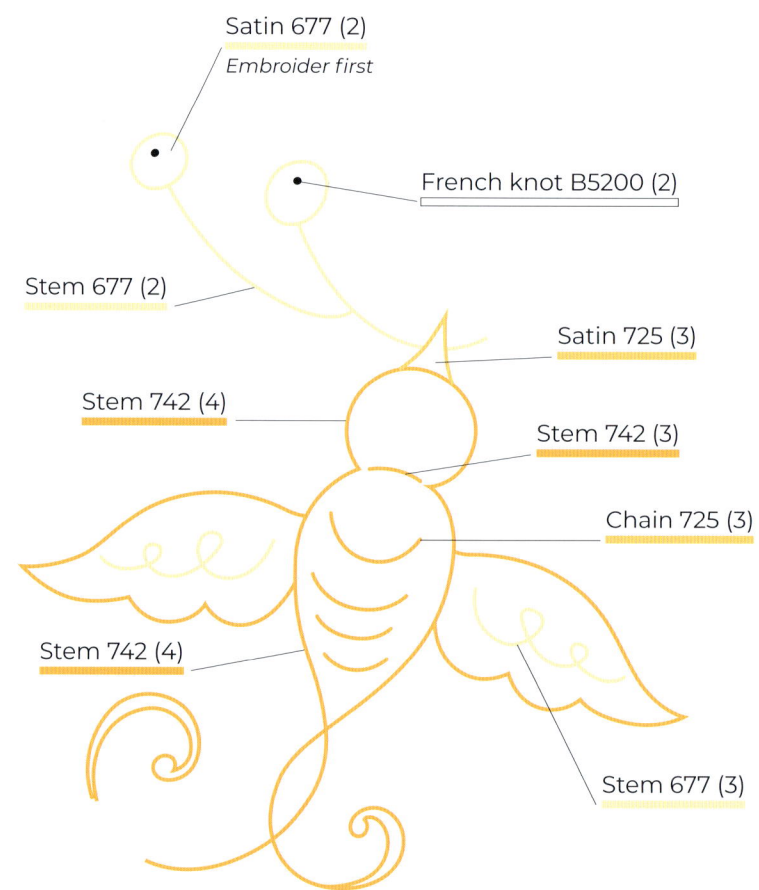

Satin 677 (2)
*Embroider first*

French knot B5200 (2)

Stem 677 (2)

Satin 725 (3)

Stem 742 (4)

Stem 742 (3)

Chain 725 (3)

Stem 742 (4)

Stem 677 (3)

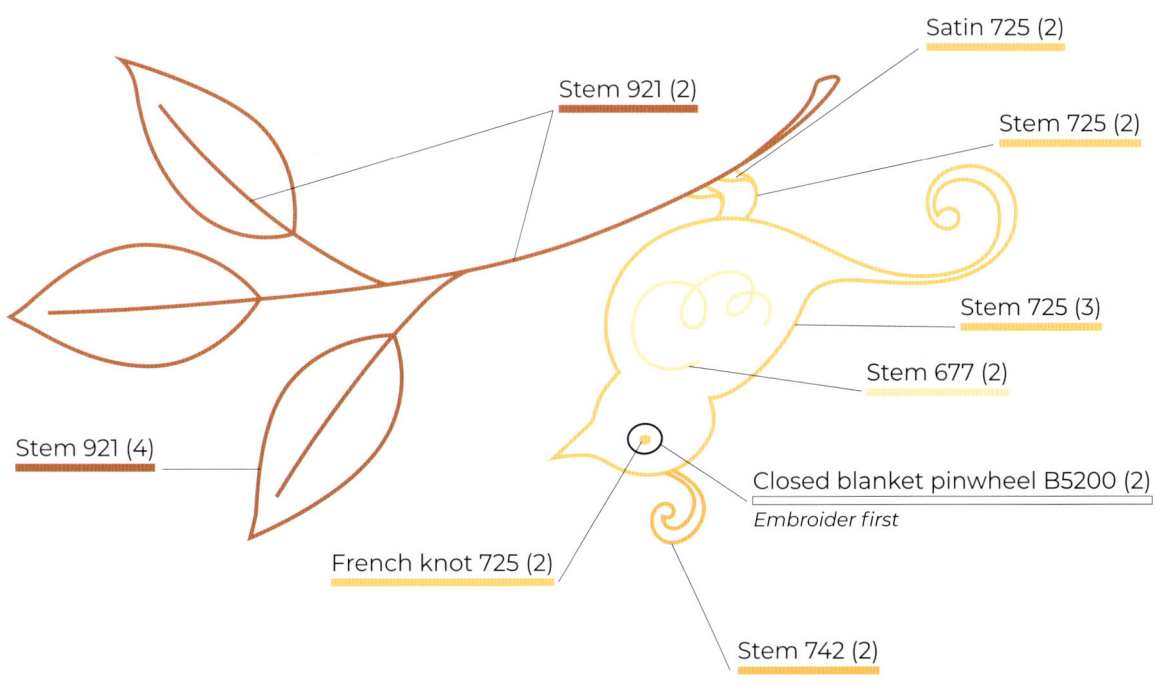

Satin 725 (2)

Stem 921 (2)

Stem 725 (2)

Stem 725 (3)

Stem 677 (2)

Closed blanket pinwheel B5200 (2)
*Embroider first*

Stem 921 (4)

French knot 725 (2)

Stem 742 (2)

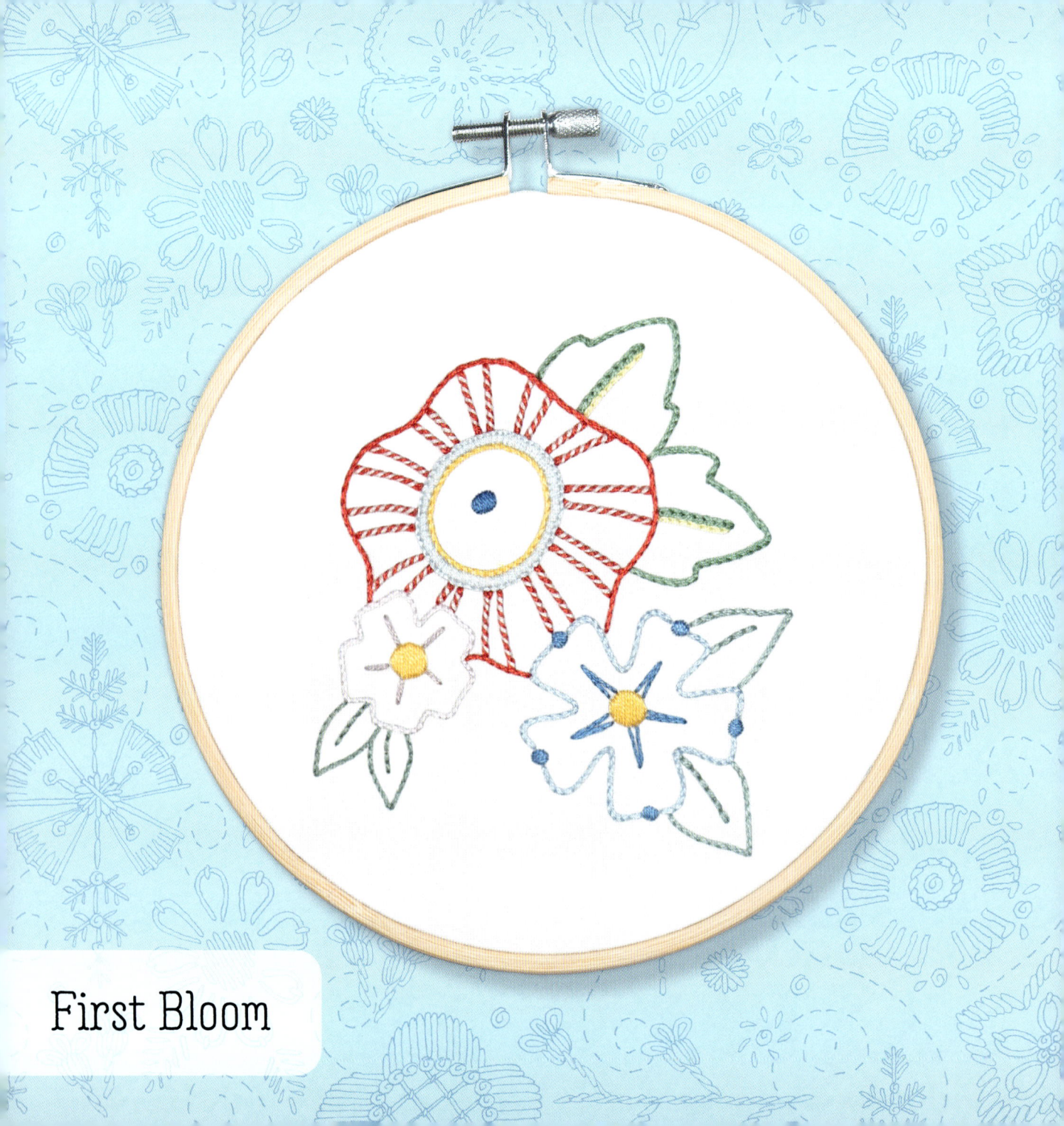

First Bloom

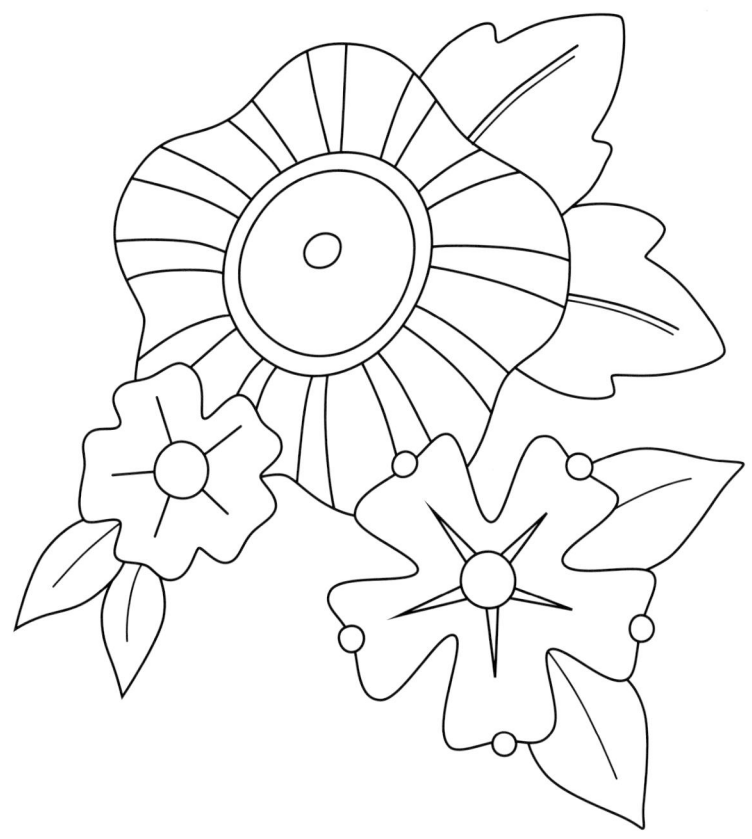

## SUPPLIES

### Fabric
12 x 12 inch (30x30cm)
ground fabric
12 x 12 inch (30x30cm)
backing fabric (optional)

### DMC six-stranded floss

| | | |
|---|---|---|
| | 11 | Lemon Drop |
| | 25 | Cornflower White |
| | 162 | Blue Water |
| | 326 | Rhubarb |
| | 502 | Almond Leaf |
| | 503 | Thyme Green |
| | 562 | Malachite |
| | 725 | Buttercup |
| | 825 | Metallic Gentian Blue |
| | 826 | Tuareg Blue |
| | 827 | Forget-Me-Knot |
| | 3042 | Silver Linings |
| | B5200 | Pearlescent White Light |

### Needles
Embroidery: size 7 and 9

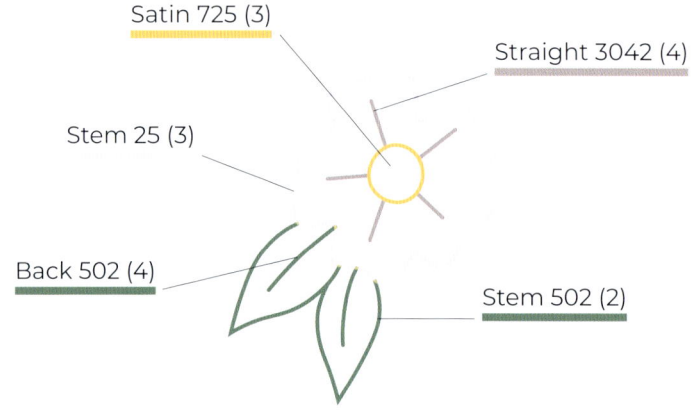

Satin 725 (3)

Straight 3042 (4)

Stem 25 (3)

Back 502 (4)

Stem 502 (2)

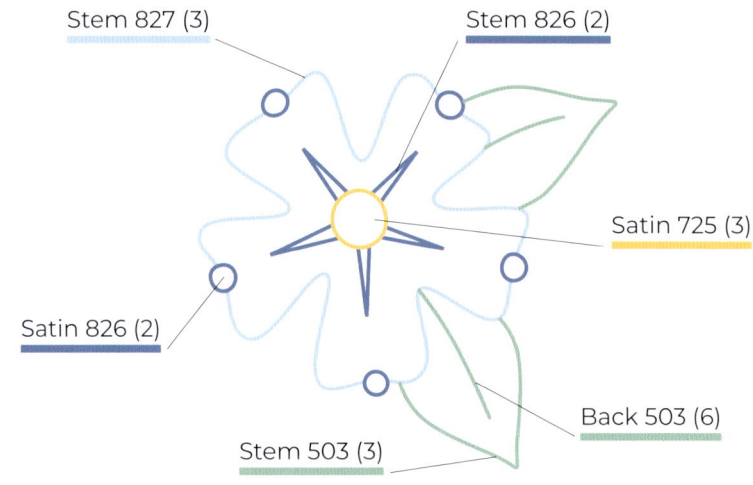

Stem 827 (3)

Stem 826 (2)

Satin 725 (3)

Satin 826 (2)

Back 503 (6)

Stem 503 (3)

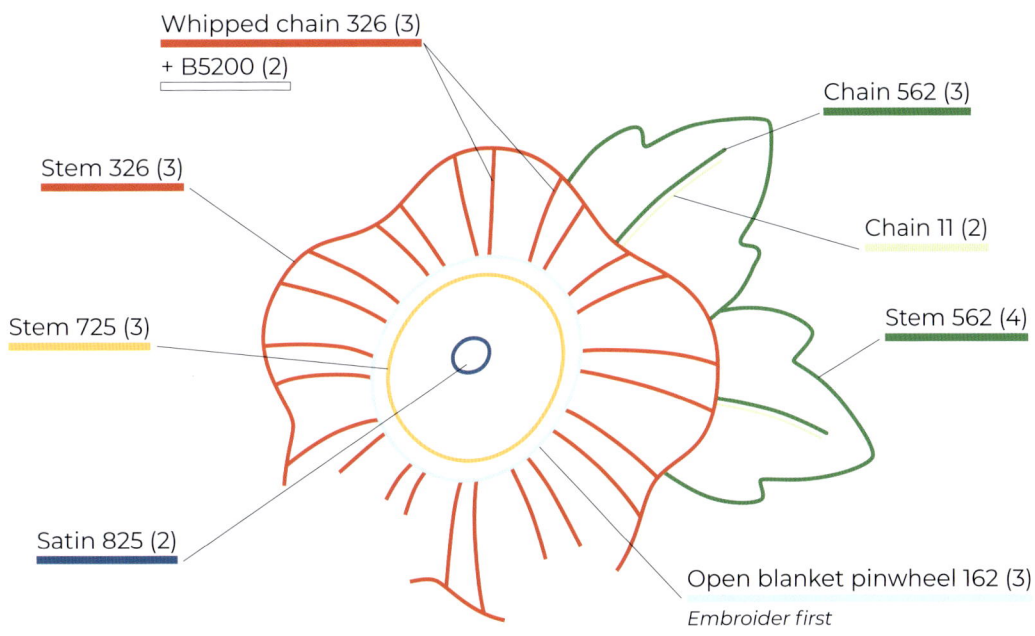

Whipped chain 326 (3)
+ B5200 (2)

Chain 562 (3)

Stem 326 (3)

Chain 11 (2)

Stem 725 (3)

Stem 562 (4)

Satin 825 (2)

Open blanket pinwheel 162 (3)
*Embroider first*

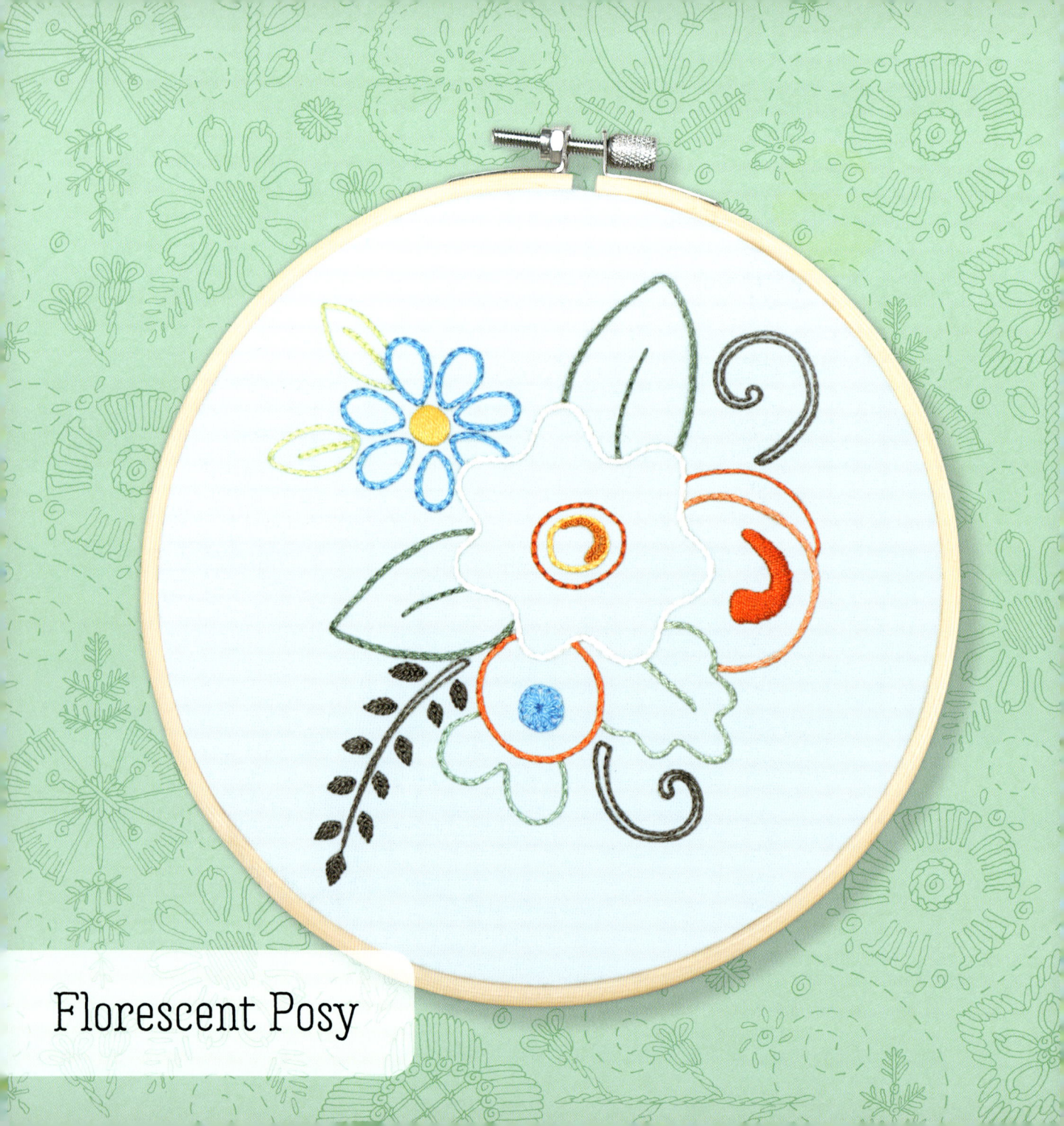

Florescent Posy

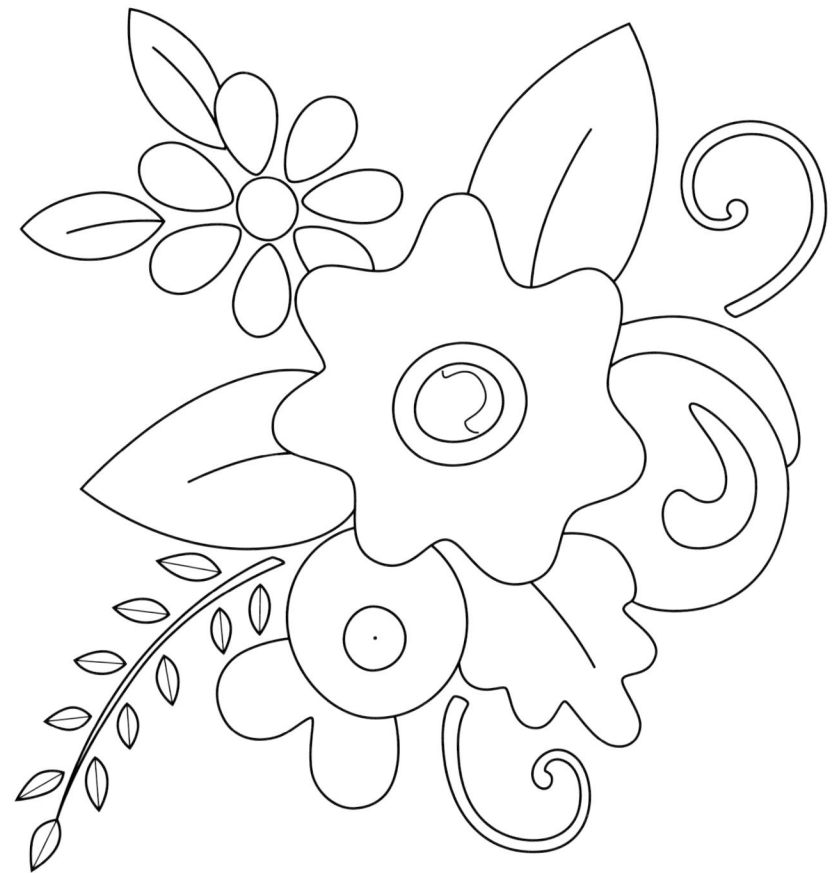

# SUPPLIES

## Fabric

12 x 12 inch (30x30cm)
ground fabric
12 x 12 inch (30x30cm)
backing fabric (optional)

## DMC six-stranded floss

| | | |
|---|---|---|
| ▨ | 15 | Spring Onion |
| ▨ | 350 | Vermillion |
| ▨ | 351 | Coral |
| ▨ | 352 | Salmon |
| ▨ | 502 | Almond Leaf |
| ▨ | 535 | Pebble |
| ▨ | 563 | Celedon |
| ▨ | 726 | Mimosa |
| ▨ | 966 | Pearlescent Soft Green |
| ▨ | 996 | Electric Blue |
| ▨ | 3853 | Copper |
| ☐ | 3865 | Edelweiss |

## Needles

Embroidery: size 7 and 9
Milliner: size 9

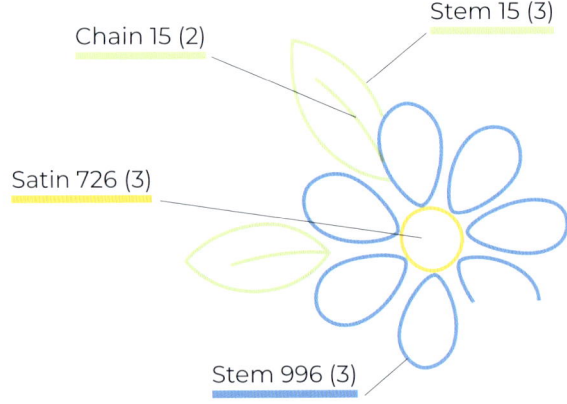

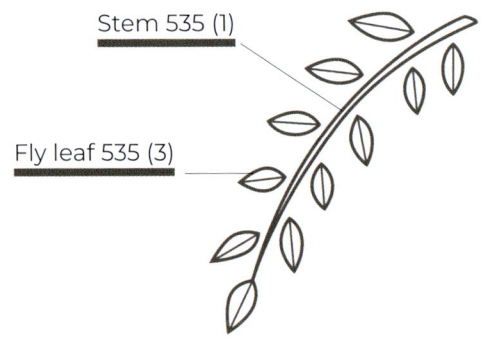

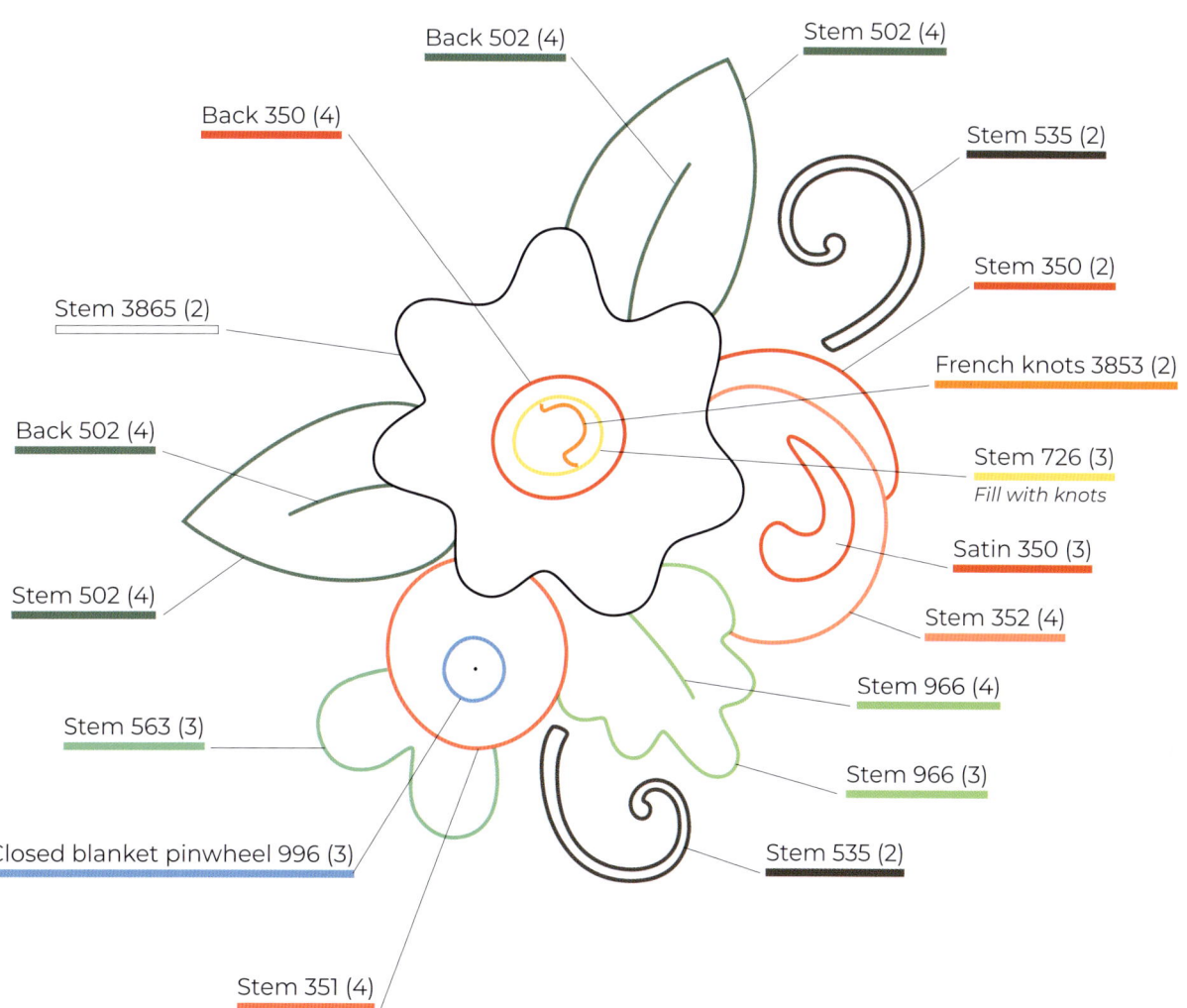

Back 502 (4)

Stem 502 (4)

Back 350 (4)

Stem 535 (2)

Stem 350 (2)

Stem 3865 (2)

French knots 3853 (2)

Back 502 (4)

Stem 726 (3)
*Fill with knots*

Satin 350 (3)

Stem 502 (4)

Stem 352 (4)

Stem 966 (4)

Stem 563 (3)

Stem 966 (3)

Closed blanket pinwheel 996 (3)

Stem 535 (2)

Stem 351 (4)

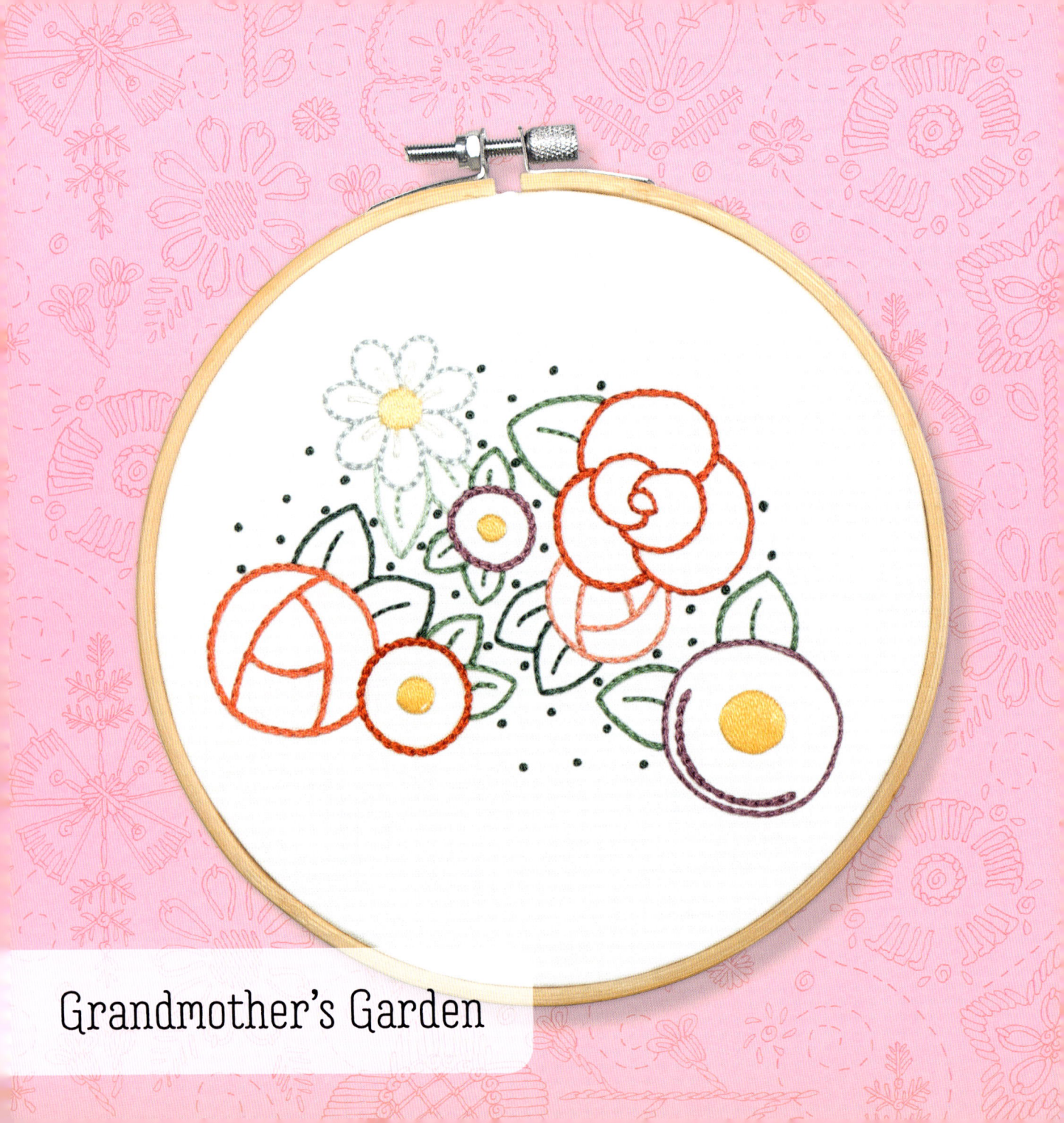

Grandmother's Garden

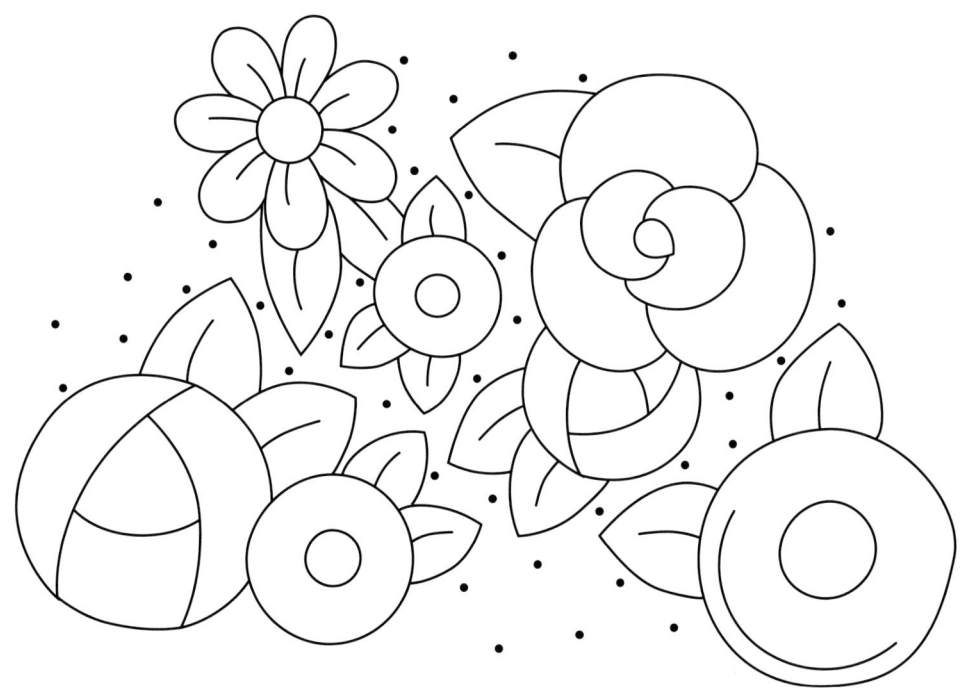

# SUPPLIES

## Fabric

12 x 12 inch (30x30cm)
ground fabric
12 x 12 inch (30x30cm)
backing fabric (optional)

## DMC six-stranded floss

| | | |
|---|---|---|
| ■ | 347 | Egyptian Red |
| ■ | 561 | Cypress Green |
| ■ | 562 | Malachite |
| ■ | 564 | Light Malachite |
| ■ | 744 | Grapefruit |
| ■ | 743 | Banana |
| | 775 | Blue Summer Rain |
| ■ | 3831 | Wild Strawberry |
| ■ | 3832 | Strawberry |
| ■ | 3833 | Strawberry Sorbet |
| ■ | 3835 | Purple Violet |
| ☐ | B5200 | Pearlescent White Light |

## Needles

Embroidery: size 7 and 9
Milliner: size 7 and 9

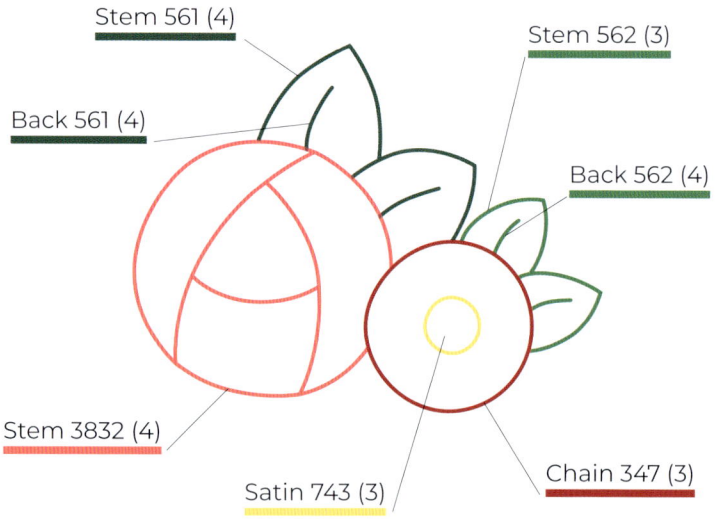

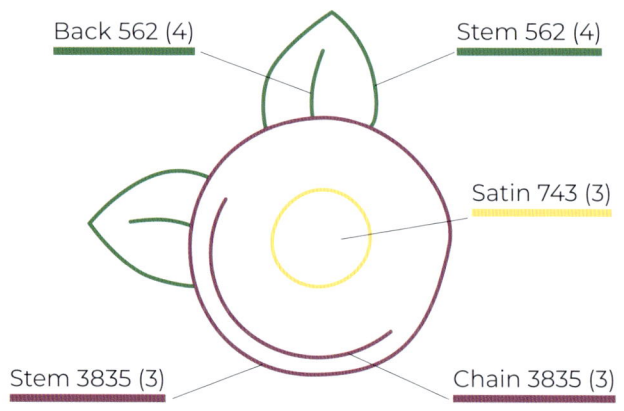

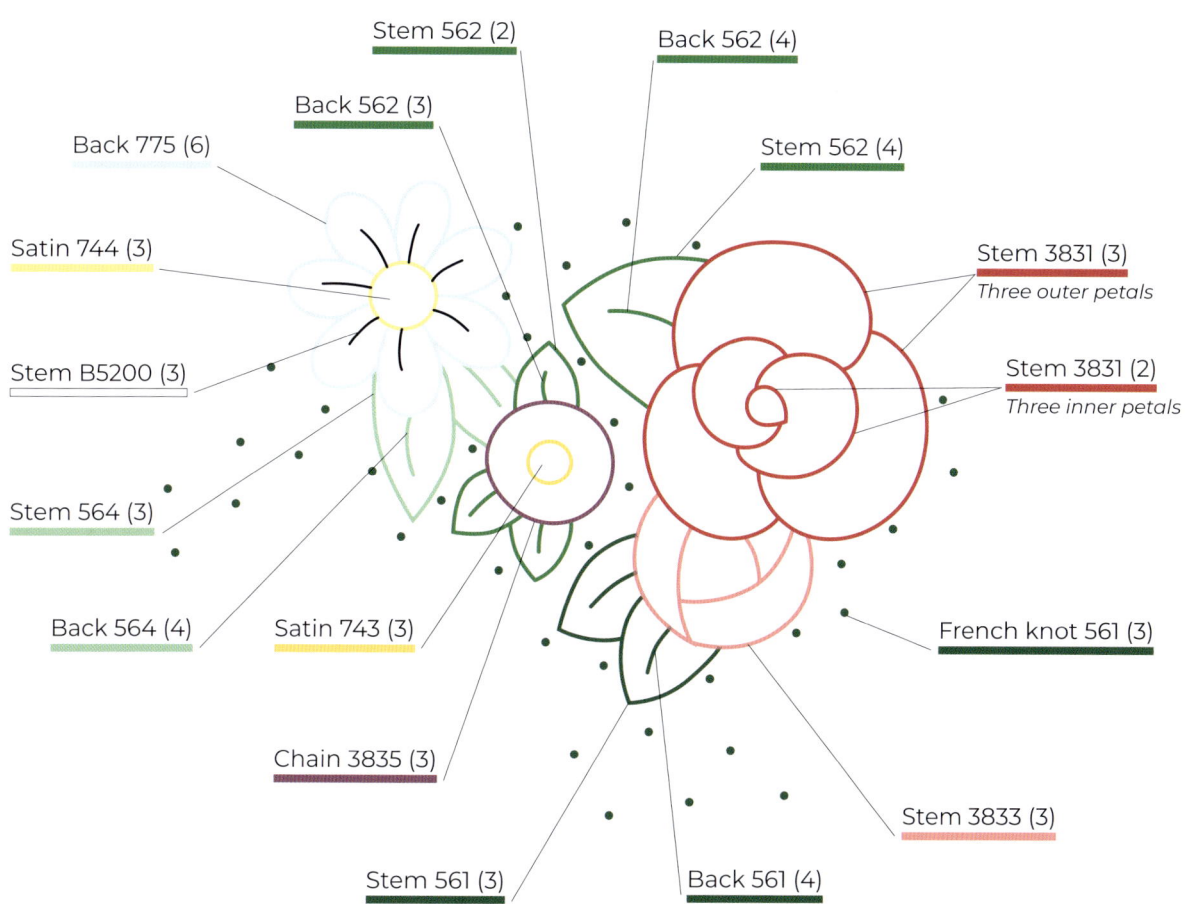

Stem 562 (2)

Back 562 (3)

Back 562 (4)

Back 775 (6)

Stem 562 (4)

Satin 744 (3)

Stem 3831 (3)
*Three outer petals*

Stem B5200 (3)

Stem 3831 (2)
*Three inner petals*

Stem 564 (3)

Back 564 (4)

Satin 743 (3)

French knot 561 (3)

Chain 3835 (3)

Stem 3833 (3)

Stem 561 (3)

Back 561 (4)

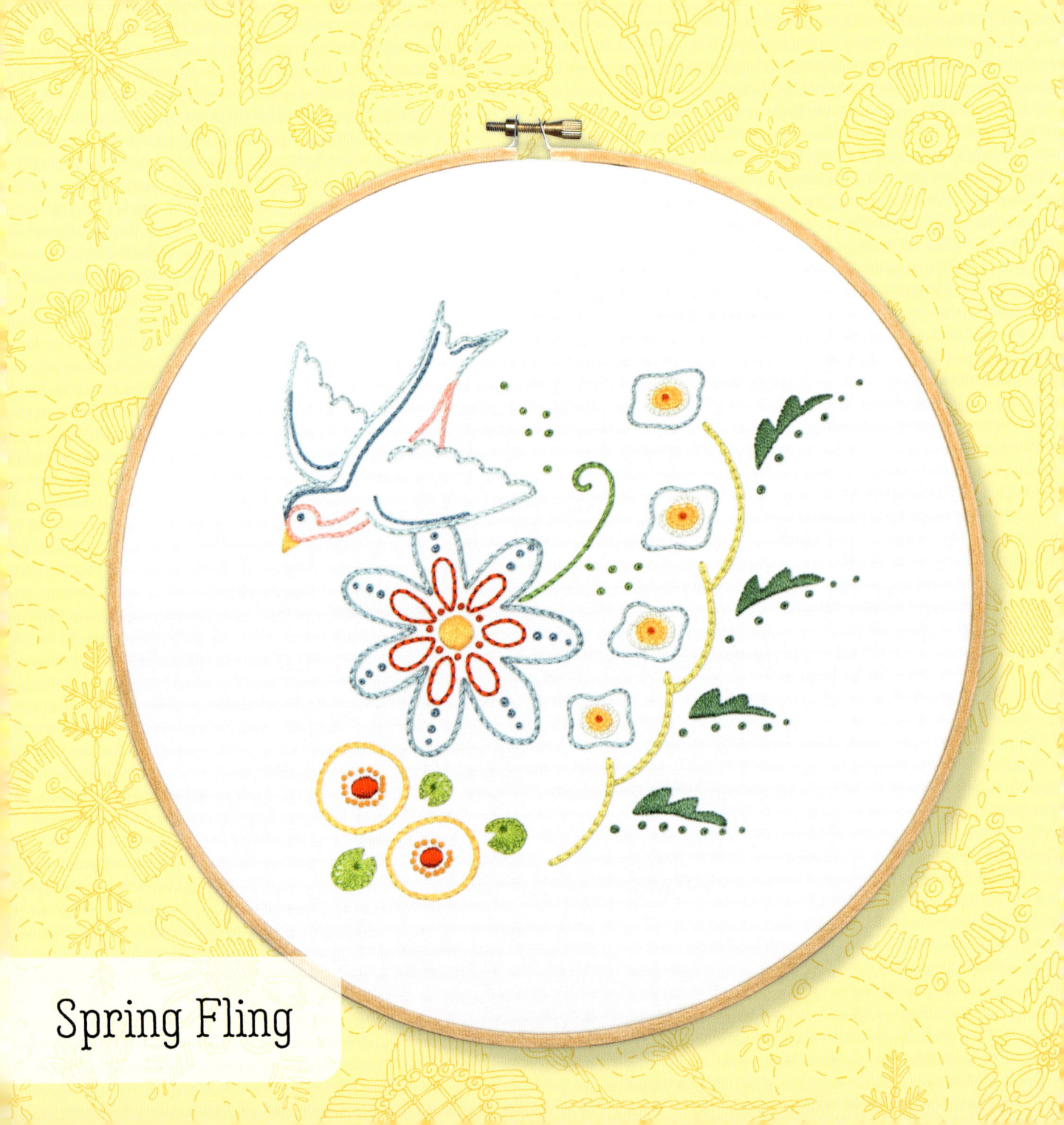

Spring Fling

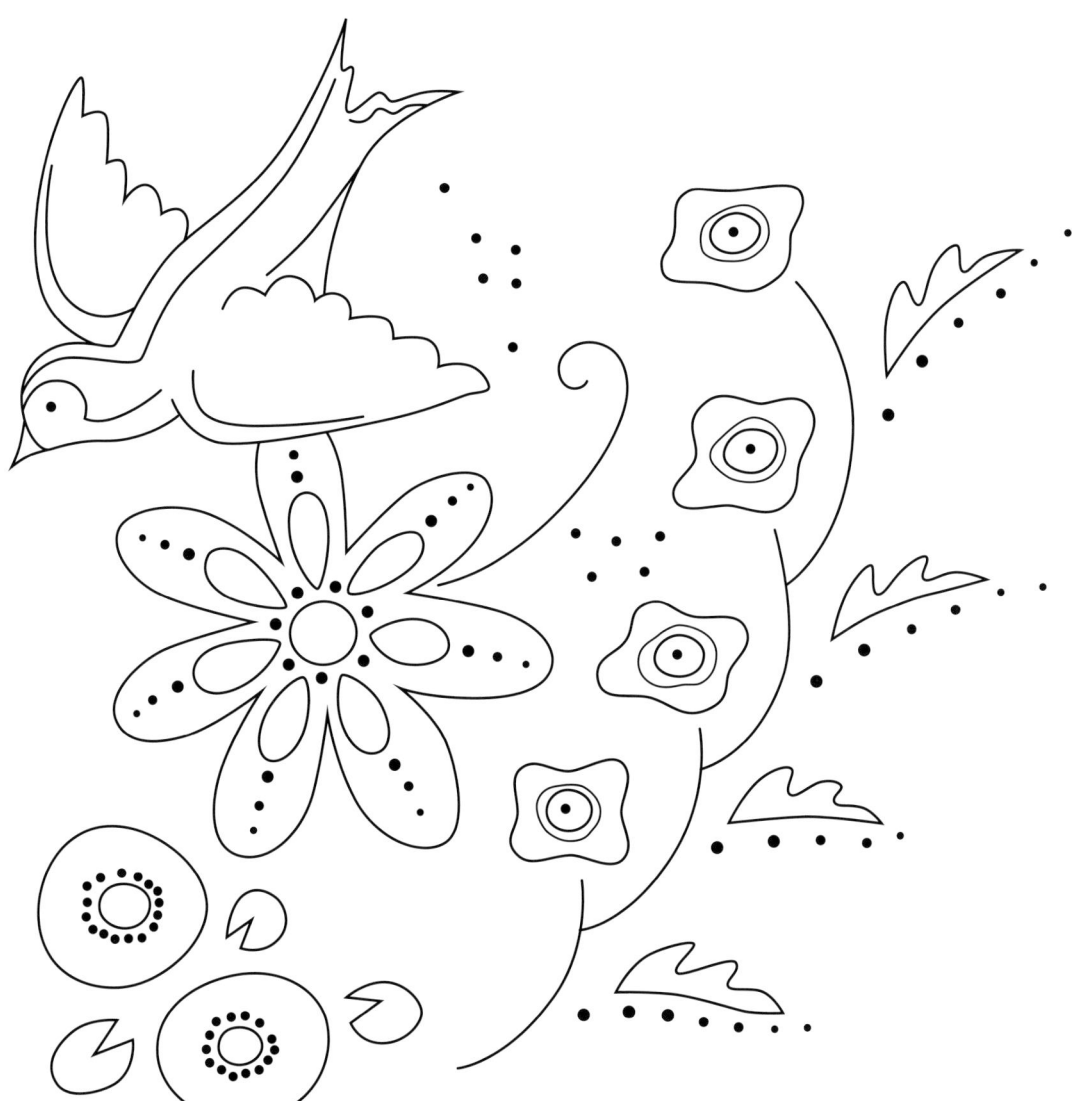

# SUPPLIES

## Fabric

12 x 12 inch (30x30cm)
ground fabric
12 x 12 inch (30x30cm)
backing fabric (optional)

## DMC six-stranded floss

| | | |
|---|---|---|
| 12 | Citrus Yellow |
| 349 | Red Pepper |
| 562 | Malachite |
| 597 | Pack Ice Blue |
| 598 | Pale Lagoon |
| 703 | Metallic Spring Green |
| 726 | Mimosa |
| 742 | Clementine |
| 907 | Granny Smith |
| 957 | Bubblegum Pink |
| 3810 | Persian Blue |
| 3811 | Blue Waterfall |
| B5200 | Pearlescent White Light |

## Needles

Embroidery: size 7 and 9
Milliner: size 7 and 9

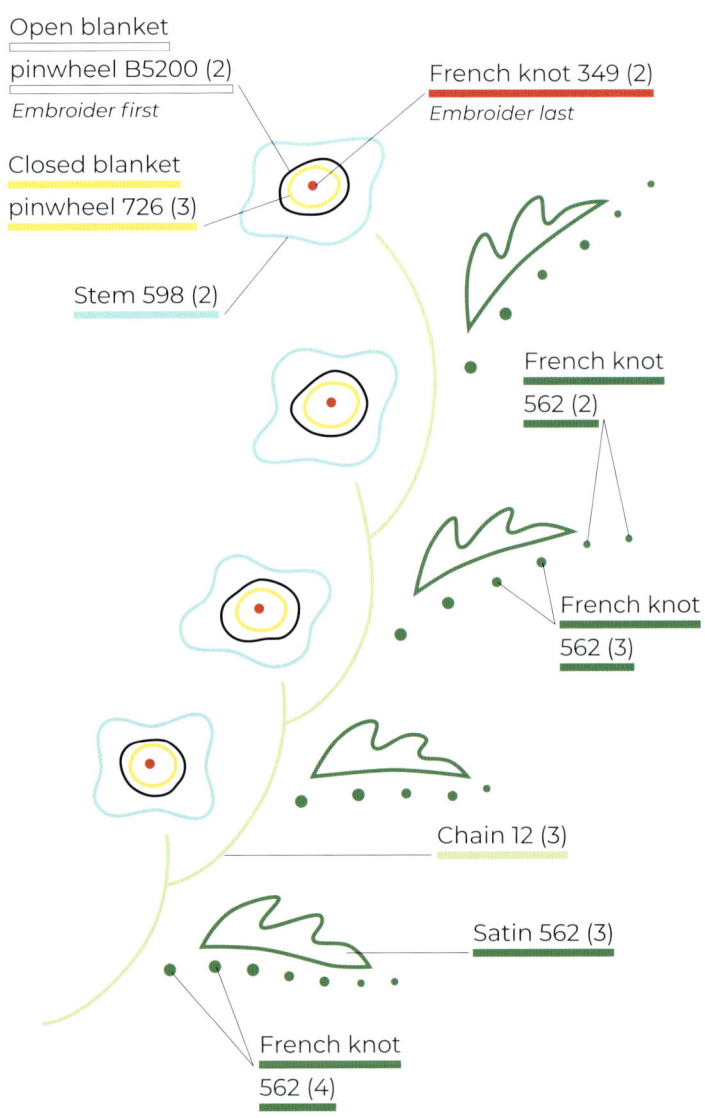

Open blanket
pinwheel B5200 (2)
*Embroider first*

French knot 349 (2)
*Embroider last*

Closed blanket
pinwheel 726 (3)

Stem 598 (2)

French knot
562 (2)

French knot
562 (3)

Chain 12 (3)

Satin 562 (3)

French knot
562 (4)

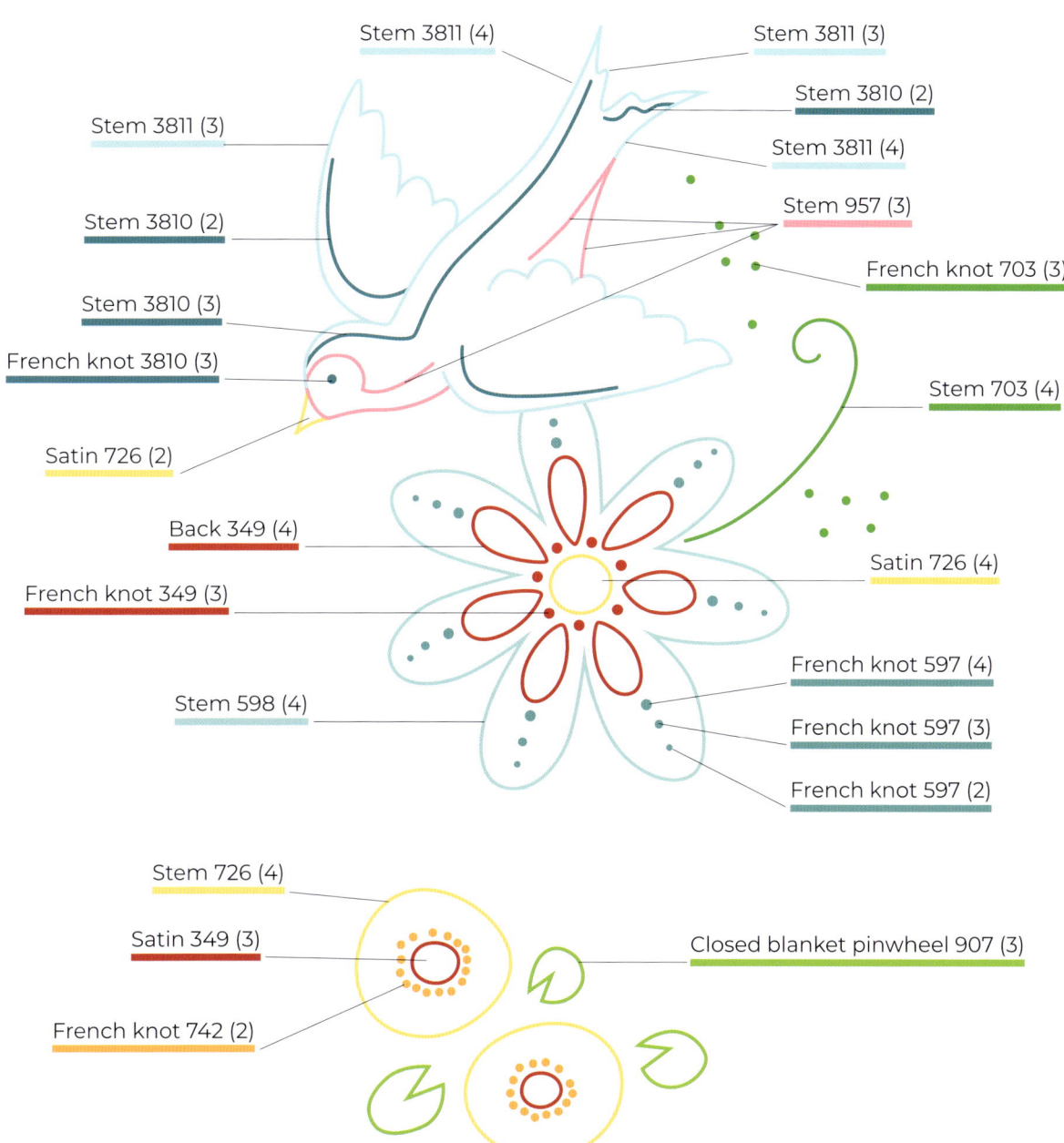

Stem 3811 (4)

Stem 3811 (3)

Stem 3810 (2)

Stem 3811 (3)

Stem 3811 (4)

Stem 3810 (2)

Stem 957 (3)

Stem 3810 (3)

French knot 703 (3)

French knot 3810 (3)

Stem 703 (4)

Satin 726 (2)

Back 349 (4)

Satin 726 (4)

French knot 349 (3)

French knot 597 (4)

French knot 597 (3)

Stem 598 (4)

French knot 597 (2)

Stem 726 (4)

Satin 349 (3)

Closed blanket pinwheel 907 (3)

French knot 742 (2)

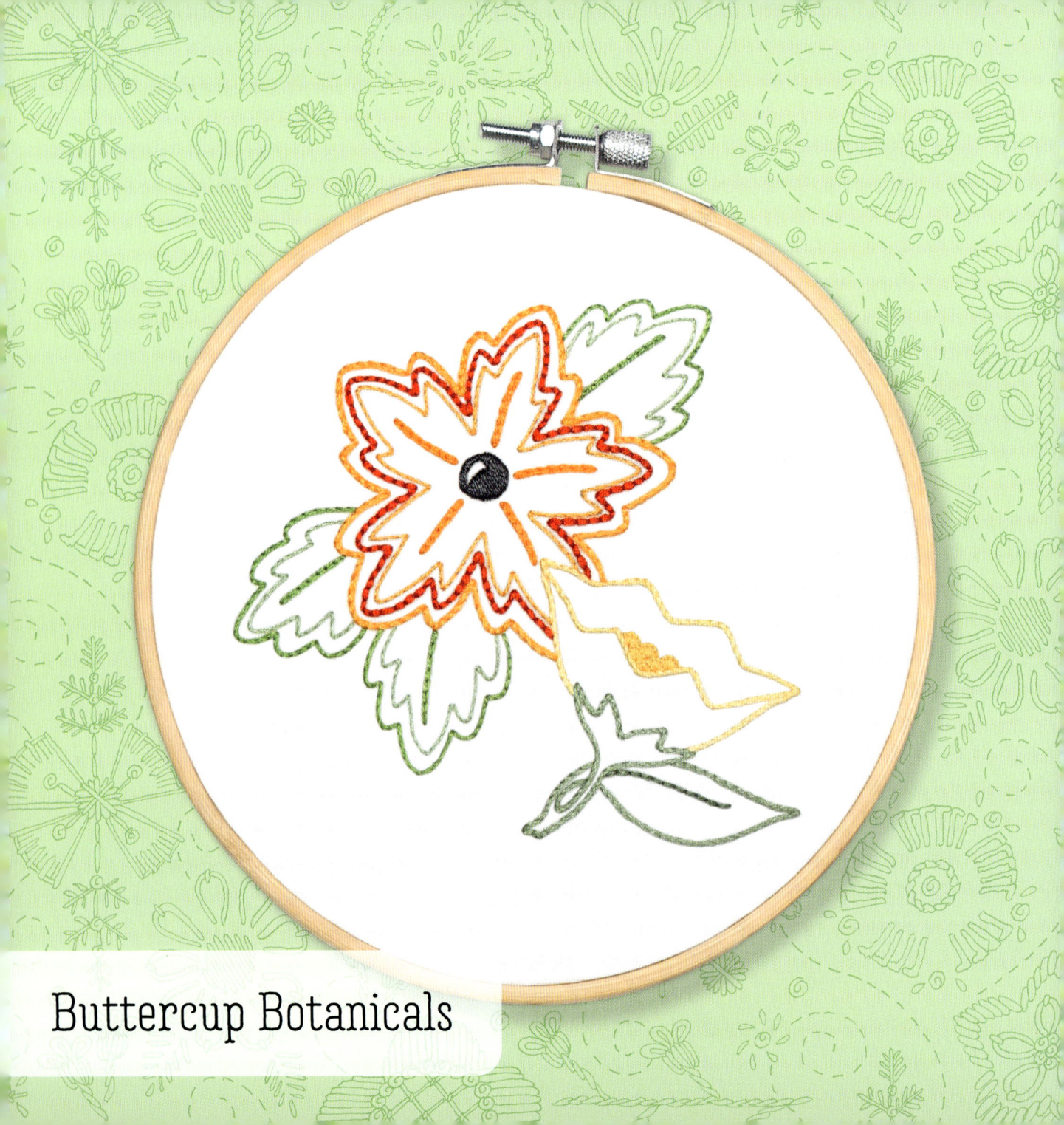

Buttercup Botanicals

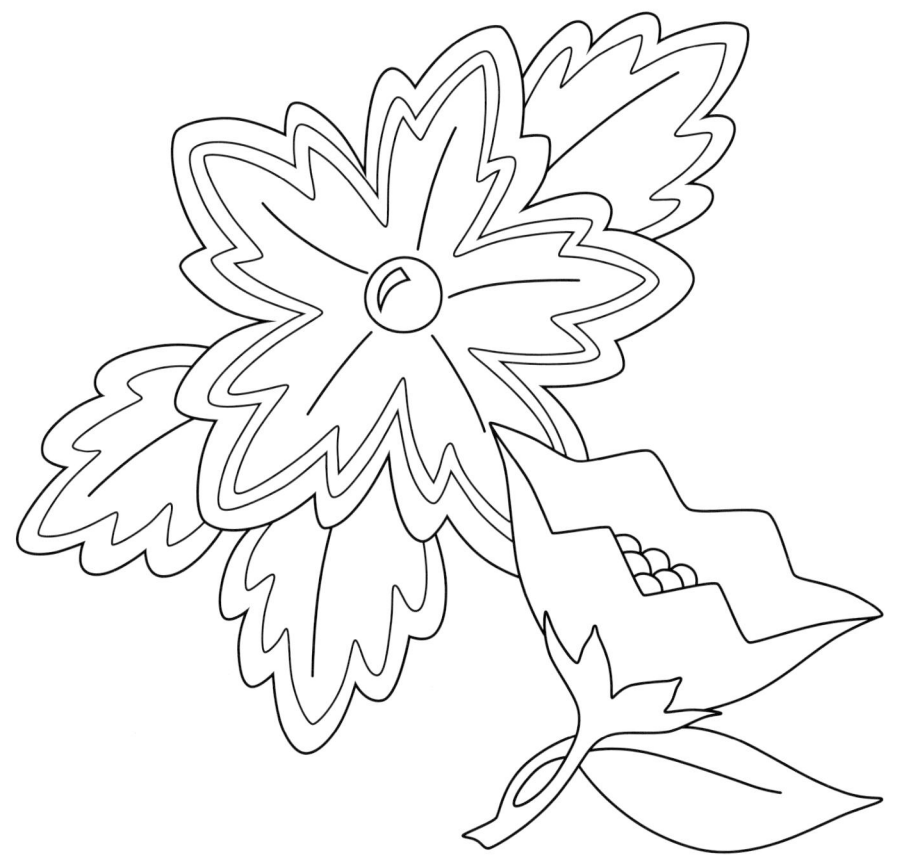

# SUPPLIES

## Fabric
12 x 12 inch (30x30cm)
ground fabric
12 x 12 inch (30x30cm)
backing fabric (optional)

## DMC six-stranded floss
- 164     Pistachio
- 320     Fern
- 349     Red Pepper
- 368     Eau de Nile
- 413     Iron
- 703     Metallic Spring Green
- 726     Mimosa
- 727     Primrose
- 741     Mandarin
- 742     Clementine

## Needles
Embroidery: size 7 and 9

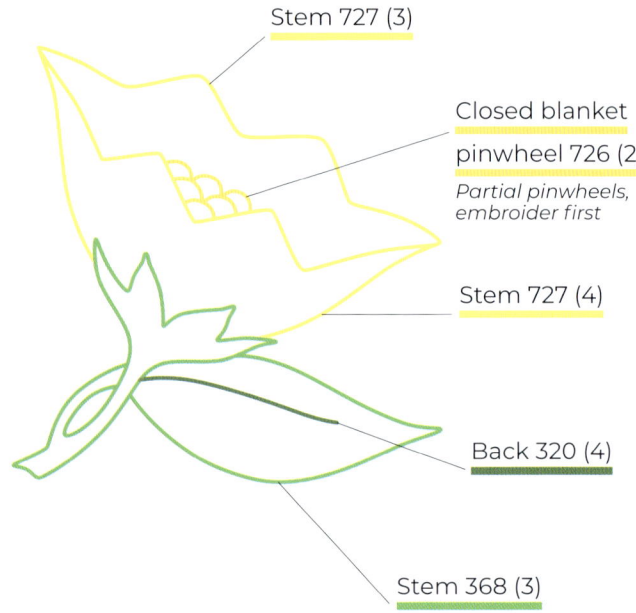

Stem 727 (3)

Closed blanket
pinwheel 726 (2)
*Partial pinwheels,
embroider first*

Stem 727 (4)

Back 320 (4)

Stem 368 (3)

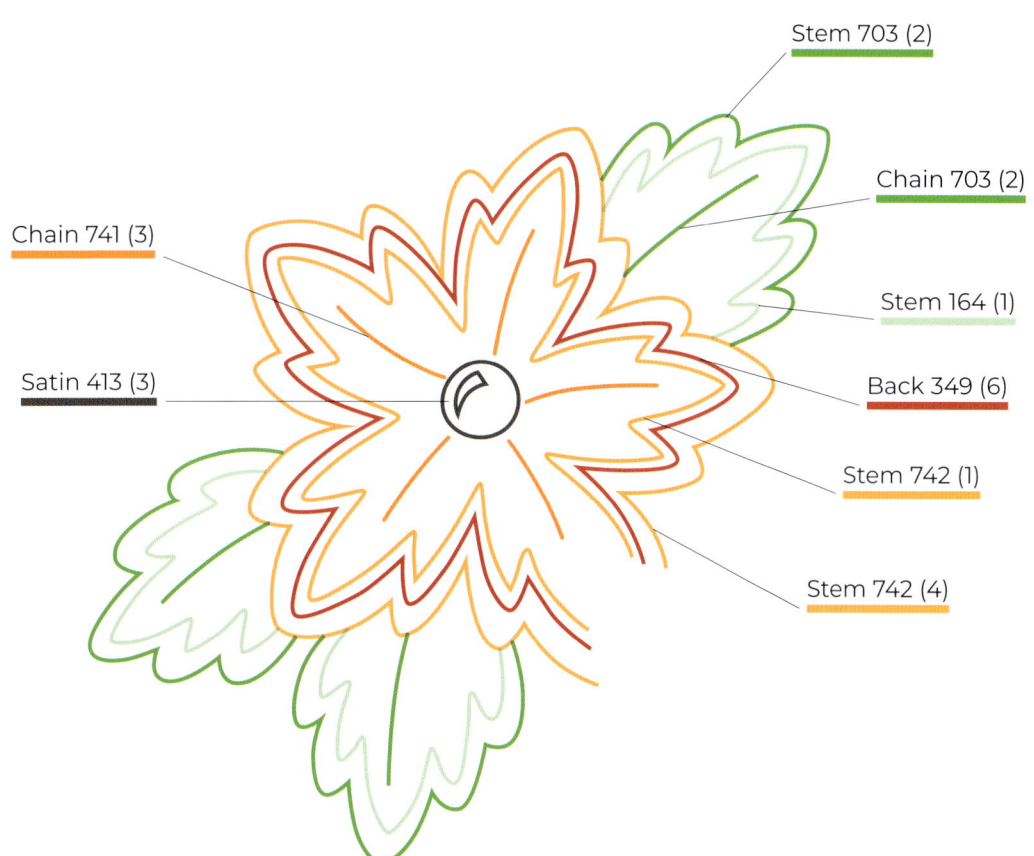

Stem 703 (2)

Chain 703 (2)

Stem 164 (1)

Back 349 (6)

Stem 742 (1)

Stem 742 (4)

Chain 741 (3)

Satin 413 (3)

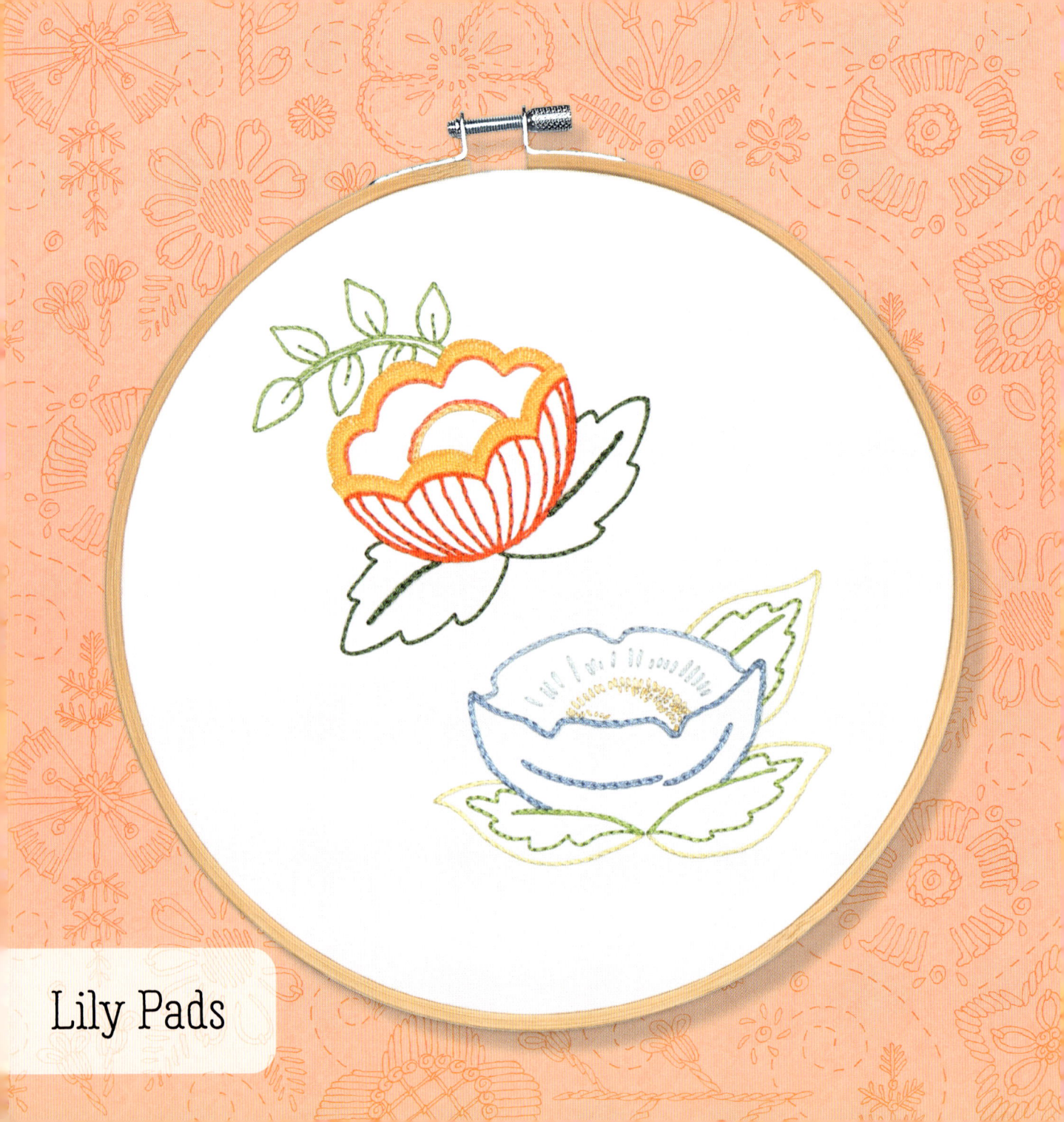

Lily Pads

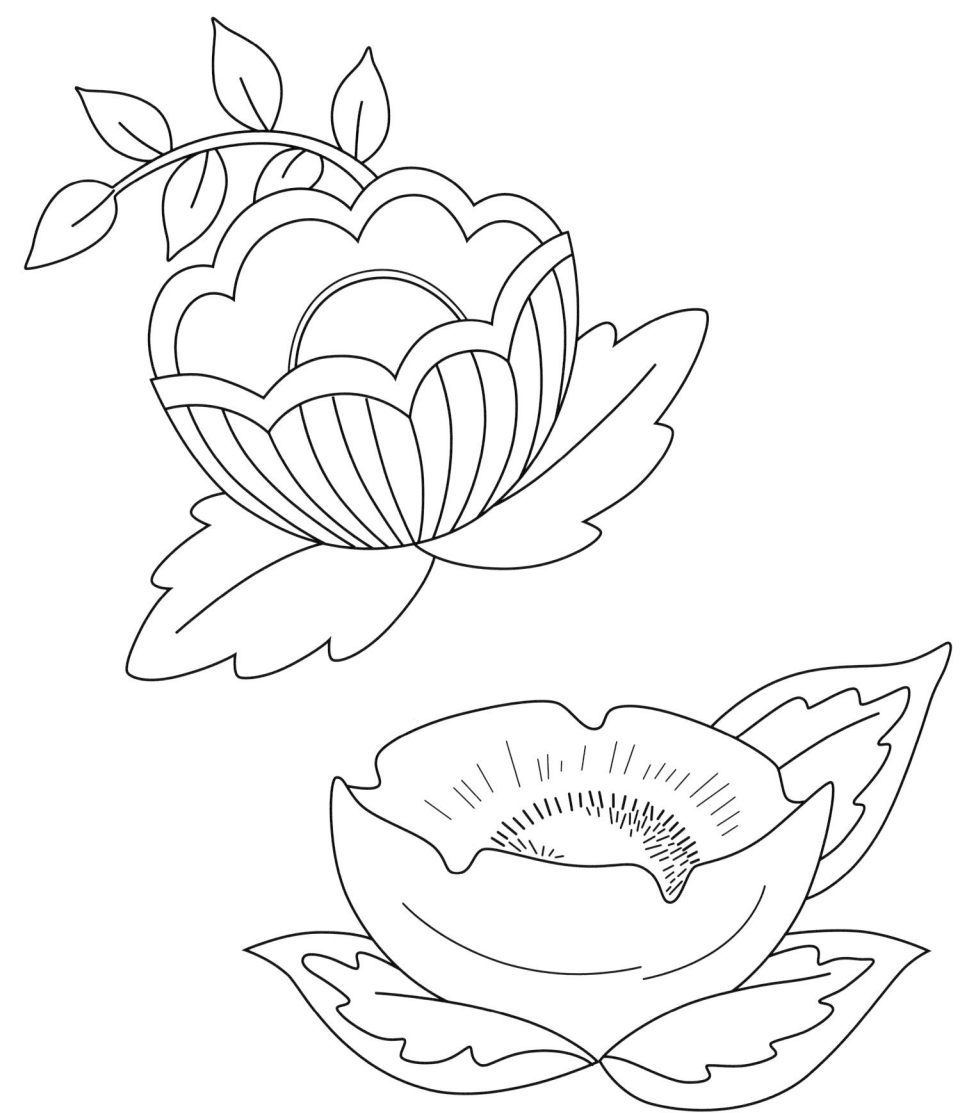

# SUPPLIES

## Fabric
12 x 12 inch (30x30cm)
ground fabric
12 x 12 inch (30x30cm)
backing fabric (optional)

## DMC six-stranded floss

| | | |
|---|---|---|
| 11 | Lemon Drop |
| 704 | Lime |
| 743 | Banana |
| 744 | Grapefruit |
| 891 | Geranium |
| 893 | Dahlia |
| 987 | Basil |
| 3325 | Arctic Blue |
| 3755 | Pastel Blue |
| 3841 | Igloo Blue |

## Needles
Embroidery: size 7 and 9

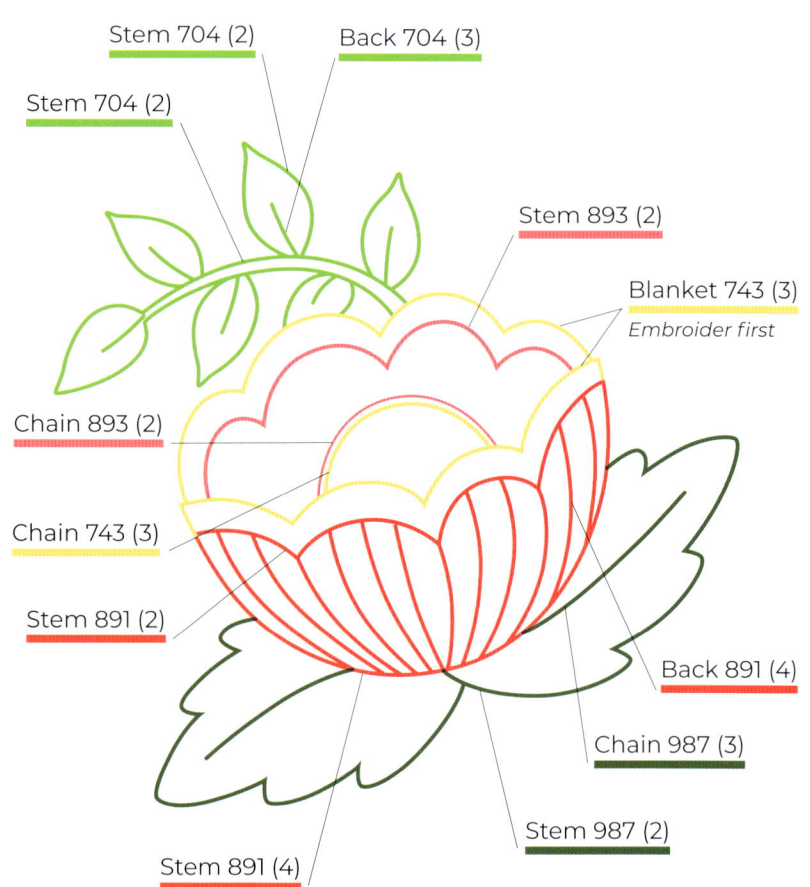

Stem 704 (2)

Stem 704 (2)

Back 704 (3)

Stem 893 (2)

Blanket 743 (3)
*Embroider first*

Chain 893 (2)

Chain 743 (3)

Stem 891 (2)

Back 891 (4)

Chain 987 (3)

Stem 987 (2)

Stem 891 (4)

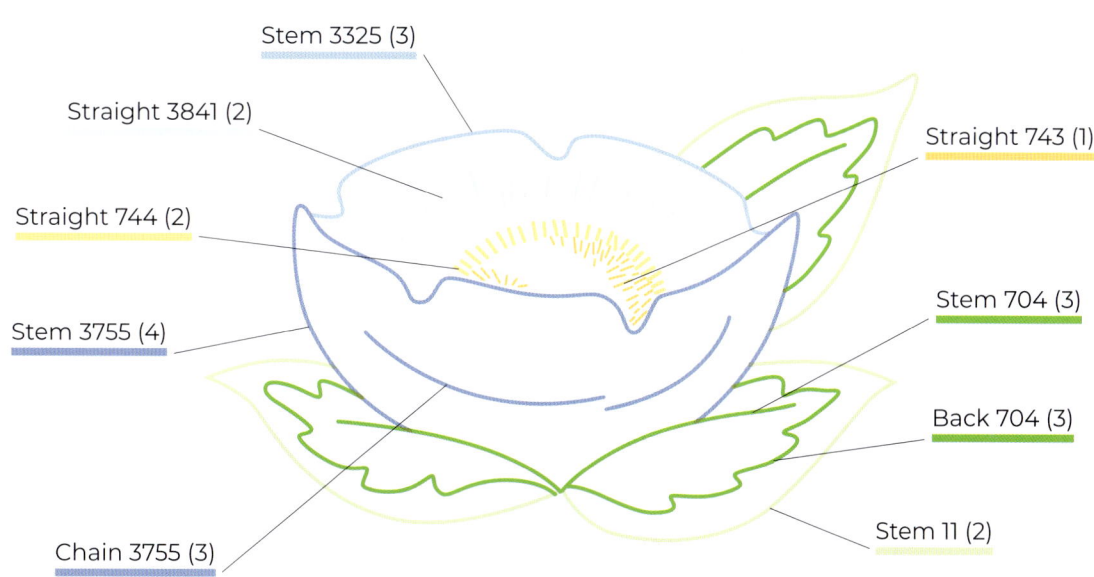

Stem 3325 (3)

Straight 3841 (2)

Straight 744 (2)

Stem 3755 (4)

Chain 3755 (3)

Straight 743 (1)

Stem 704 (3)

Back 704 (3)

Stem 11 (2)

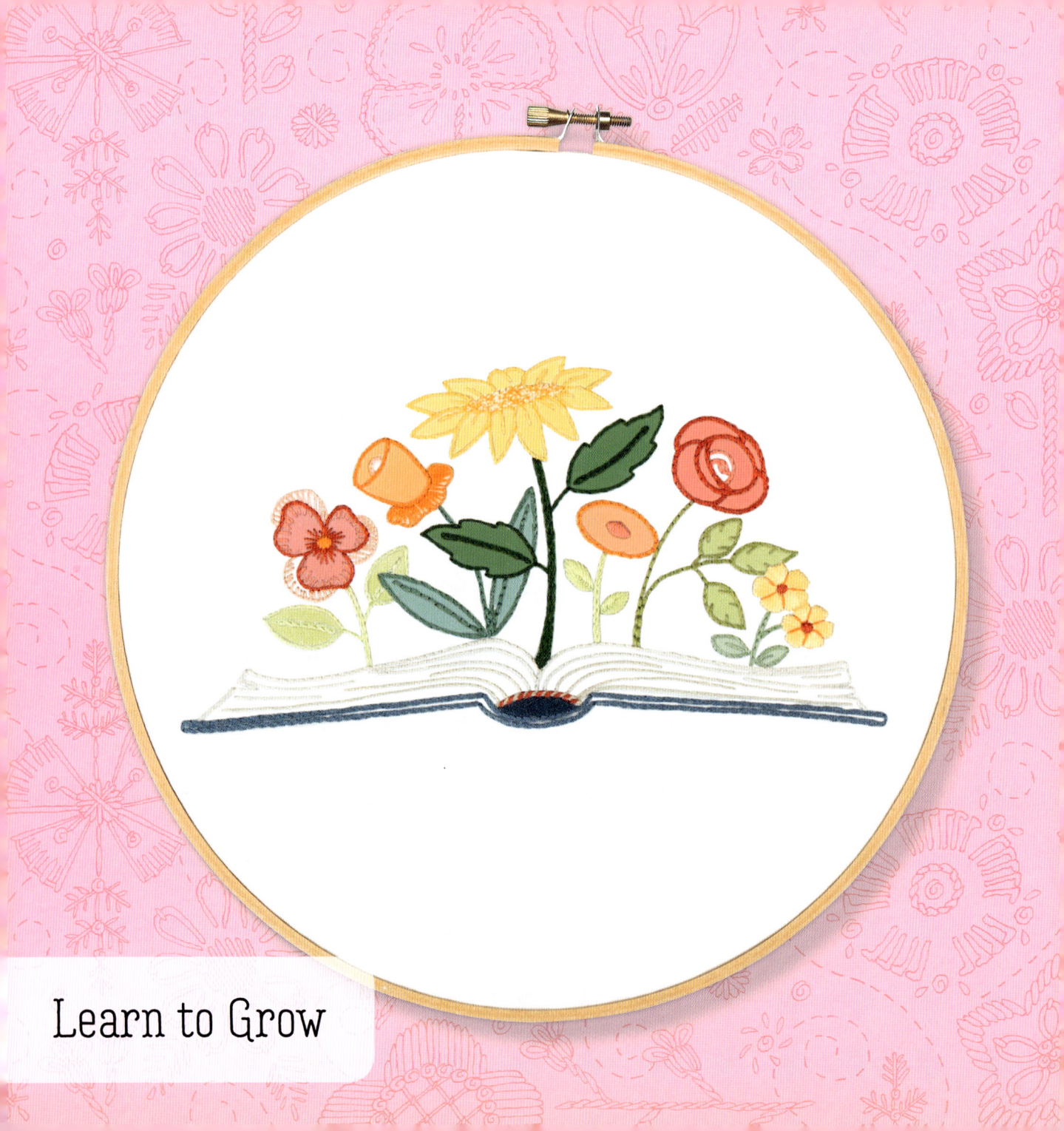

Learn to Grow

# SUPPLIES

## Fabric
12 x 12 inch (30x30cm)
ground fabric
12 x 12 inch (30x30cm)
backing fabric (optional)

## DMC six-stranded floss

| | | |
|---|---|---|
| | 15 | Spring Onion |
| | 163 | Eucalyptus |
| | 368 | Eau de Nile |
| | 471 | Tarragon |
| | 613 | Twine |
| | 742 | Clementine |
| | 743 | Banana |
| | 744 | Grapefruit |
| | 930 | Slate Grey |
| | 931 | Blue Grey |
| | 986 | Boxwood |
| | 3779 | Burnished Pink |
| | 3831 | Wild Strawberry |
| | 3833 | Strawberry Sorbet |
| | 3853 | Copper |
| | 3866 | Garlic White |
| | B5200 | Pearlescent White Light |

## Needles
Embroidery: size 7 and 9
Milliner: size 9

## Optional Fabric Marker Colors
Yellow, Orange, Red, and Greens
See page 92 for color placement.

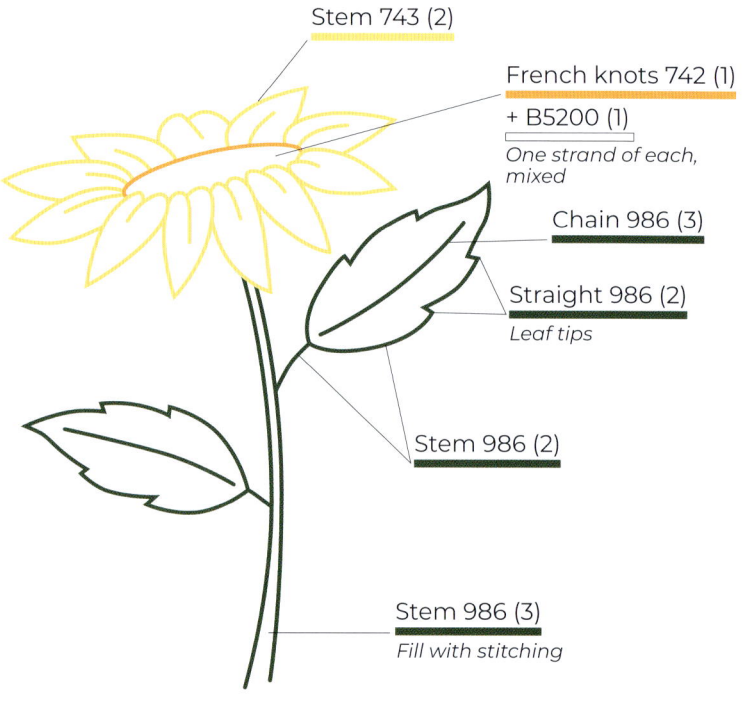

Stem 743 (2)

French knots 742 (1)
+ B5200 (1)
*One strand of each, mixed*

Chain 986 (3)

Straight 986 (2)
*Leaf tips*

Stem 986 (2)

Stem 986 (3)
*Fill with stitching*

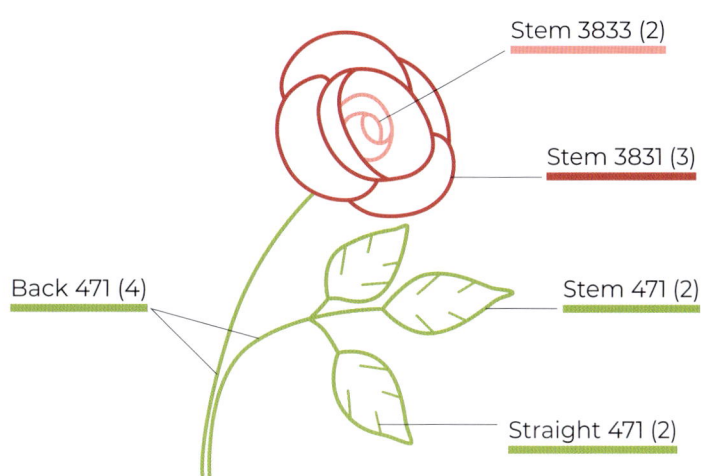

Stem 3833 (2)

Stem 3831 (3)

Back 471 (4)

Stem 471 (2)

Straight 471 (2)

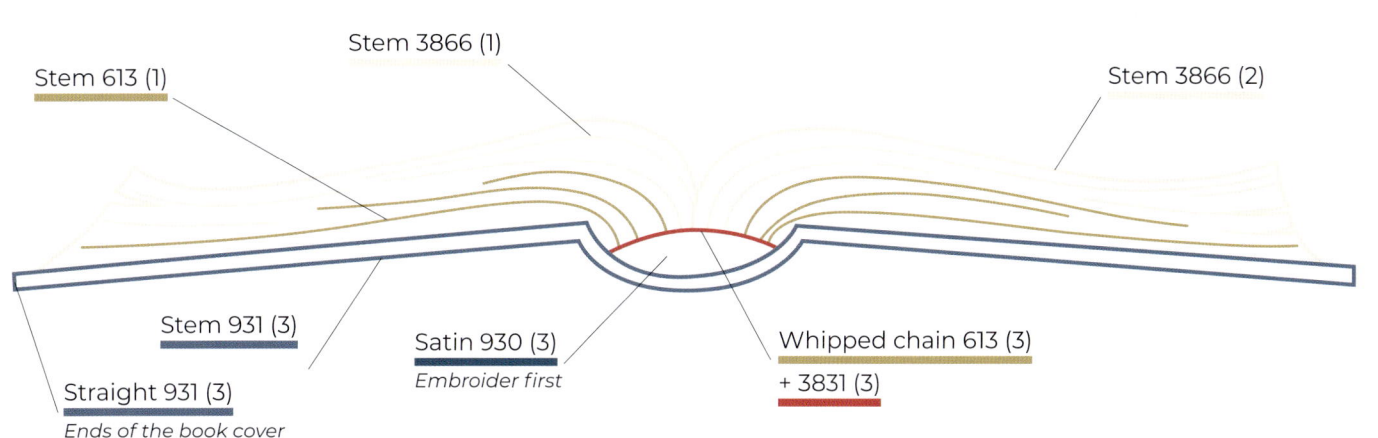

Stem 3866 (1)

Stem 613 (1)

Stem 3866 (2)

Stem 931 (3)

Satin 930 (3)
*Embroider first*

Whipped chain 613 (3)
+ 3831 (3)

Straight 931 (3)
*Ends of the book cover*

Chain 3853 (2)

Satin 3833 (2)

Fly leaf 15 (2)

Stem 15 (2)

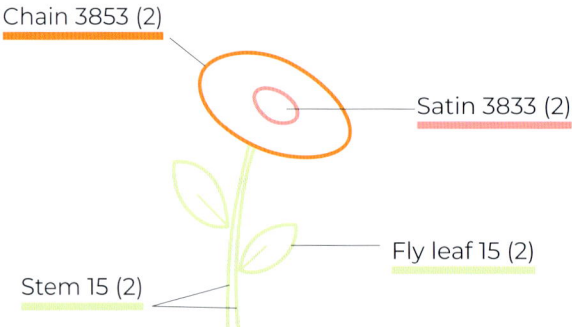

Chain 3779 (2)

Stem 3853 (2)

Blanket 3853 (2)

Chain 163 (2)

Back 163 (6)

Stem 163 (3)

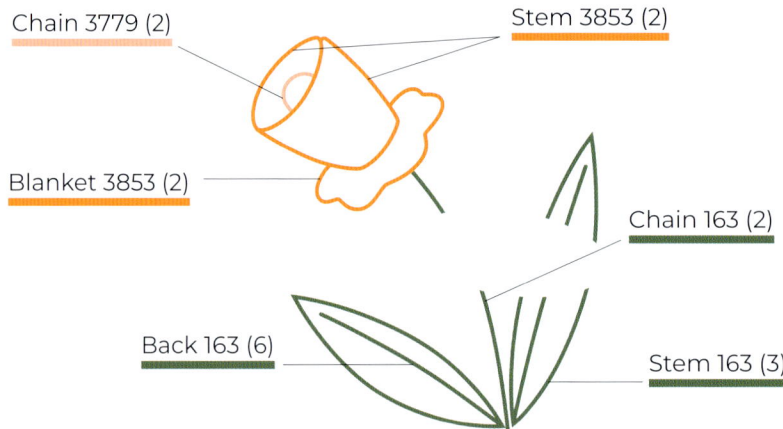

Satin 3831 (2)

Straight 3853 (2)

Chain 368 (2)

Stem 368 (2)

Satin 744 (3)
*Embroider first*

Stem 368 (1)

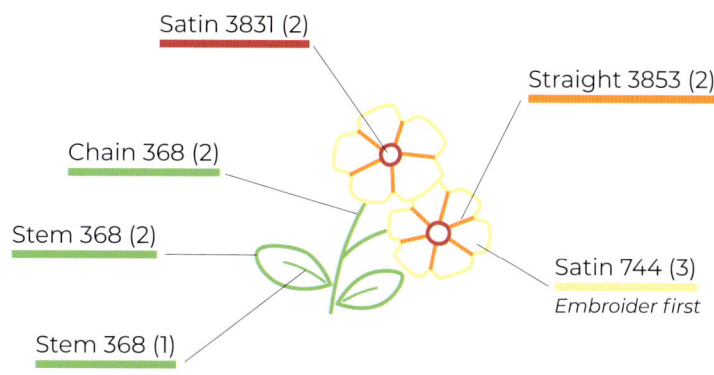

Satin 3853 (2)

Stem 3831 (2)

Blanket 3779 (2)
*Embroider first*

Straight 3831 (2)

Chain 15 (3)

Stem 15 (2)

Straight 3833 (2)
*Embroider second*

Stem 15 (2)

Stem 15 (2)

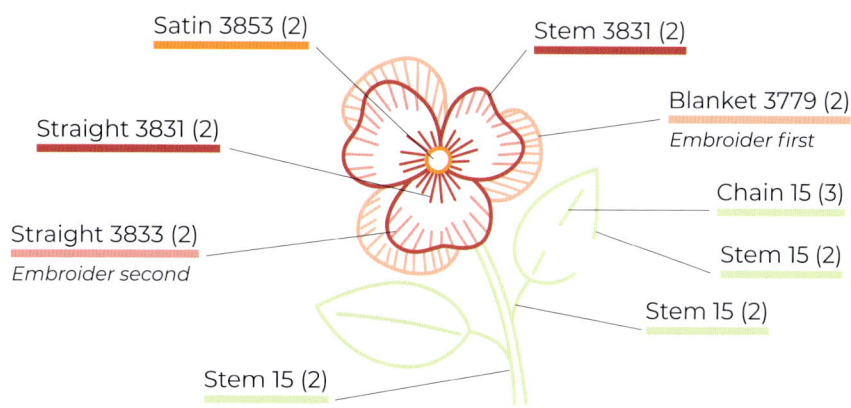

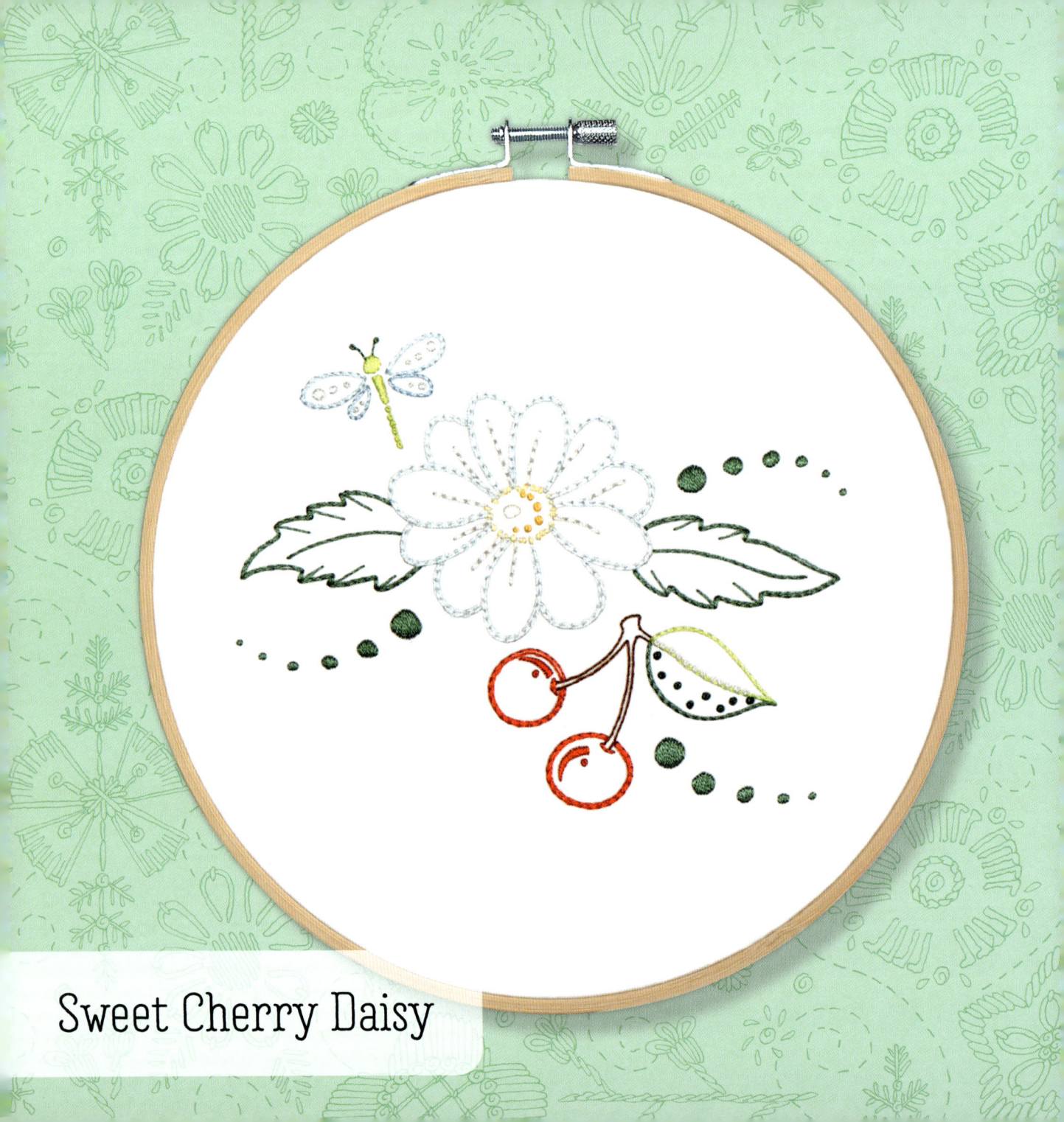

Sweet Cherry Daisy

# SUPPLIES

## Fabric
12 x 12 inch (30x30cm)
ground fabric
12 x 12 inch (30x30cm)
backing fabric (optional)

## DMC six-stranded floss
☐ 01      Rain
▧ 16      Sprout
▧ 163     Eucalyptus
▧ 347     Egyptian Red
▧ 561     Cypress Green
▧ 726     Mimosa
▧ 727     Primrose
  775     Blue Summer Rain
▧ 801     Mink
▧ 3325    Arctic Blue
▧ 3815    Almond Green
  3841    Igloo Blue
☐ B5200   Pearlescent White
          Light

## Needles
Embroidery: size 7 and 9
Milliner: size 7 and 9

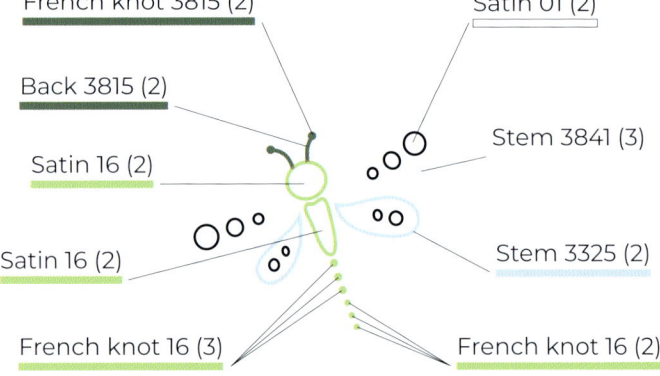

French knot 3815 (2)

Back 3815 (2)

Satin 16 (2)

Satin 16 (2)

French knot 16 (3)

Satin 01 (2)

Stem 3841 (3)

Stem 3325 (2)

French knot 16 (2)

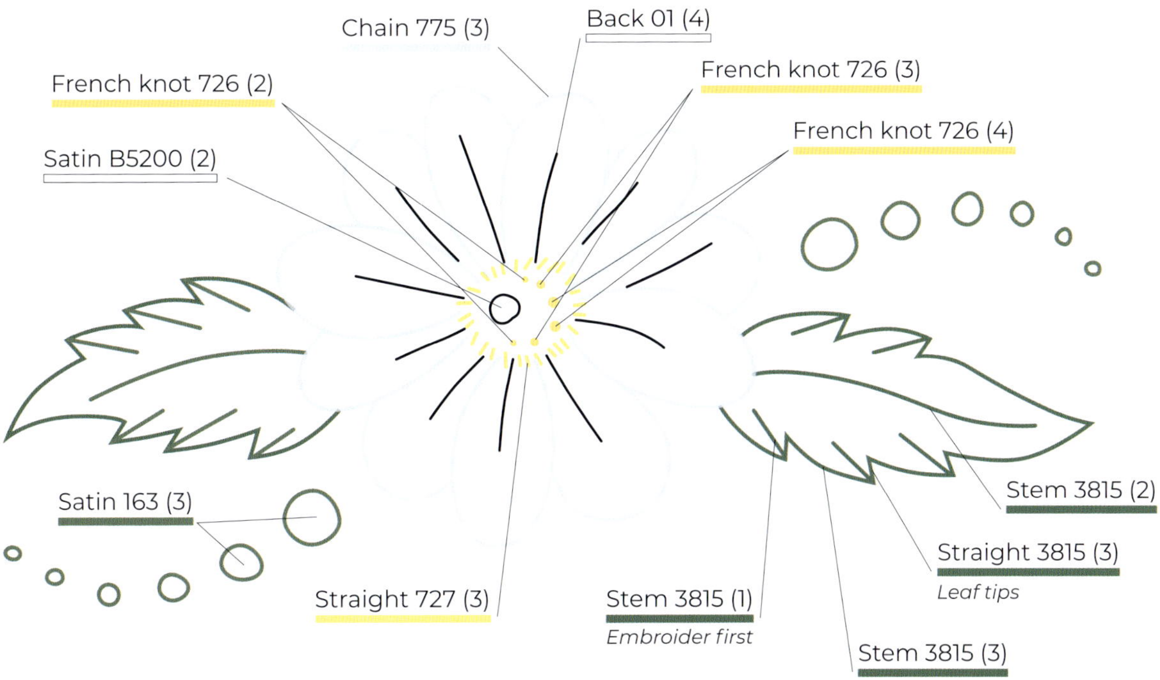

Chain 775 (3)

Back 01 (4)

French knot 726 (2)

French knot 726 (3)

French knot 726 (4)

Satin B5200 (2)

Satin 163 (3)

Straight 727 (3)

Stem 3815 (1)
*Embroider first*

Stem 3815 (3)

Stem 3815 (2)

Straight 3815 (3)
*Leaf tips*

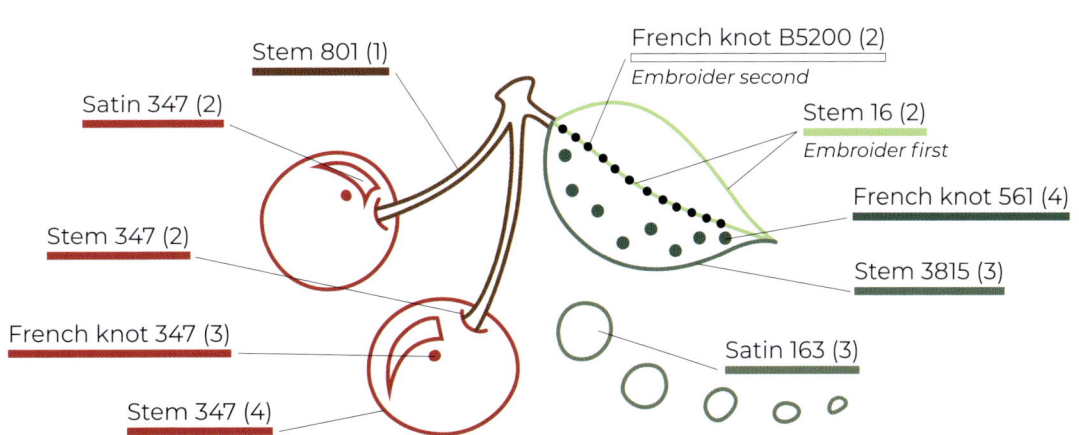

Stem 801 (1)

French knot B5200 (2)
*Embroider second*

Satin 347 (2)

Stem 16 (2)
*Embroider first*

French knot 561 (4)

Stem 347 (2)

Stem 3815 (3)

French knot 347 (3)

Satin 163 (3)

Stem 347 (4)

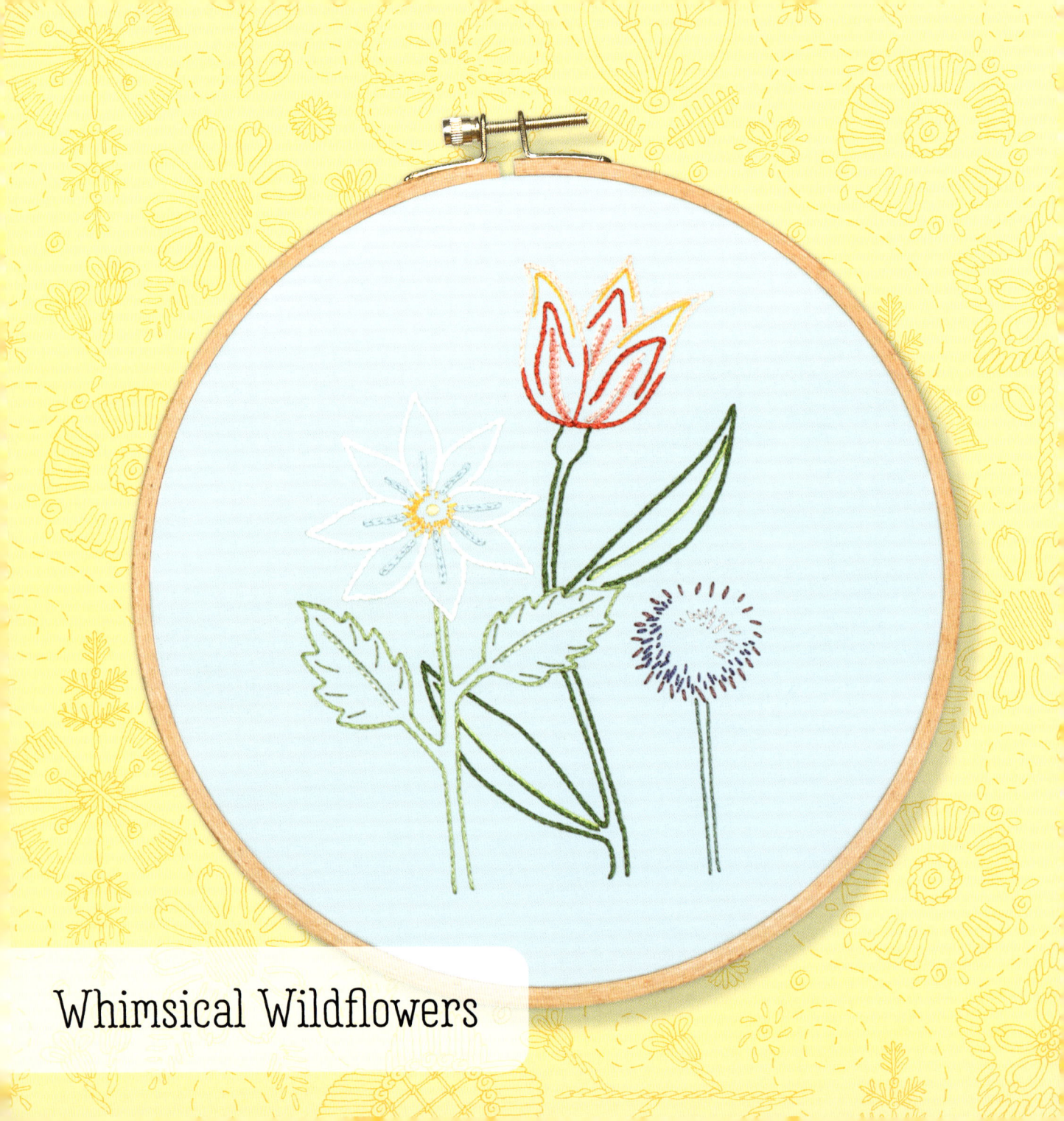

Whimsical Wildflowers

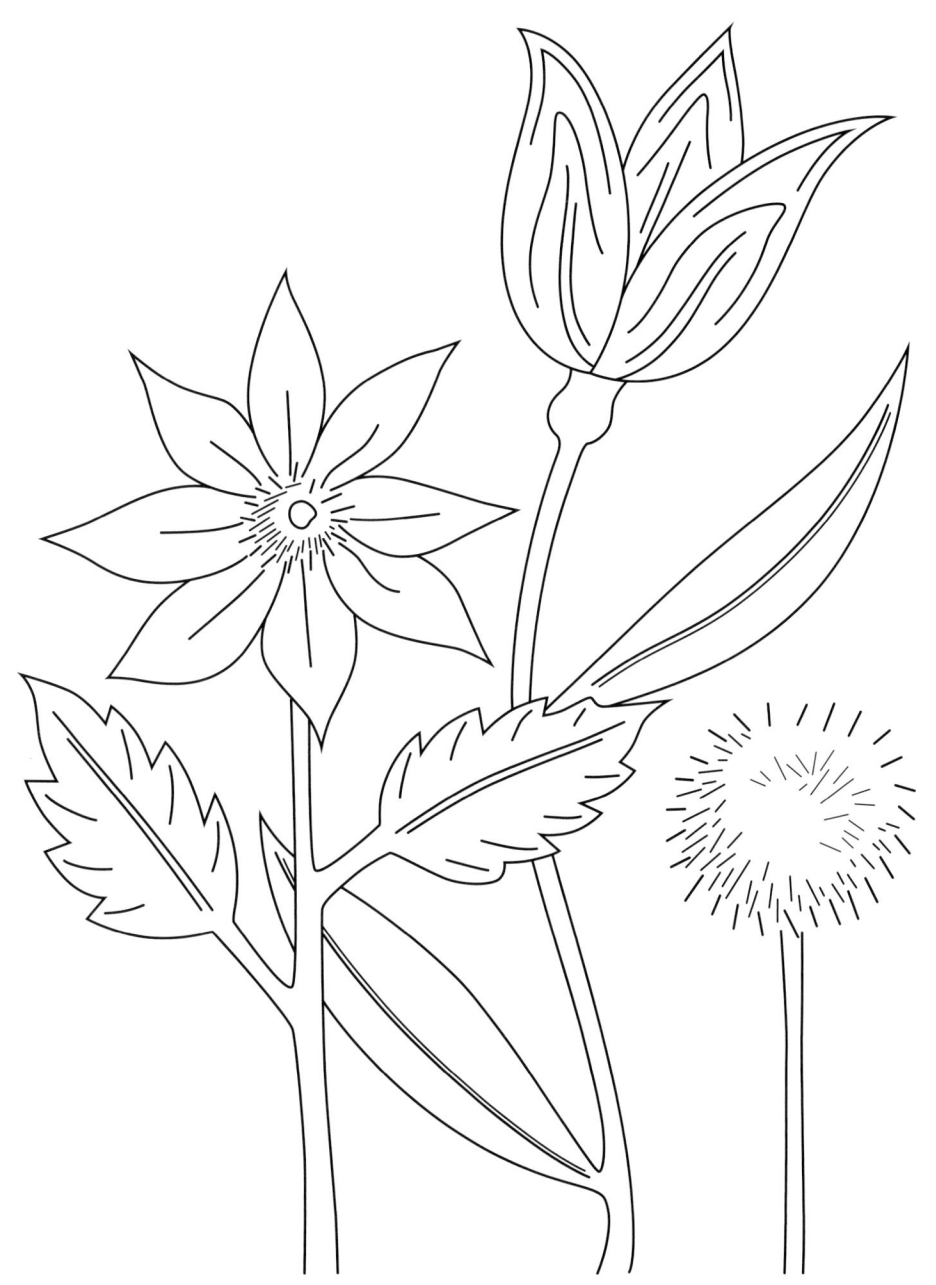

# SUPPLIES

## Fabric

12 x 12 inch (30x30cm) ground fabric

12 x 12 inch (30x30cm) backing fabric (optional)

## DMC six-stranded floss

| | | |
|---|---|---|
| 16 | Sprout | |
| 158 | Ultramarine Blue | |
| 164 | Pistachio | |
| 561 | Cypress Green | |
| 725 | Buttercup | |
| 727 | Primrose | |
| 747 | Pearlescent Blue Sea Mist | |
| 967 | Pearlescent Tutu | |
| 972 | Curry | |
| 986 | Boxwood | |
| 987 | Basil | |
| 989 | Fennel | |
| 3042 | Silver Linings | |
| 3713 | Rose Quartz | |
| 3740 | Gun Metal | |
| 3831 | Wild Strawberry | |
| 3833 | Strawberry Sorbet | |
| B5200 | Pearlescent White Light | |

## Needles

Embroidery: size 7 and 9

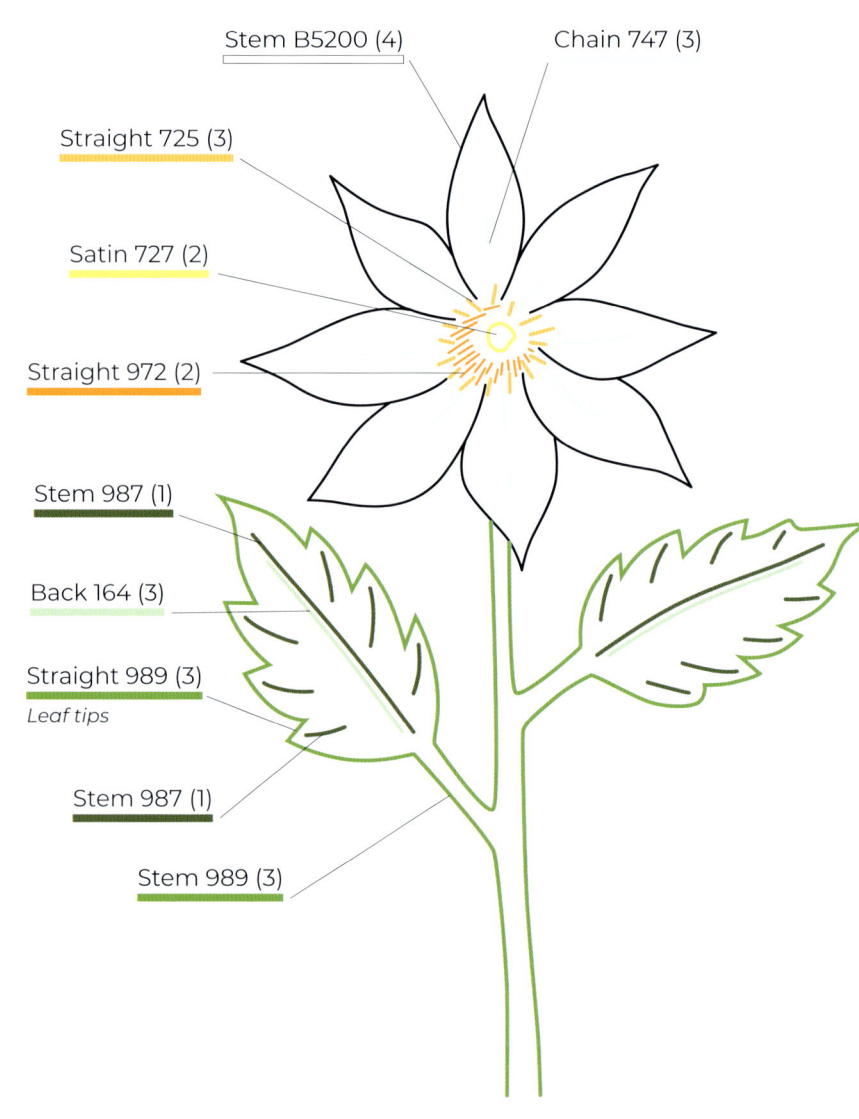

Stem B5200 (4)

Chain 747 (3)

Straight 725 (3)

Satin 727 (2)

Straight 972 (2)

Stem 987 (1)

Back 164 (3)

Straight 989 (3)

*Leaf tips*

Stem 987 (1)

Stem 989 (3)

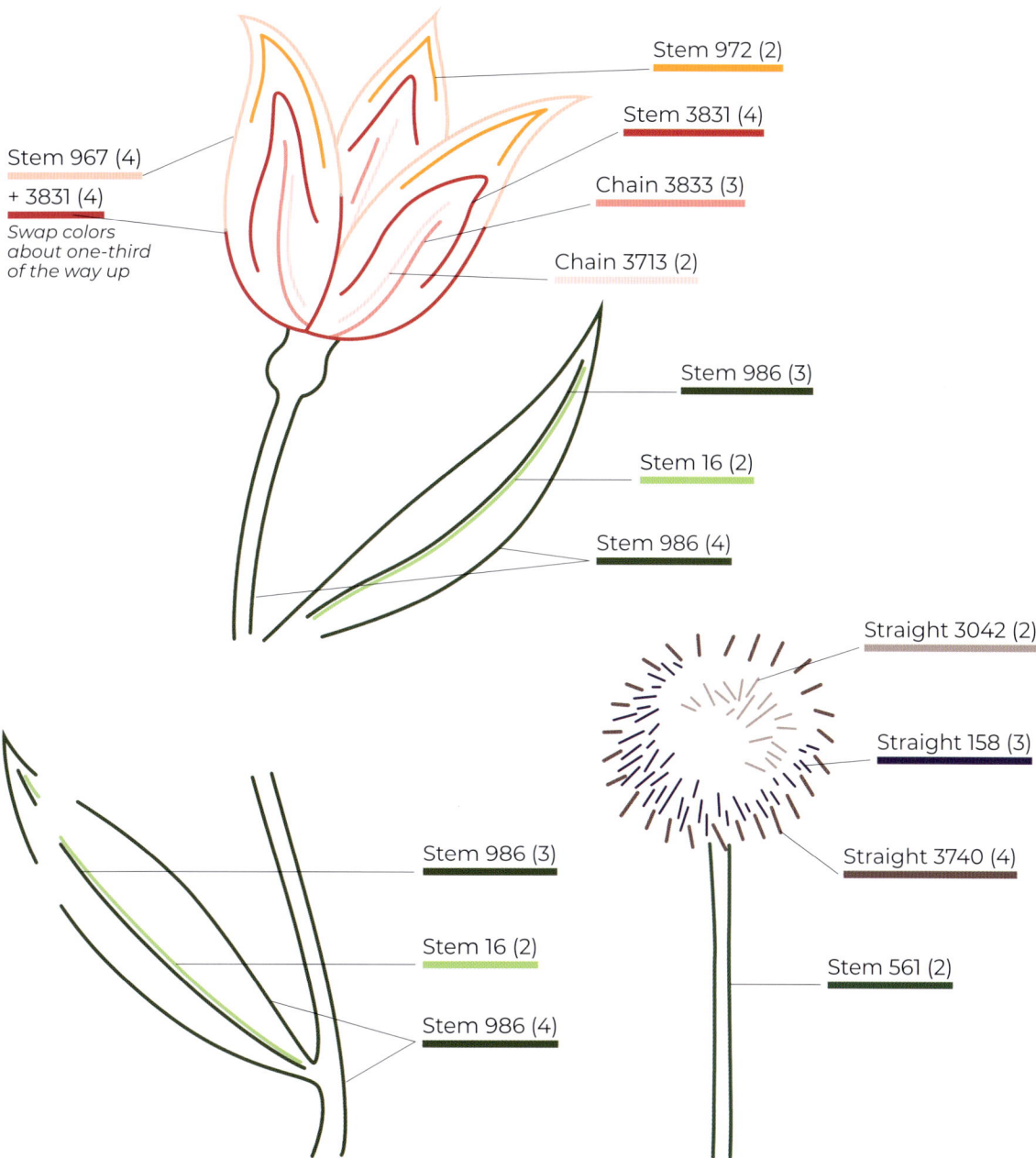

Stem 972 (2)

Stem 3831 (4)

Chain 3833 (3)

Chain 3713 (2)

Stem 967 (4)
+ 3831 (4)

*Swap colors about one-third of the way up*

Stem 986 (3)

Stem 16 (2)

Stem 986 (4)

Straight 3042 (2)

Straight 158 (3)

Straight 3740 (4)

Stem 561 (2)

Stem 986 (3)

Stem 16 (2)

Stem 986 (4)

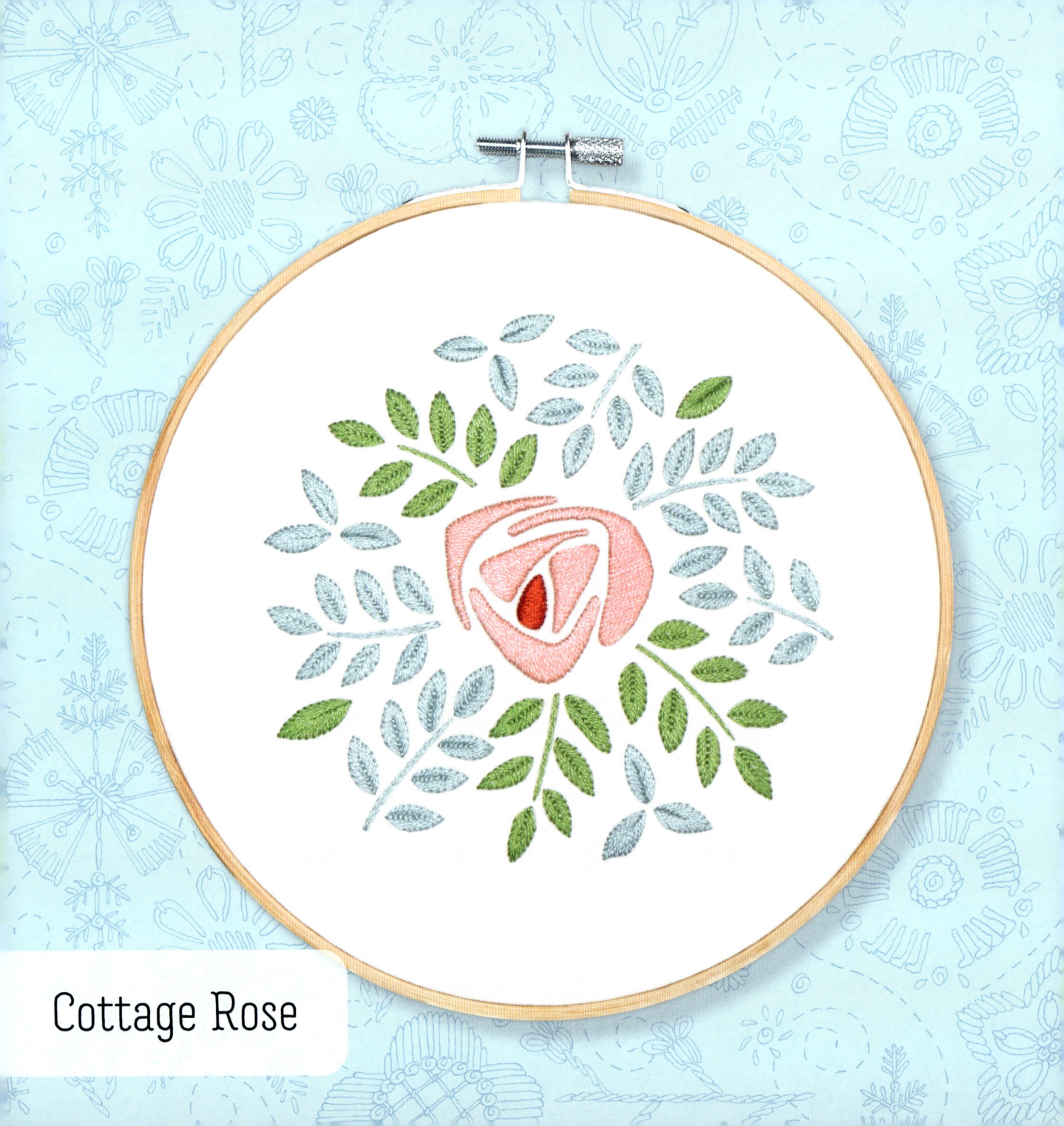

Cottage Rose

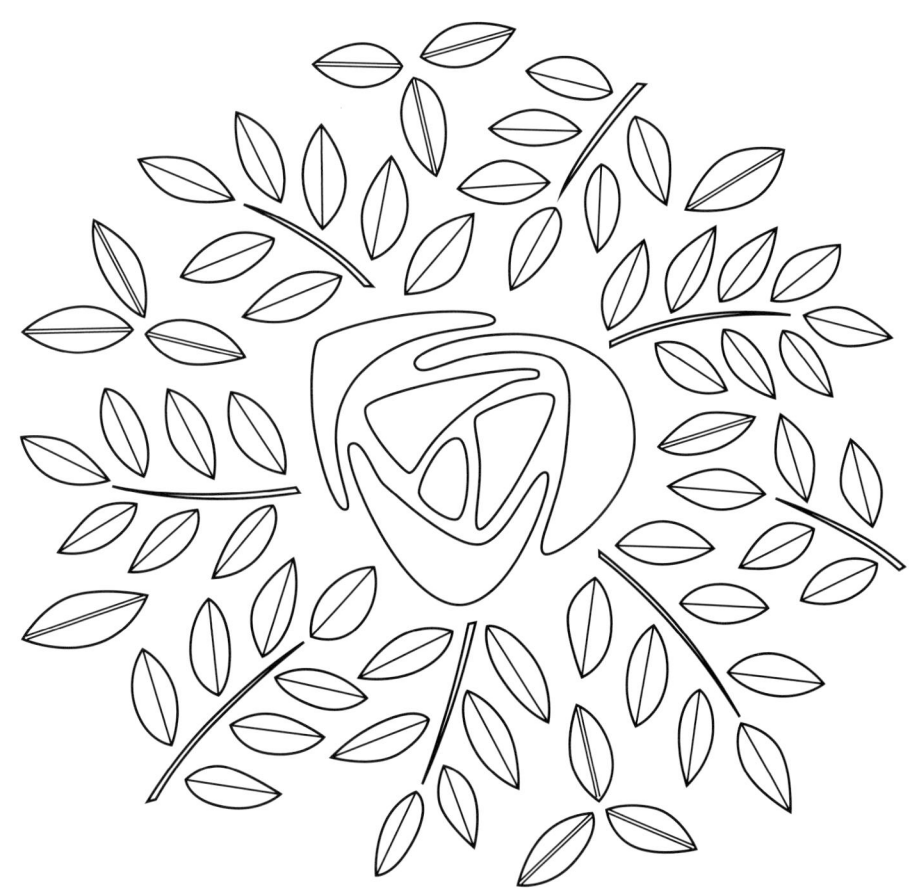

## SUPPLIES

### Fabric
12 x 12 inch (30x30cm)
ground fabric
12 x 12 inch (30x30cm)
backing fabric (optional)

### DMC six-stranded floss
- 326      Rhubarb
- 598      Pale Lagoon
- 703      Metallic Spring Green
- 3326     Wild Rose

### Needles
Embroidery: size 7 and 9

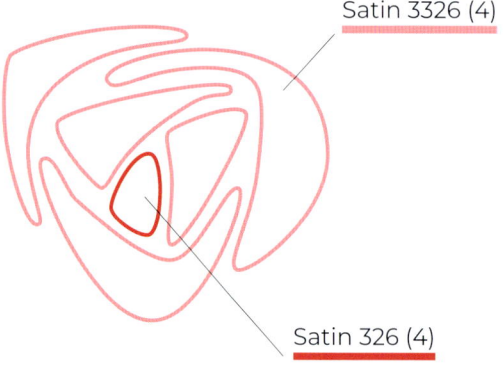

Satin 3326 (4)

Satin 326 (4)

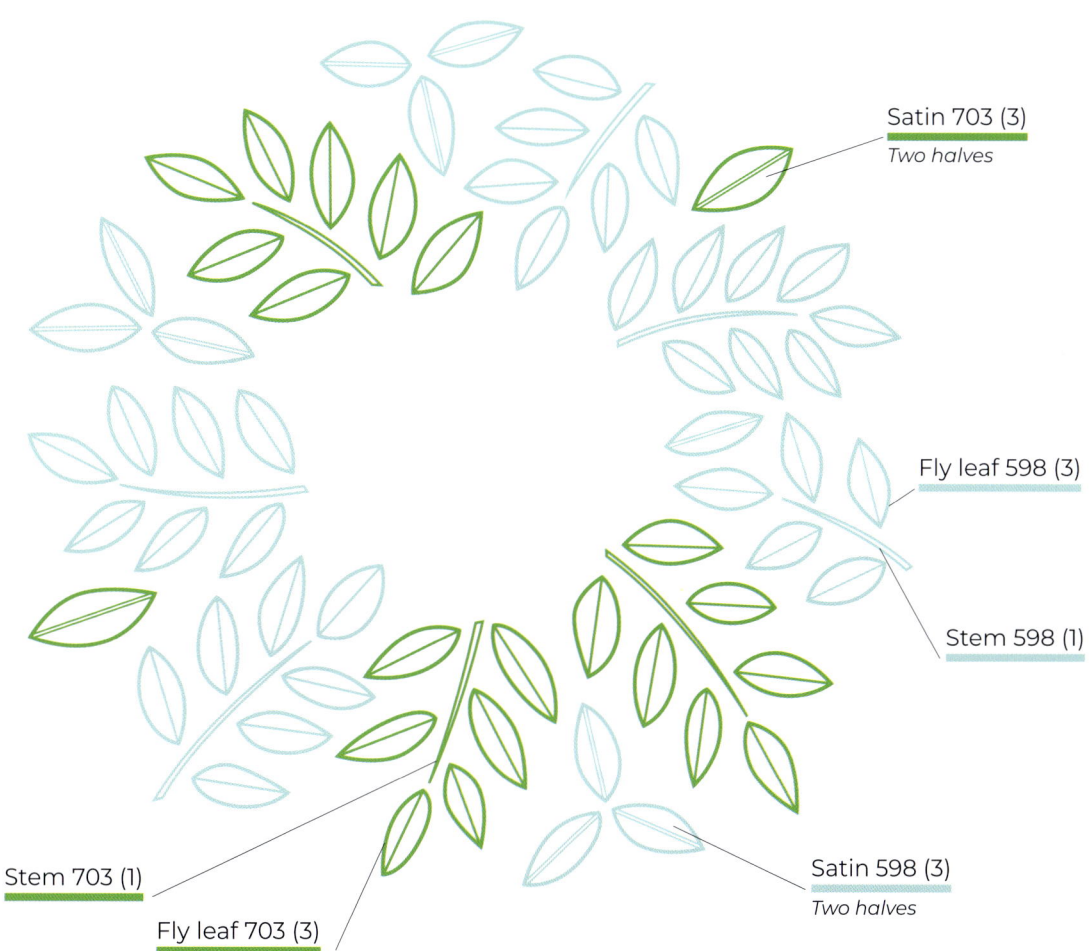

Satin 703 (3)
*Two halves*

Fly leaf 598 (3)

Stem 598 (1)

Satin 598 (3)
*Two halves*

Stem 703 (1)

Fly leaf 703 (3)

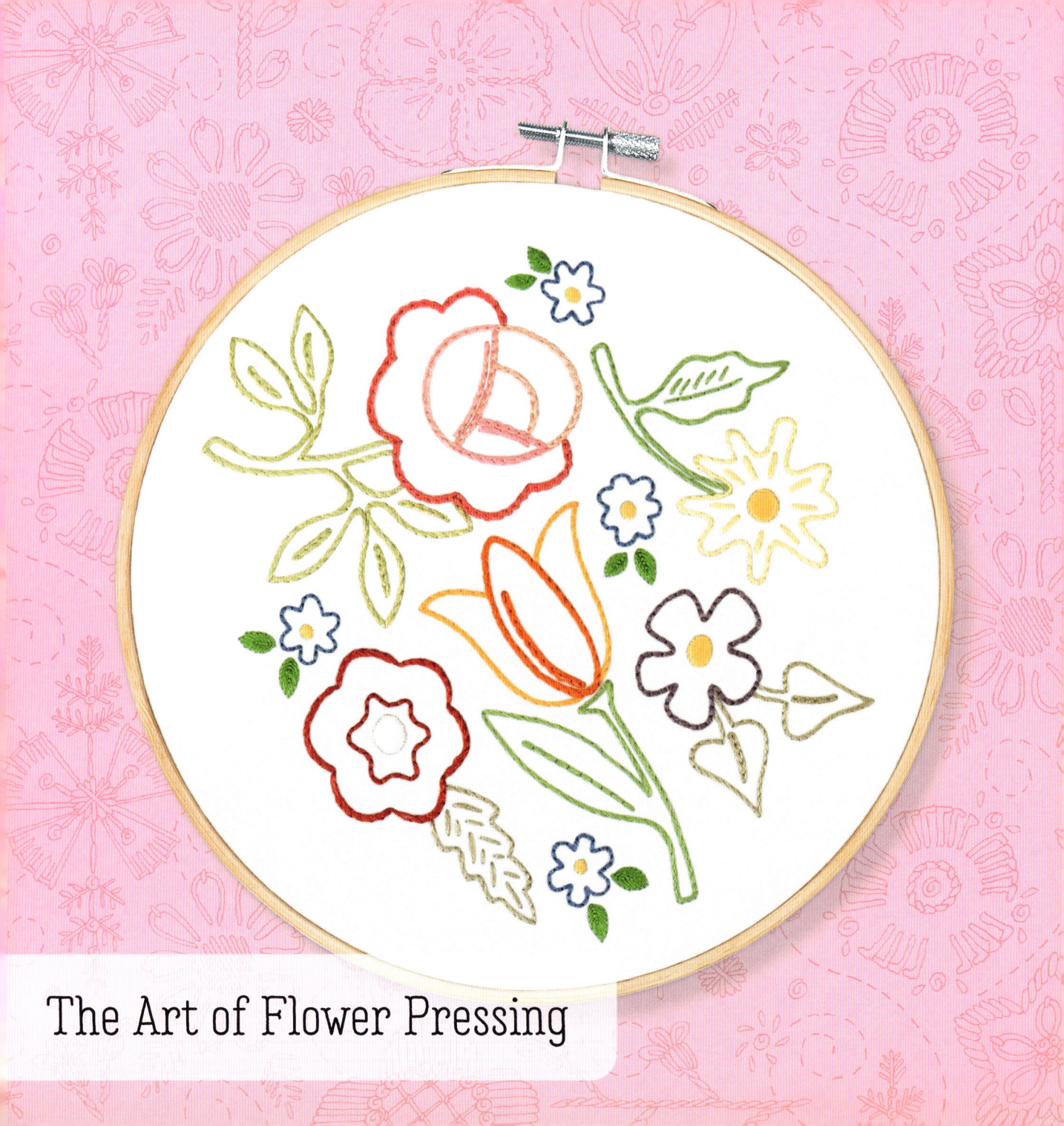

The Art of Flower Pressing

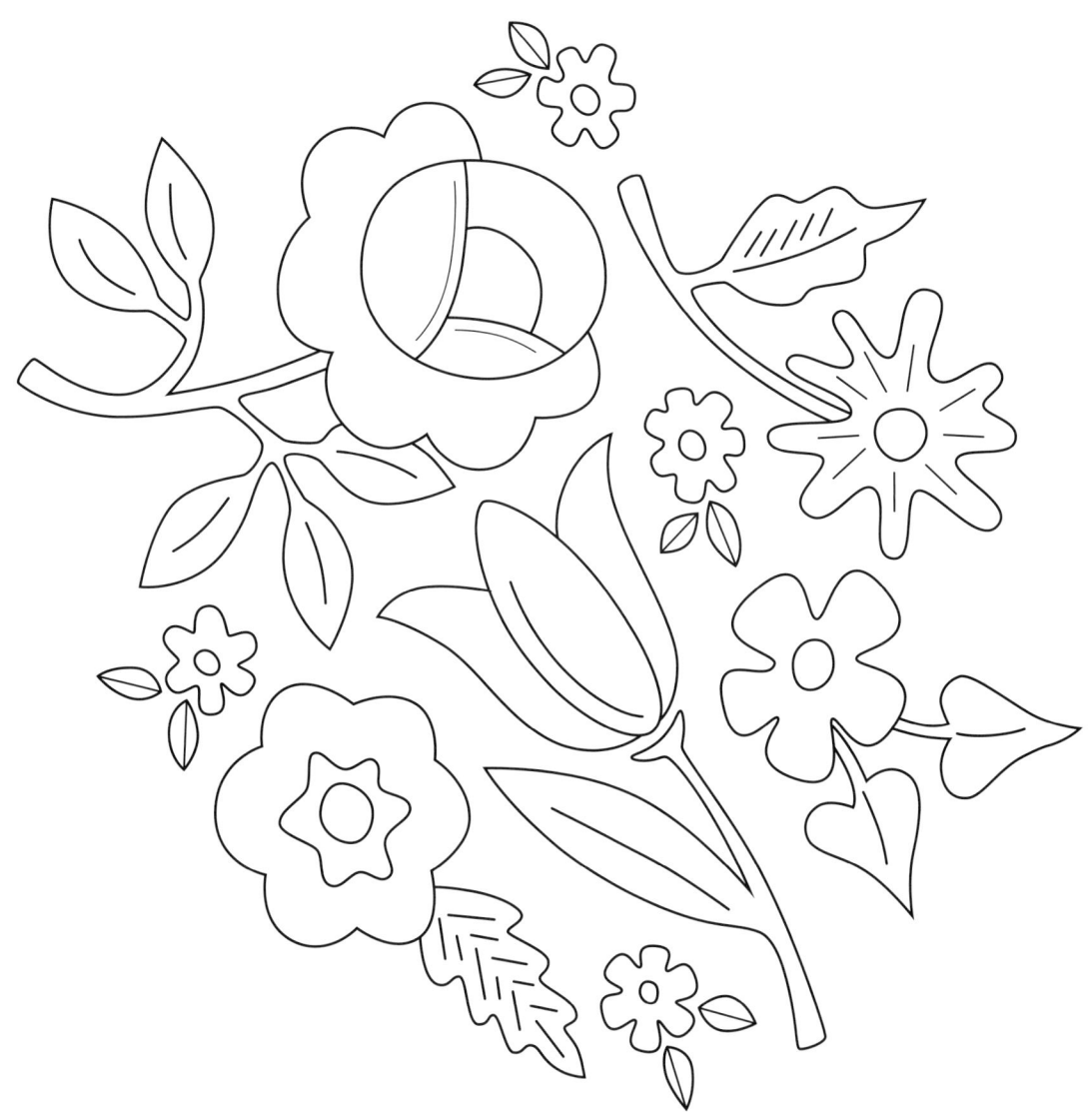

# SUPPLIES

## Fabric
12 x 12 inch (30x30cm)
ground fabric
12 x 12 inch (30x30cm)
backing fabric (optional)

## DMC six-stranded floss

| | | |
|---|---|---|
| ■ | 326 | Rhubarb |
| ■ | 472 | Green Bud |
| ■ | 602 | Pink Verbena |
| ■ | 604 | Pink Hyacinth |
| ■ | 704 | Lime |
| ■ | 720 | Rust |
| ■ | 726 | Mimosa |
| ■ | 727 | Primrose |
| ■ | 742 | Clementine |
| ■ | 826 | Tuareg Blue |
| ■ | 906 | Mistletoe |
| ■ | 3013 | Green Oyster |
| ■ | 3041 | Purple Slate |
| ■ | 3326 | Wild Rose |
| ■ | 3779 | Burnished Pink |
| □ | B5200 | Pearlescent White Light |

## Needles
Embroidery: size 7 and 9

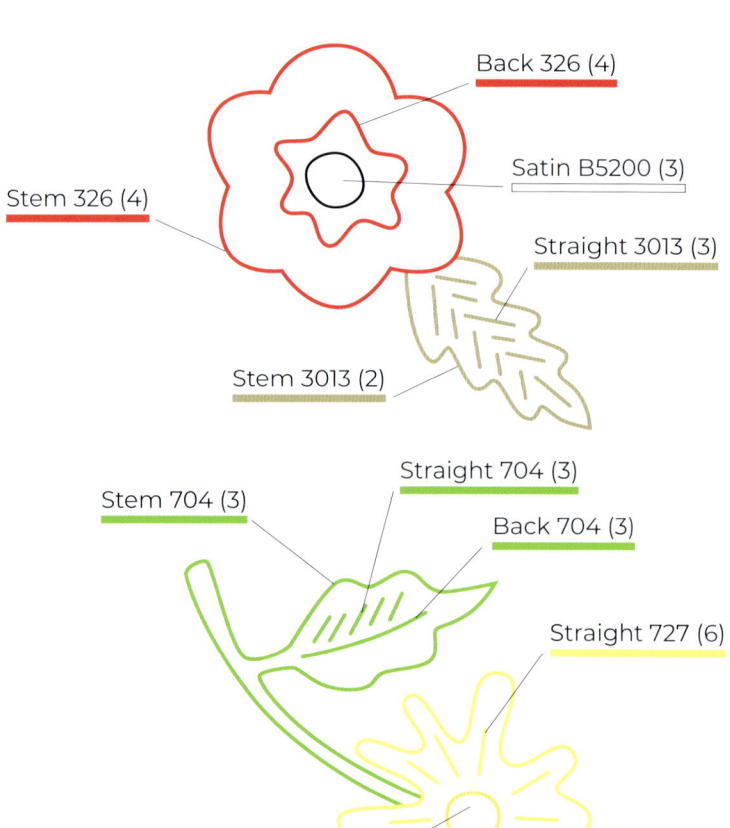

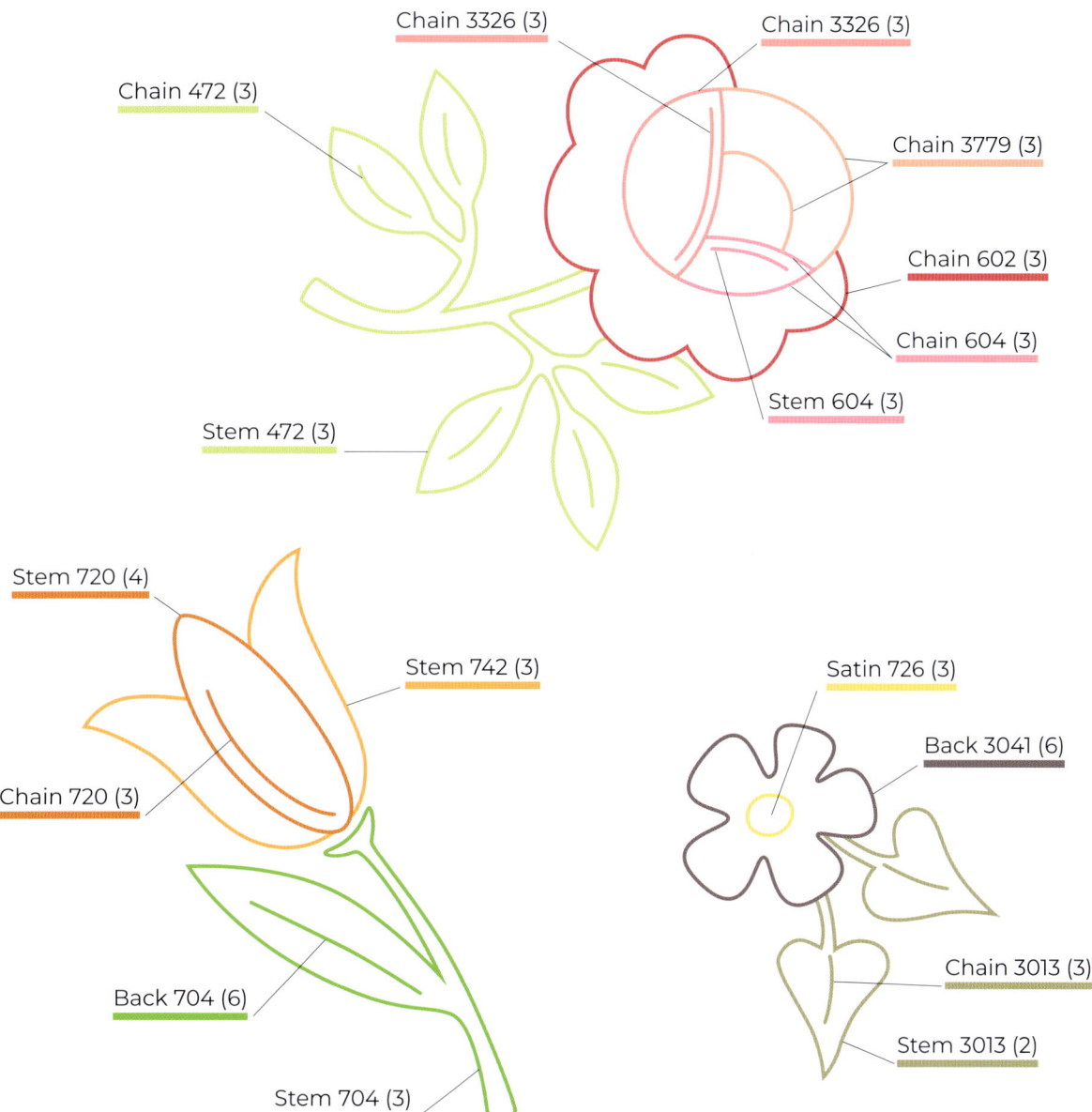

Chain 3326 (3)

Chain 3326 (3)

Chain 472 (3)

Chain 3779 (3)

Chain 602 (3)

Chain 604 (3)

Stem 604 (3)

Stem 472 (3)

Stem 720 (4)

Stem 742 (3)

Satin 726 (3)

Back 3041 (6)

Chain 720 (3)

Chain 3013 (3)

Back 704 (6)

Stem 3013 (2)

Stem 704 (3)

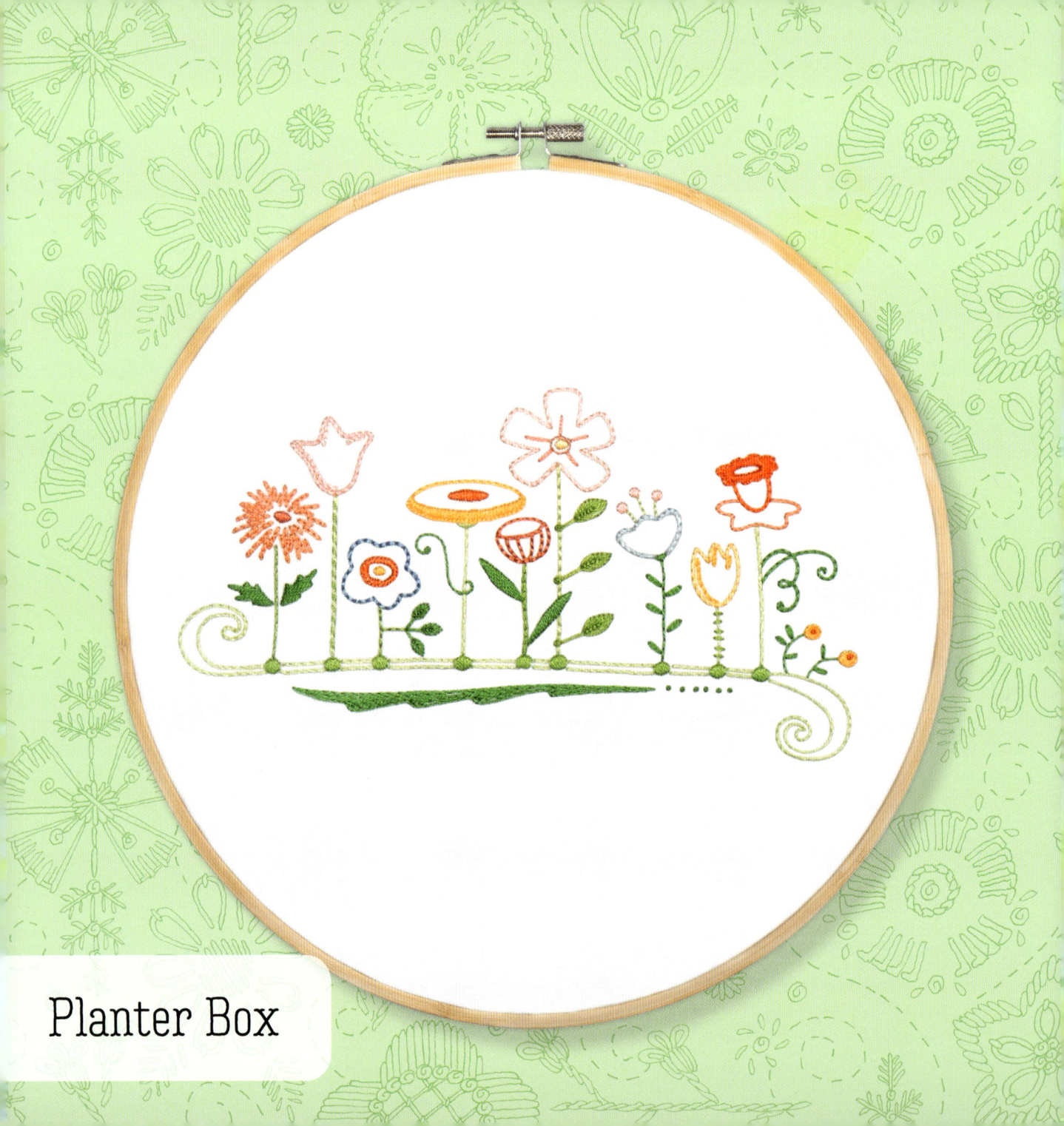

Planter Box

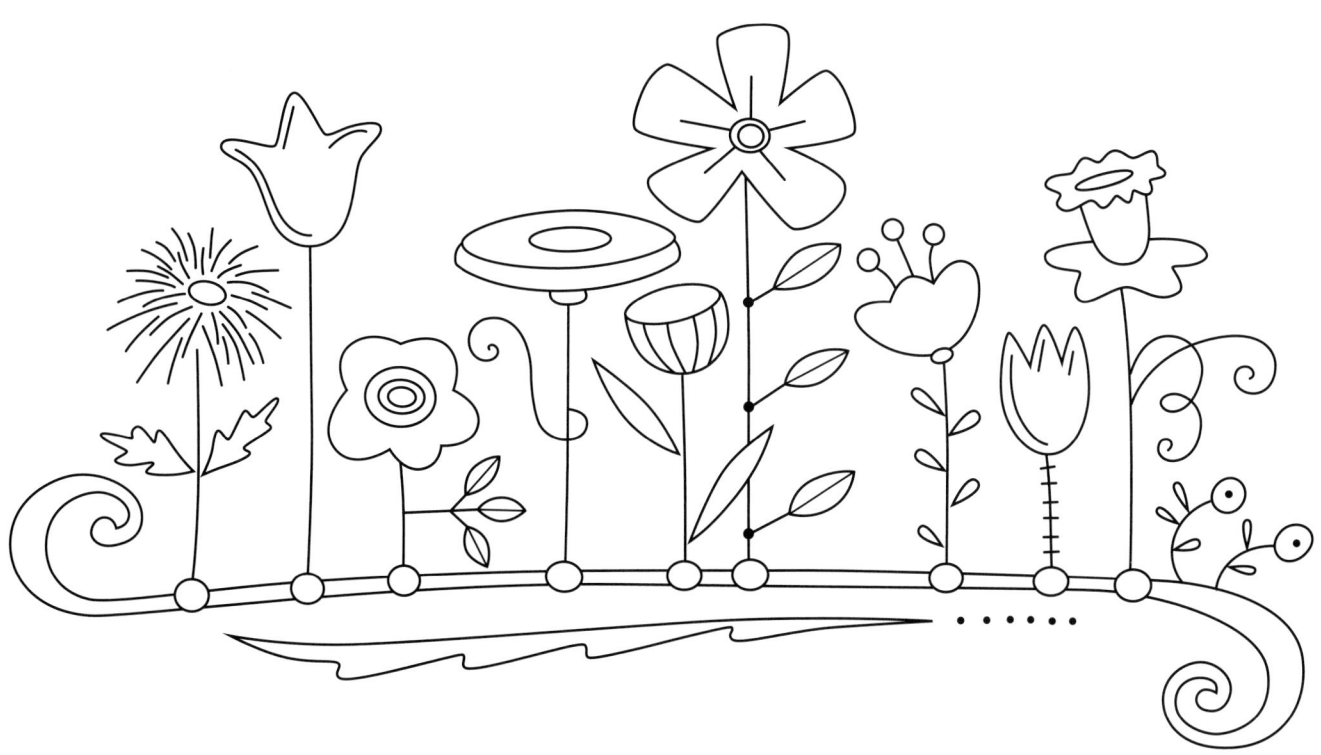

# SUPPLIES

## Fabric
12 x 12 inch (30x30cm)
ground fabric
12 x 12 inch (30x30cm)
backing fabric (optional)

## DMC six-stranded floss

| | | |
|---|---|---|
| 15 | Spring Onion |
| 351 | Coral |
| 352 | Salmon |
| 702 | Spring Lawn |
| 704 | Lime |
| 743 | Banana |
| 744 | Grapefruit |
| 760 | Dusty Pink |
| 761 | Rose Dawn |
| 3712 | Blush |
| 3713 | Rose Quartz |
| 3755 | Pastel Blue |
| 3841 | Igloo Blue |

## Needles
Embroidery: size 7 and 9
Milliner: size 7 and 9

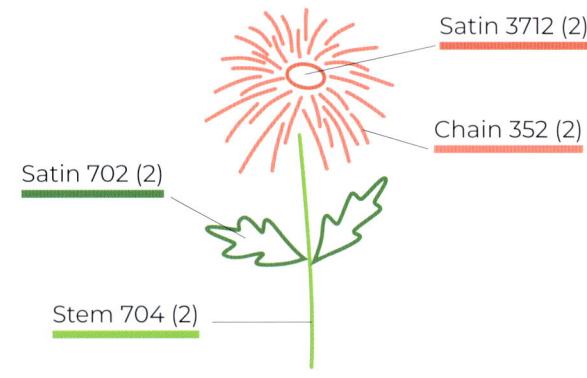

Satin 3712 (2)

Chain 352 (2)

Satin 702 (2)

Stem 704 (2)

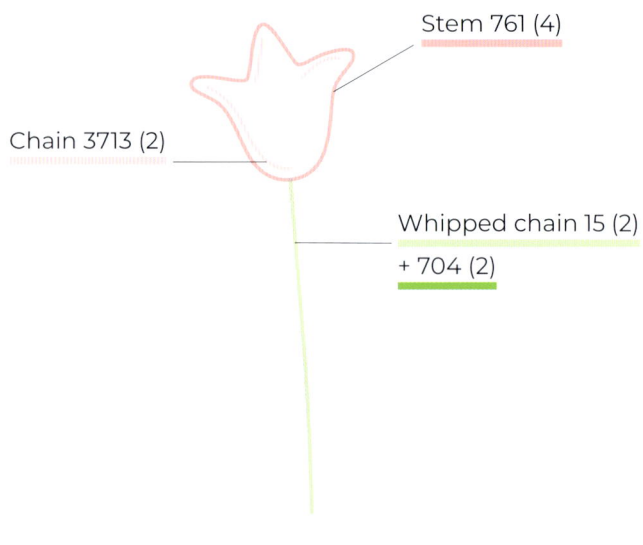

Stem 761 (4)

Chain 3713 (2)

Whipped chain 15 (2)
+ 704 (2)

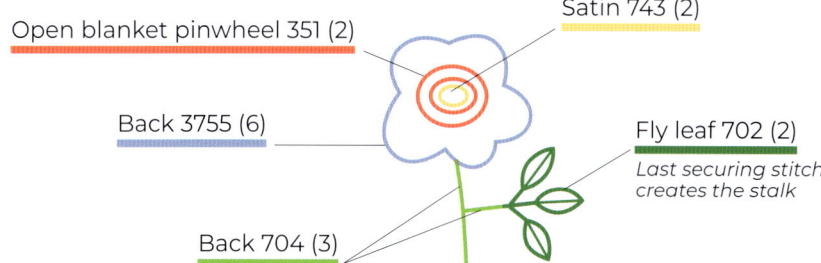

Satin 743 (2)

Open blanket pinwheel 351 (2)

Back 3755 (6)

Fly leaf 702 (2)
*Last securing stitch creates the stalk*

Back 704 (3)

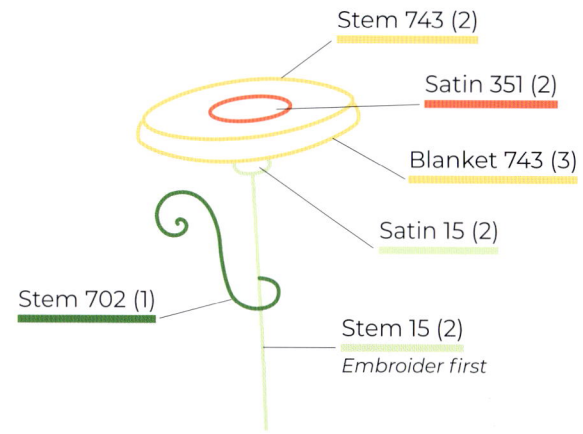

Stem 743 (2)

Satin 351 (2)

Blanket 743 (3)

Satin 15 (2)

Stem 702 (1)

Stem 15 (2)
*Embroider first*

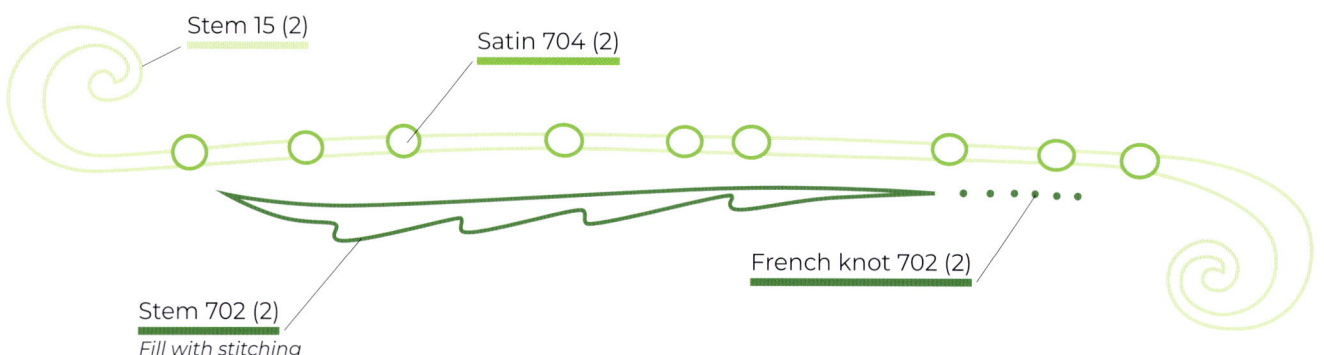

Stem 15 (2)

Satin 704 (2)

French knot 702 (2)

Stem 702 (2)
*Fill with stitching*

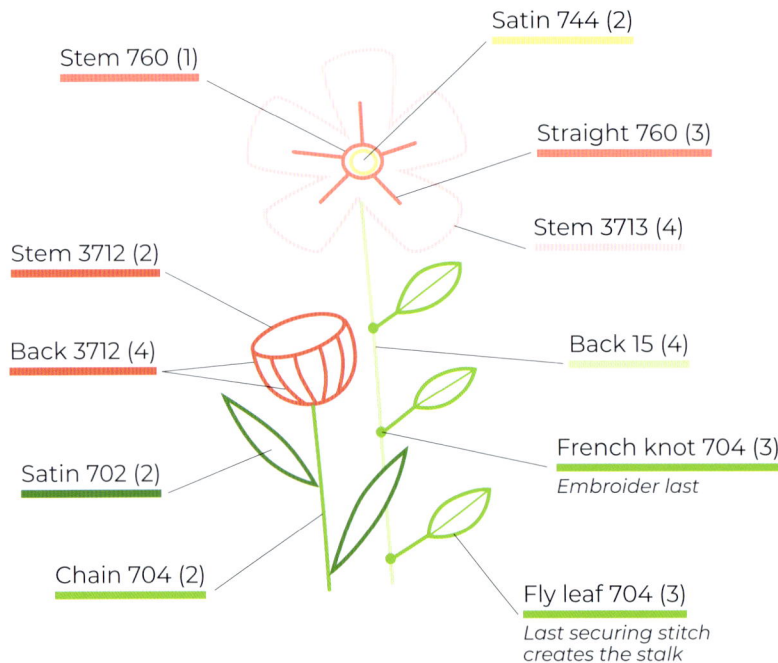

Stem 760 (1)

Satin 744 (2)

Straight 760 (3)

Stem 3713 (4)

Stem 3712 (2)

Back 3712 (4)

Back 15 (4)

Satin 702 (2)

French knot 704 (3)

*Embroider last*

Chain 704 (2)

Fly leaf 704 (3)

*Last securing stitch creates the stalk*

Satin 761 (2)

Back 15 (2)

Stem 3841 (4)

Satin 702 (2)

Back 702 (2)

Detached chain 702 (2)

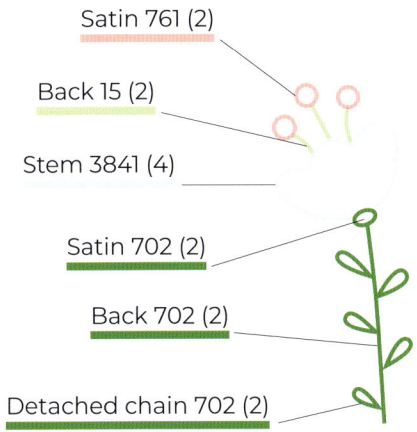

Stem 744 (3)

Chain 743 (2)

Straight 704 (3)

Stem 15 (1)
*Embroider first*

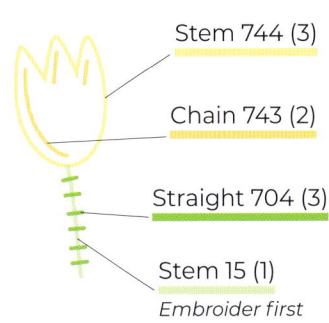

Open blanket
pinwheel 351 (2)

Stem 351 (3)

Stem 352 (2)

Stem 15 (3)

Stem 702 (2)

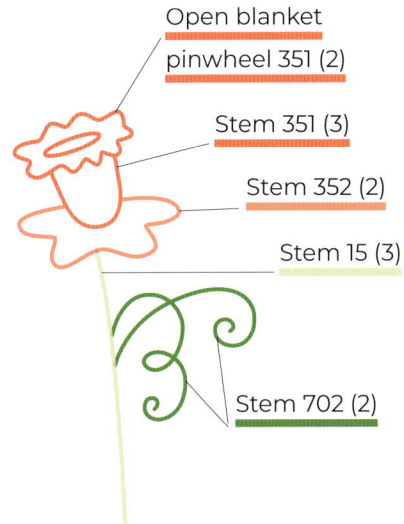

Detached chain 702 (2)

French knot 351 (2)
*Embroider last*

Closed blanket
pinwheel 743 (2)
*Embroider first*

Stem 702 (1)

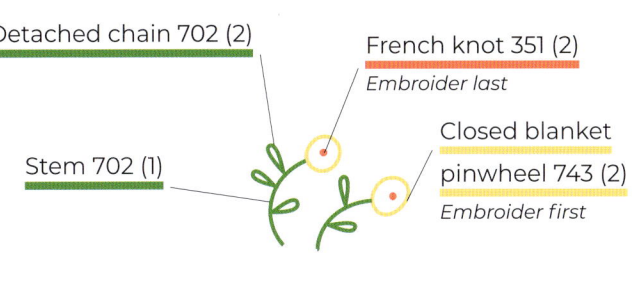

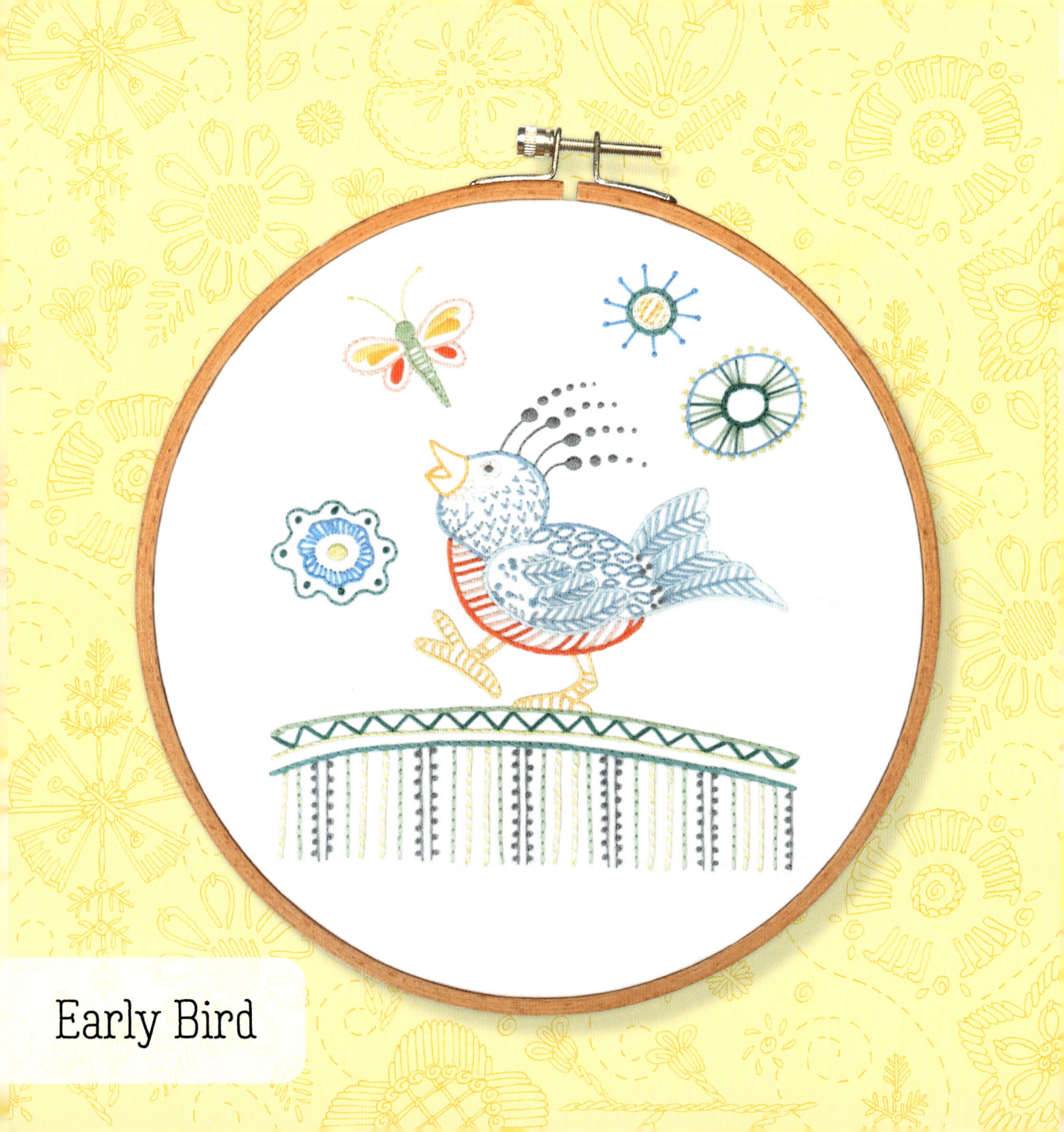

Early Bird

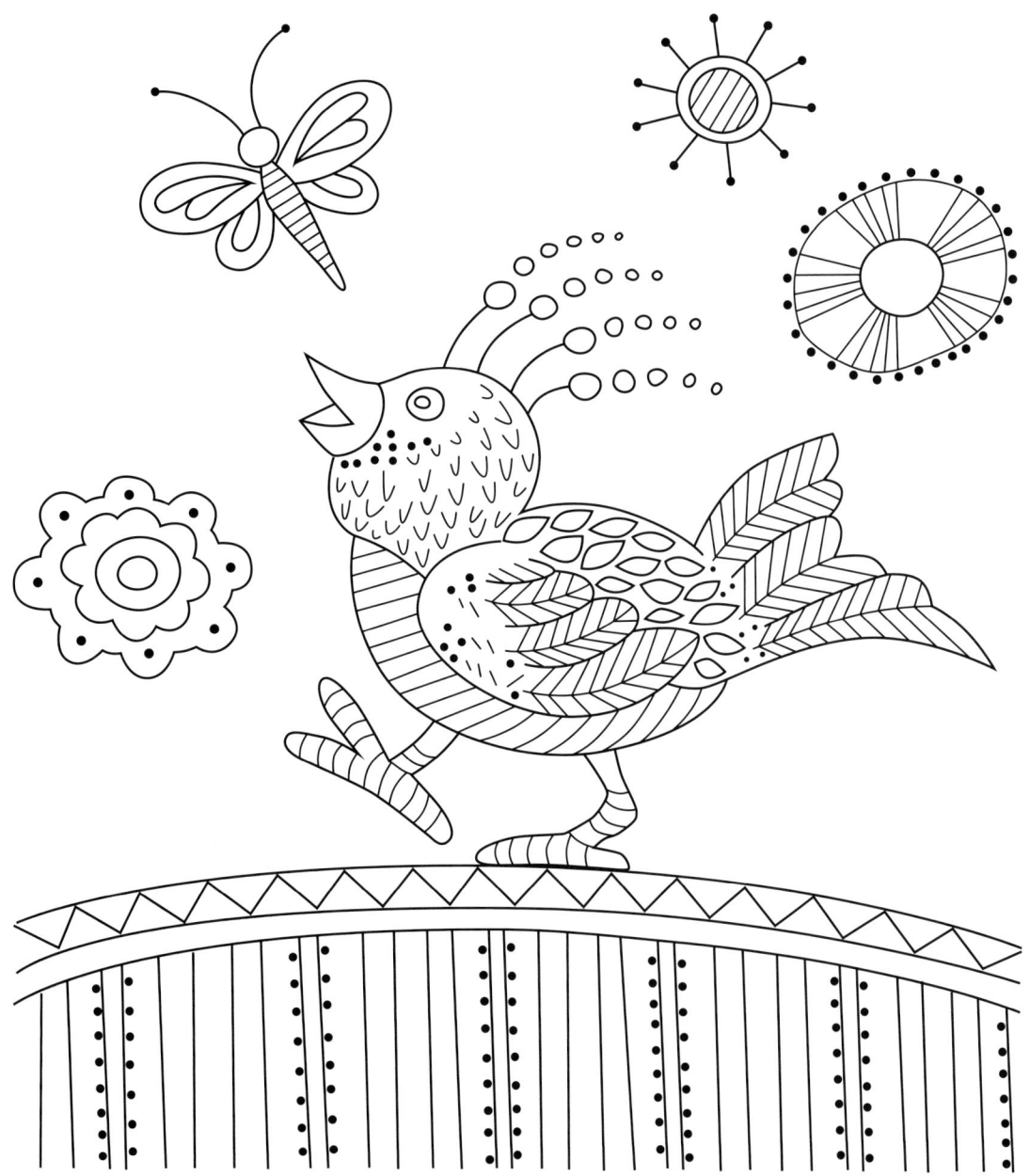

## SUPPLIES

### Fabric
12 x 12 inch (30x30cm)
ground fabric
12 x 12 inch (30x30cm)
backing fabric (optional)

### DMC six-stranded floss

| | | |
|---|---|---|
| 11 | Lemon Drop |
| 164 | Pistachio |
| 169 | Tin |
| 743 | Banana |
| 744 | Grapefruit |
| 747 | Pearlescent Blue Sea Mist |
| 996 | Electric Blue |
| 3713 | Rose Quartz |
| 3766 | Blue Green |
| 3832 | Strawberry |
| 3850 | Emerald |
| 3851 | Emerald Shard |
| B5200 | Pearlescent White Light |

### Needles
Embroidery: size 7 and 9
Milliner: size 7 and 9

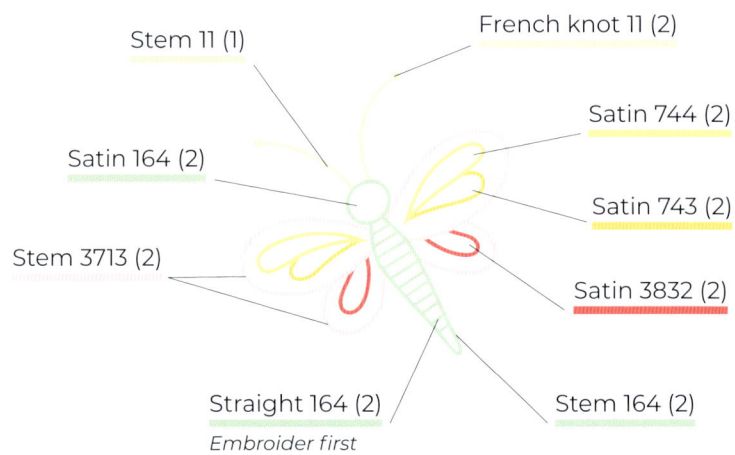

Stem 11 (1)

French knot 11 (2)

Satin 744 (2)

Satin 164 (2)

Satin 743 (2)

Stem 3713 (2)

Satin 3832 (2)

Straight 164 (2)

*Embroider first*

Stem 164 (2)

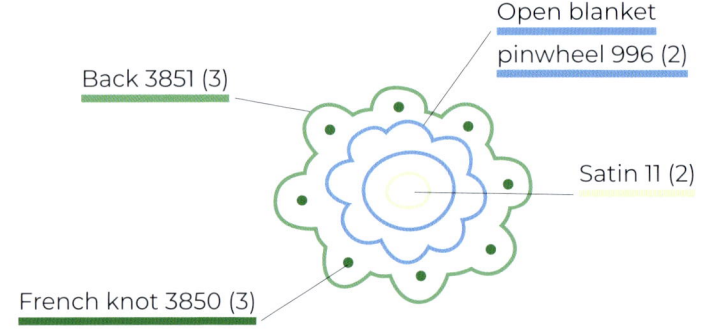

Open blanket

pinwheel 996 (2)

Back 3851 (3)

Satin 11 (2)

French knot 3850 (3)

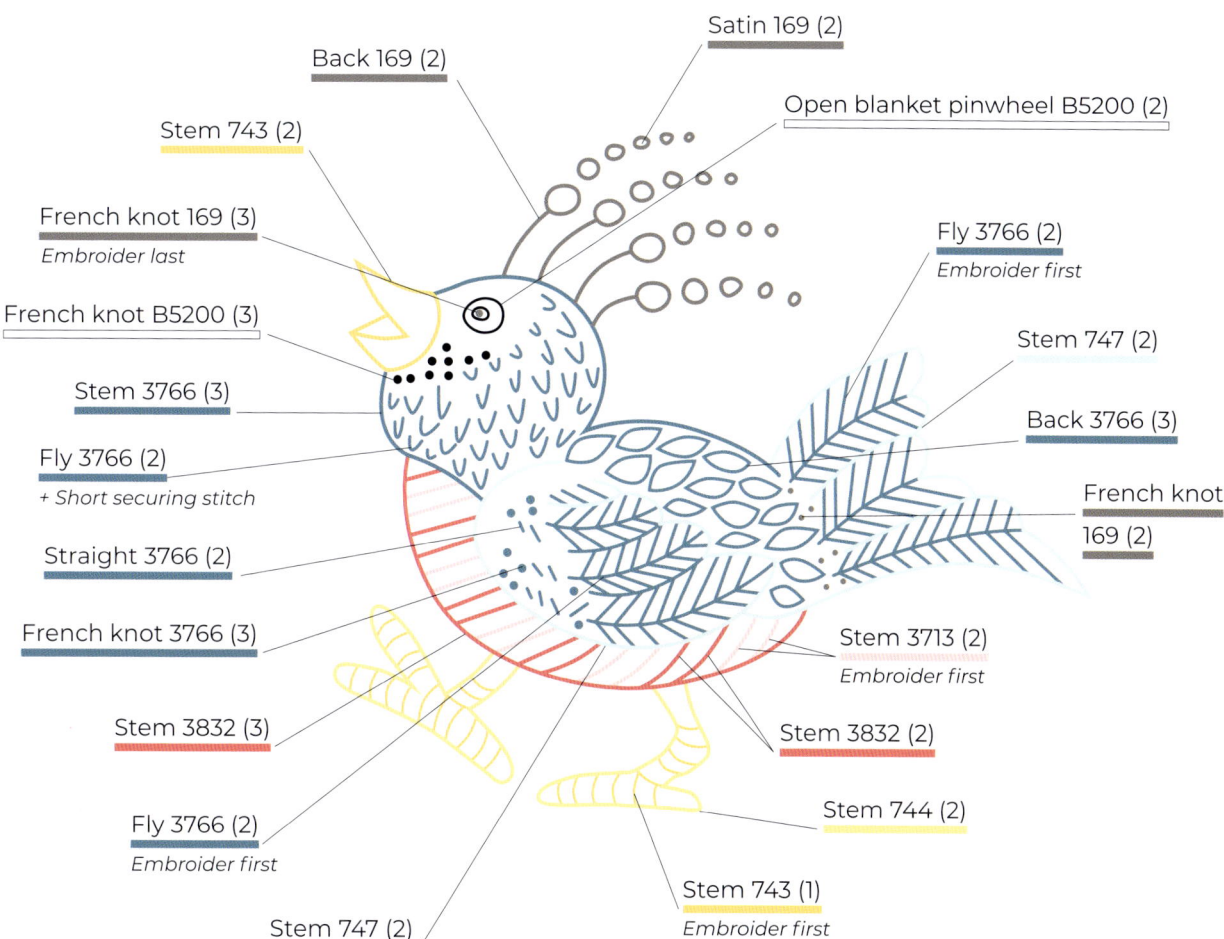

Satin 169 (2)

Back 169 (2)

Open blanket pinwheel B5200 (2)

Stem 743 (2)

Fly 3766 (2)
*Embroider first*

French knot 169 (3)
*Embroider last*

Stem 747 (2)

French knot B5200 (3)

Back 3766 (3)

Stem 3766 (3)

French knot 169 (2)

Fly 3766 (2)
*+ Short securing stitch*

Straight 3766 (2)

Stem 3713 (2)
*Embroider first*

French knot 3766 (3)

Stem 3832 (3)

Stem 3832 (2)

Fly 3766 (2)
*Embroider first*

Stem 744 (2)

Stem 747 (2)

Stem 743 (1)
*Embroider first*

Back 743 (3)
*Embroider first*

Straight 996 (2)

Chain B5200 (2)

Back 744 (3)
*Embroider first*

Chain 3851 (3)

French knot 996 (2)

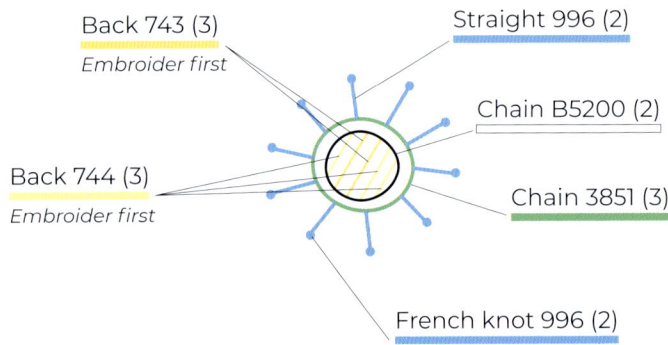

French knot 11 (2)

Stem 996 (1)

Straight 3850 (2)

Chain 3850 (2)

Straight 164 (2)

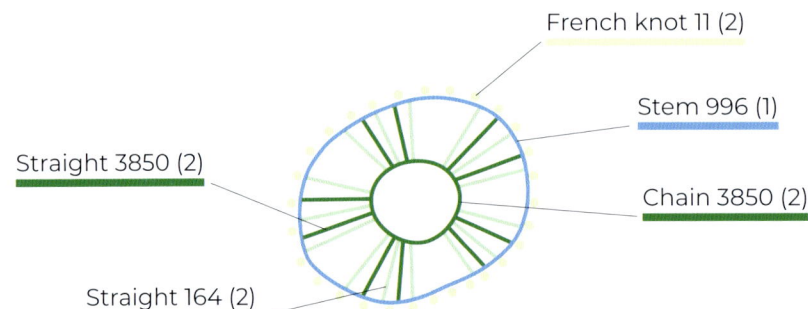

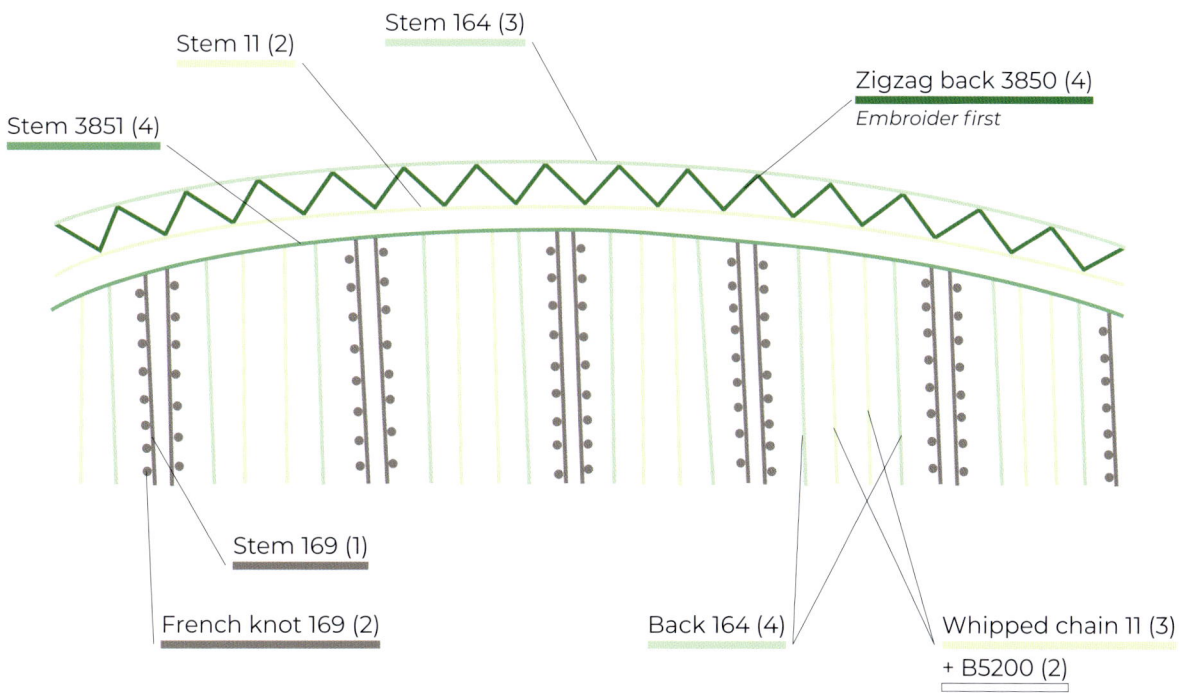

Stem 11 (2)

Stem 164 (3)

Zigzag back 3850 (4)
*Embroider first*

Stem 3851 (4)

Stem 169 (1)

French knot 169 (2)

Back 164 (4)

Whipped chain 11 (3)

+ B5200 (2)

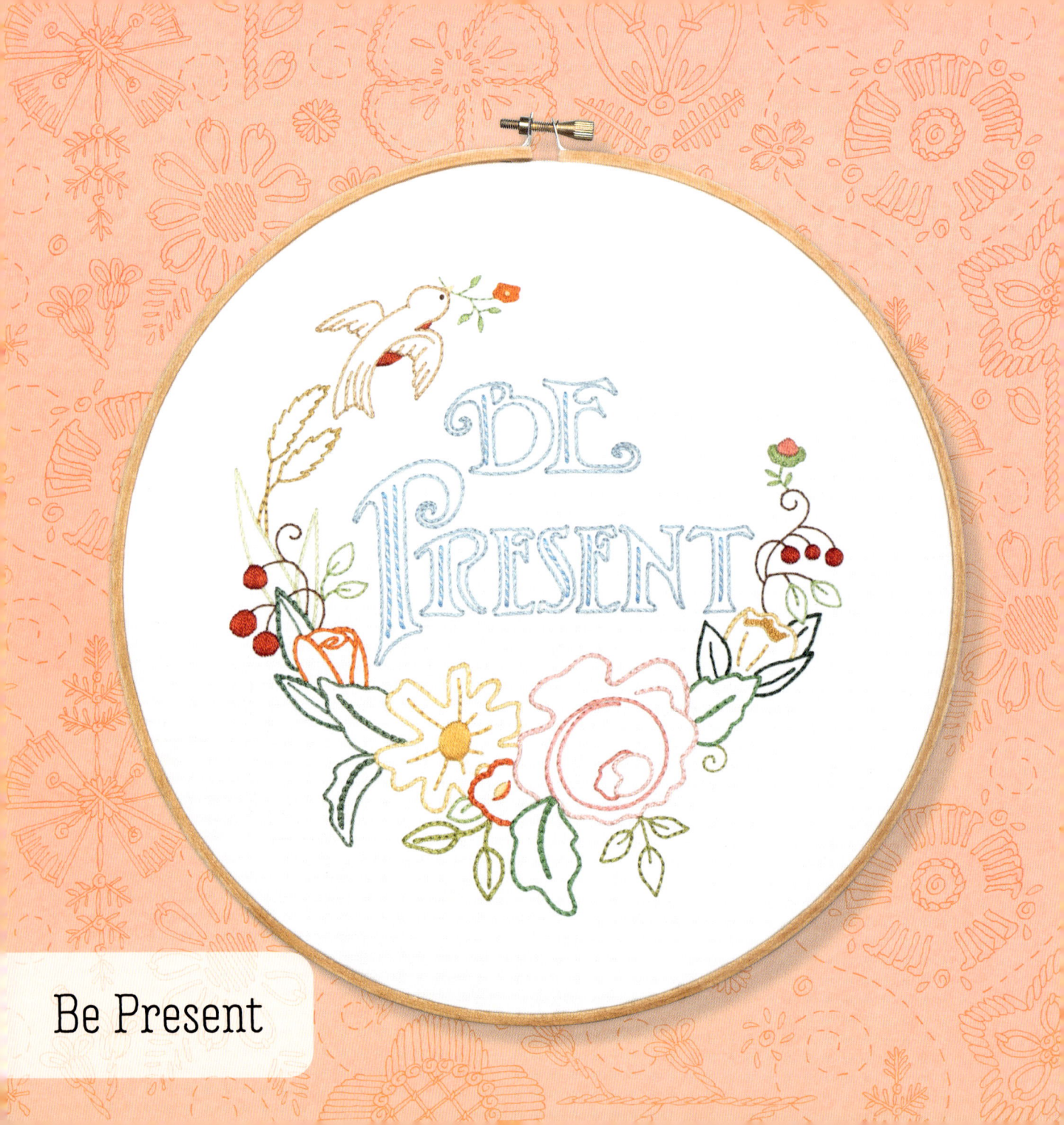

Be Present

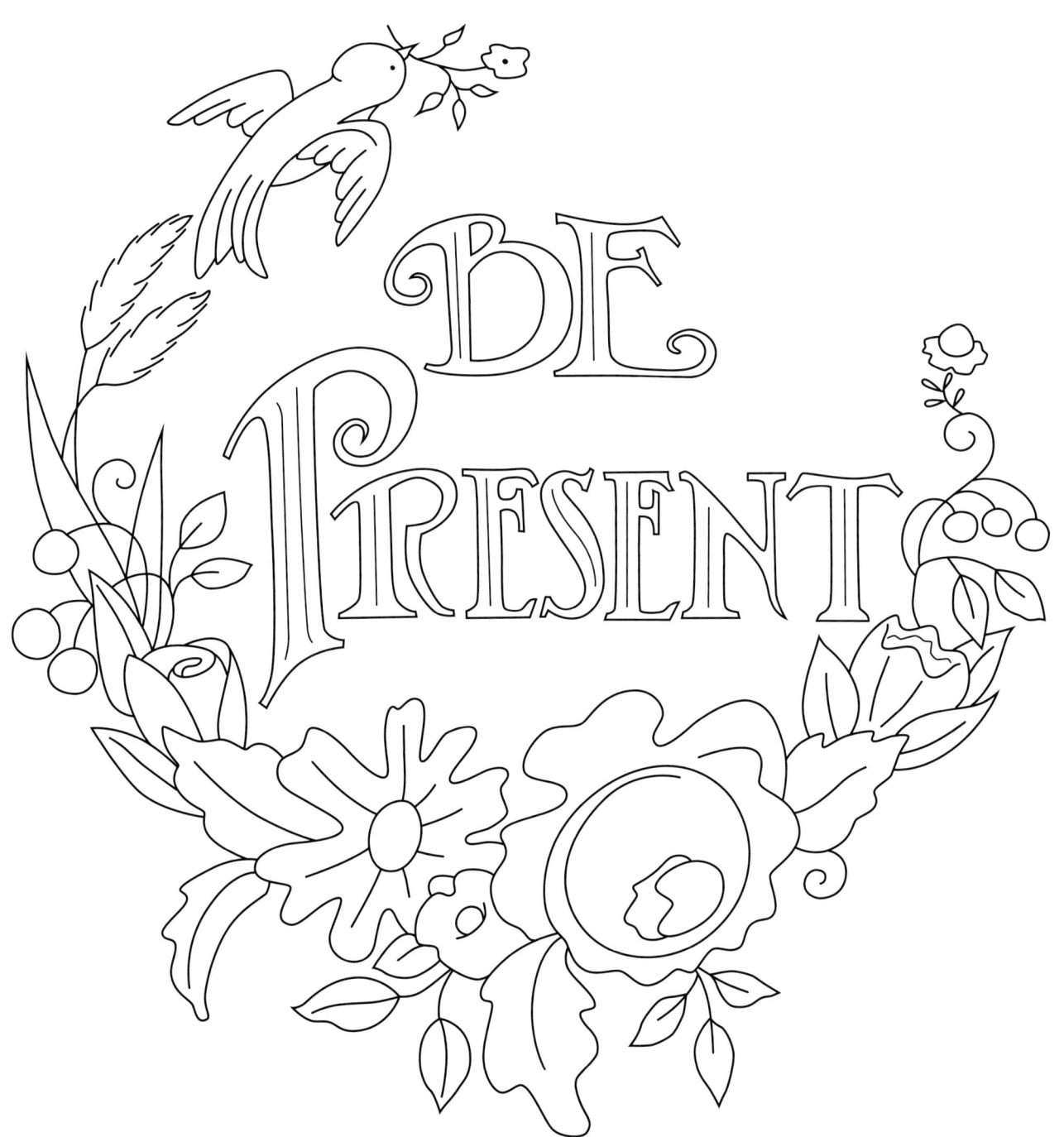

# SUPPLIES

## Fabric
12 x 12 inch (30x30cm) ground fabric
12 x 12 inch (30x30cm) backing fabric (optional)

## DMC six-stranded floss
| | | |
|---|---|---|
| 15 | Spring Onion |
| 304 | Chinese Lacquer |
| 319 | Shaded Green |
| 335 | Dark Pink |
| 350 | Vermillion |
| 367 | Laurel |
| 422 | Light Oak |
| 505 | Pinewood |
| 519 | Bluish Spray |
| 581 | Grasshopper |
| 701 | Grass |
| 704 | Lime |
| 720 | Rust |
| 727 | Primrose |
| 801 | Mink |
| 833 | Brass |
| 899 | Watermelon |
| 996 | Electric Blue |
| 3326 | Wild Rose |
| 3820 | Sunshine |
| 3821 | Metallic Mango |
| 3822 | Corn Husk |
| B5200 | Pearlescent White Light |

## Needles
Embroidery: size 7 and 9
Milliner: size 9

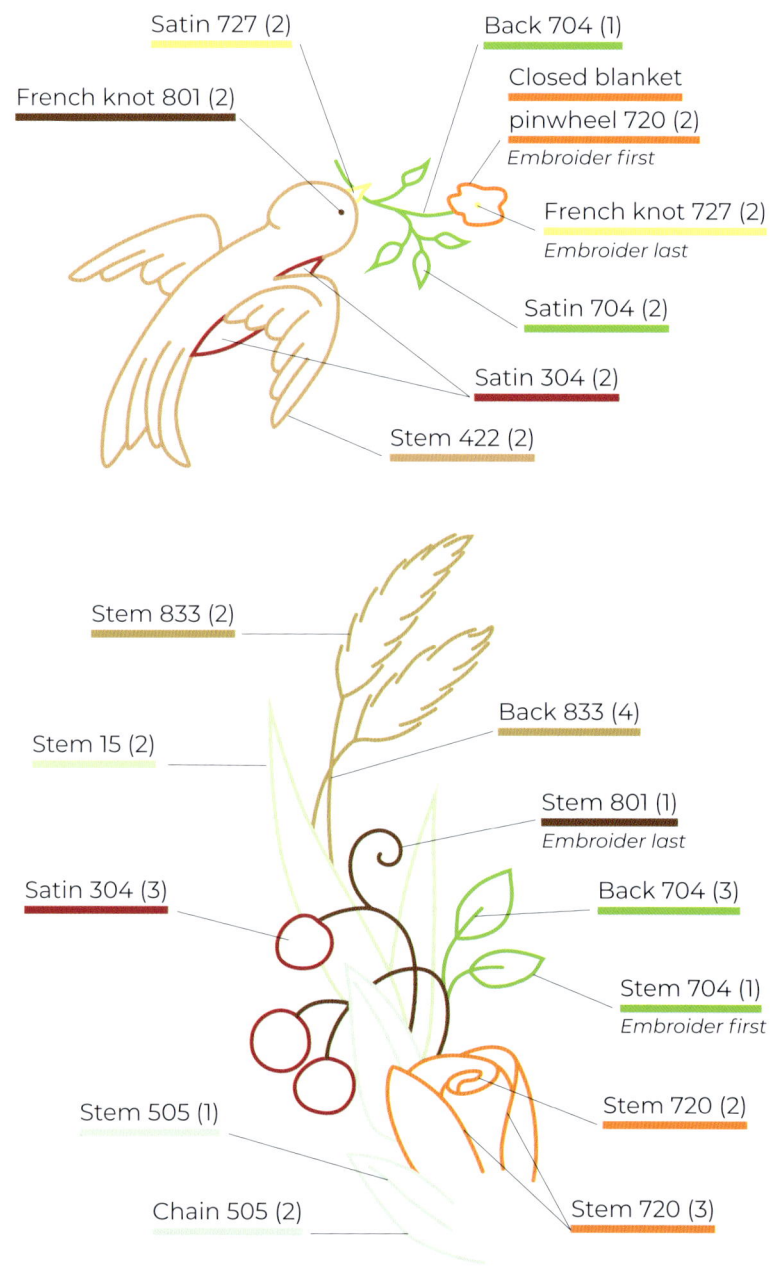

Satin 727 (2)

Back 704 (1)

French knot 801 (2)

Closed blanket pinwheel 720 (2)
*Embroider first*

French knot 727 (2)
*Embroider last*

Satin 704 (2)

Satin 304 (2)

Stem 422 (2)

Stem 833 (2)

Back 833 (4)

Stem 15 (2)

Stem 801 (1)
*Embroider last*

Satin 304 (3)

Back 704 (3)

Stem 704 (1)
*Embroider first*

Stem 505 (1)

Stem 720 (2)

Chain 505 (2)

Stem 720 (3)

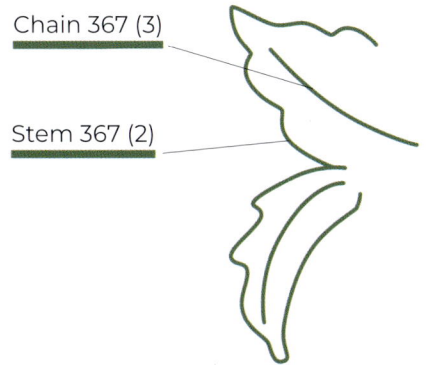

Chain 367 (3)

Stem 367 (2)

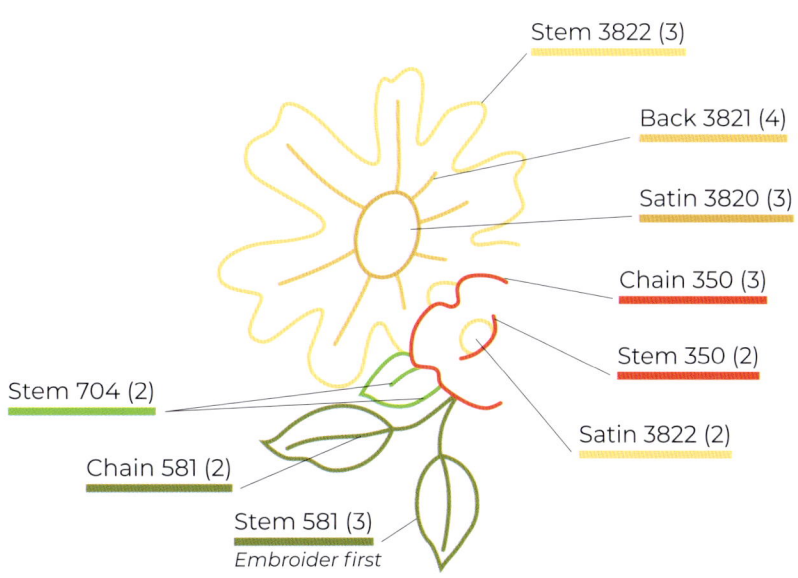

Stem 3822 (3)

Back 3821 (4)

Satin 3820 (3)

Chain 350 (3)

Stem 350 (2)

Satin 3822 (2)

Stem 704 (2)

Chain 581 (2)

Stem 581 (3)
*Embroider first*

Stem 3326 (4)

Stem 335 (2)

Stem 899 (3)

Stem 3326 (3)

Chain 701 (3)

Stem 701 (3)

Stem 581 (1)

Stem 3326 (2)

Stem 581 (2)

Back 581 (4)
*Embroider first*

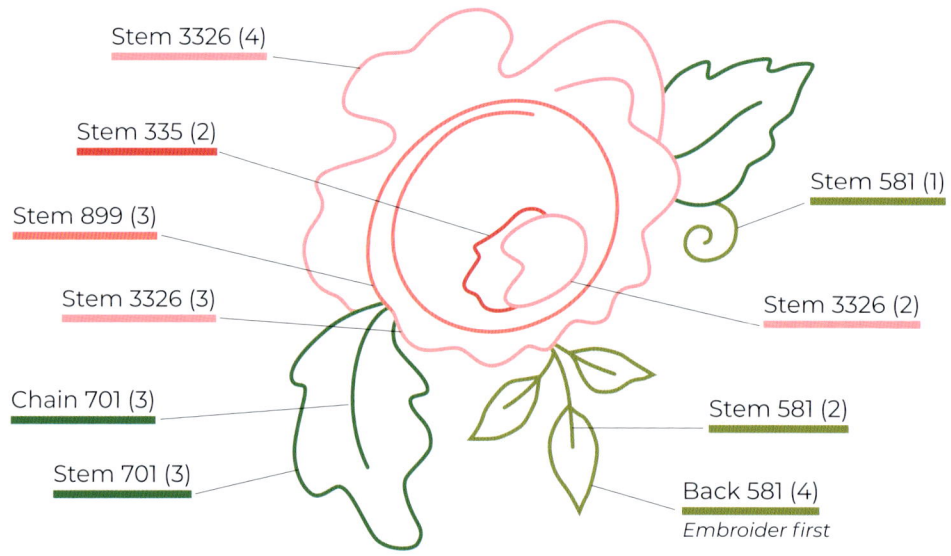

Stem 3822 (1)

French knots 3820 (2)

Back 3821 (3)

Stem 3822 (3)

Back 319 (3)

Stem 319 (2)

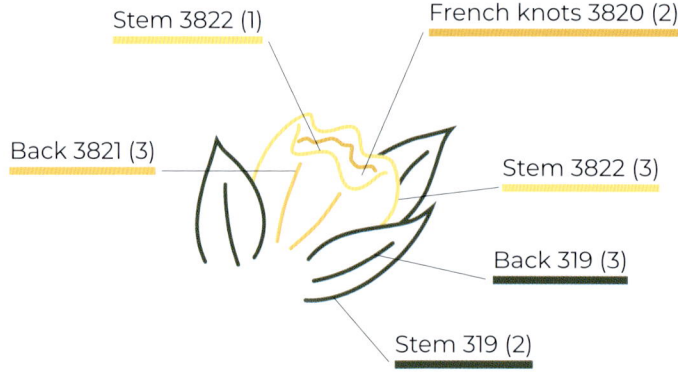

Blanket 704 (2)

Satin 335 (2)

Back 704 (2)

Detached chain 704 (2)

Stem 801 (1)

Satin 304 (3)

Back 704 (3)

Stem 704 (1)

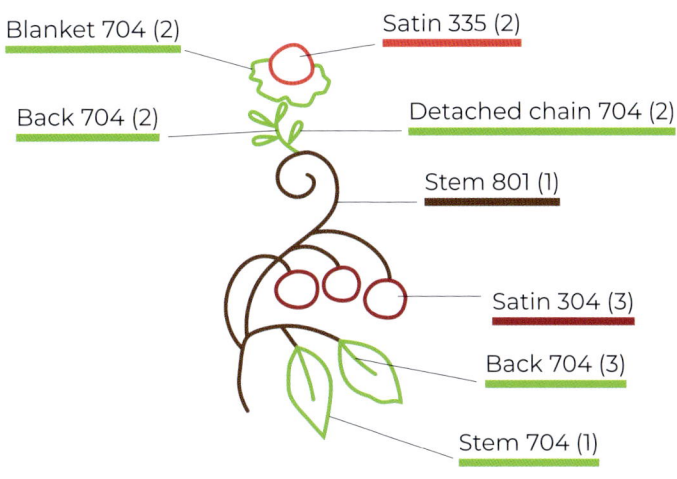

Whipped chain 996 (2)
+ B5200 (2)

Stem 519 (2)

Straight 519 (2)
*Letterform tips*

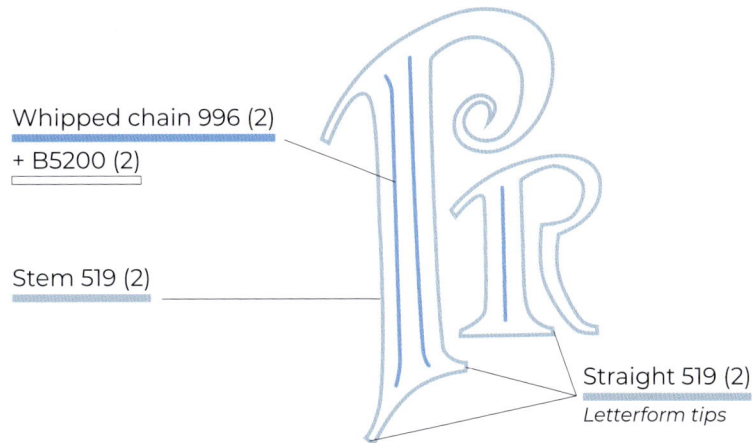

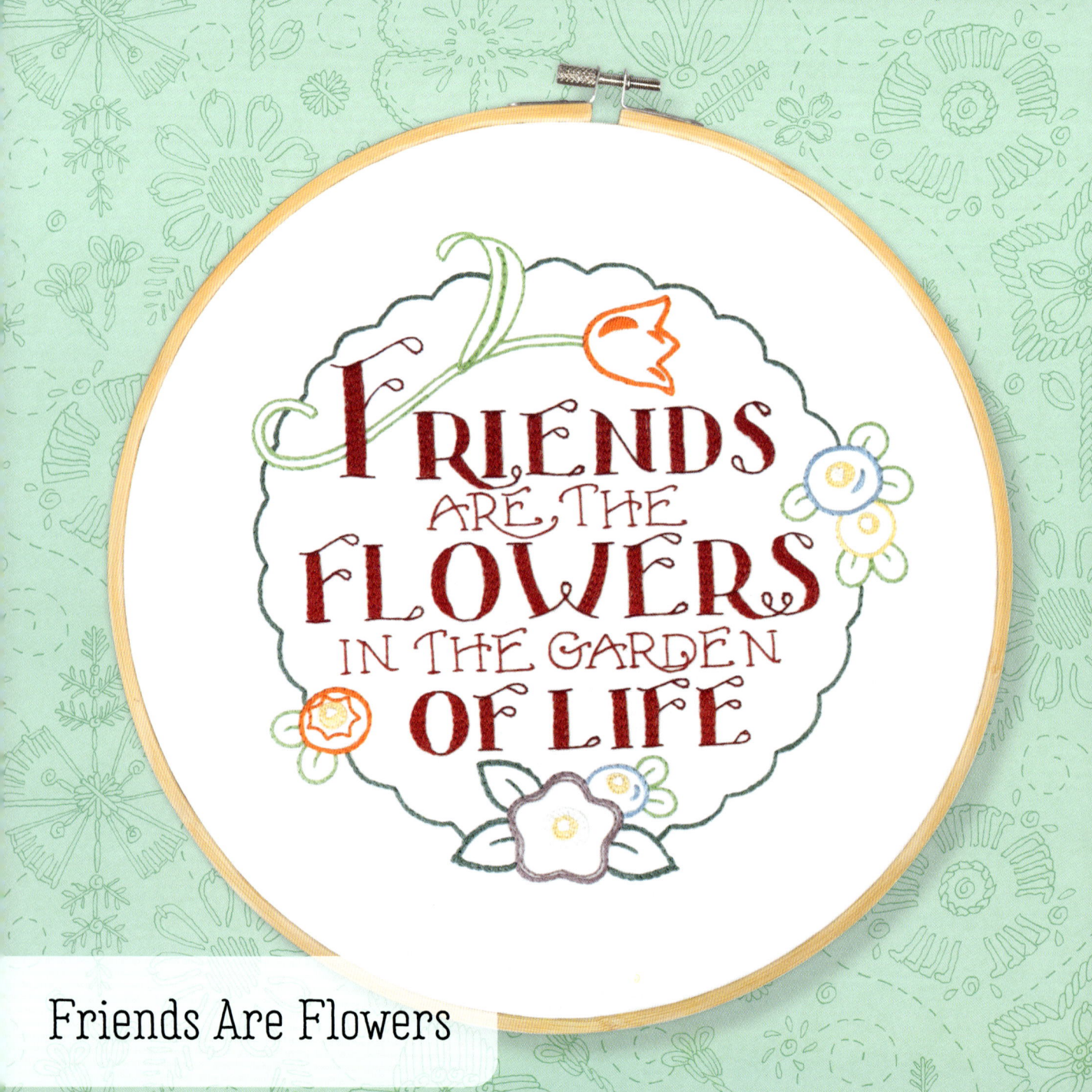

Friends Are Flowers

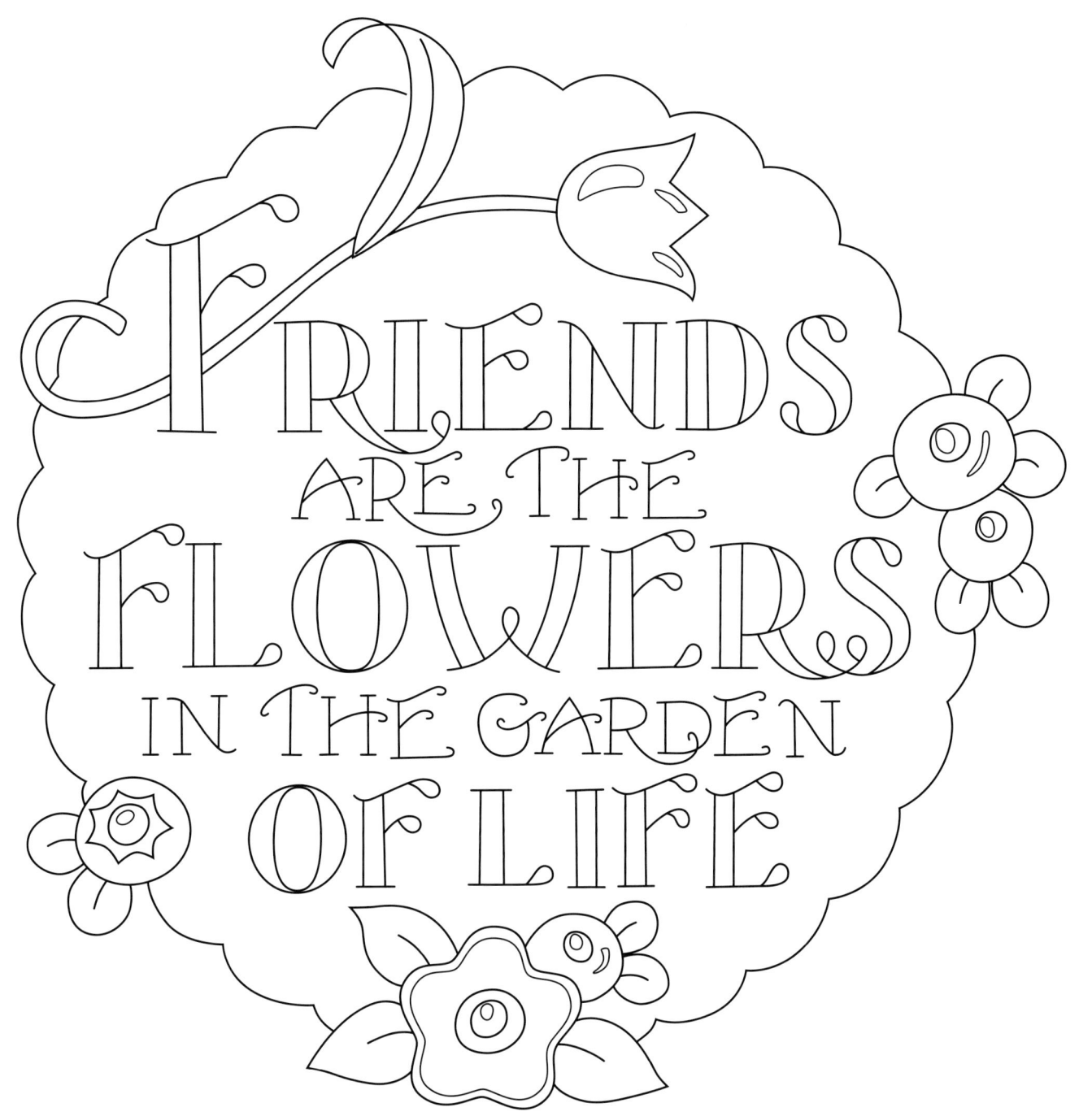

# SUPPLIES

## Fabric

12 x 12 inch (30x30cm)
ground fabric
12 x 12 inch (30x30cm)
backing fabric (optional)

## DMC six-stranded floss

- 501 — Pond Green
- 703 — Metallic Spring Green
- 720 — Rust
- 777 — Wine
- 813 — Gallic Blue
- 814 — Vin Rouge
- 3041 — Purple Slate
- 3822 — Corn Husk
- B5200 — Pearlescent White Light

## Needles

Embroidery: size 7 and 9
Milliner: size 9

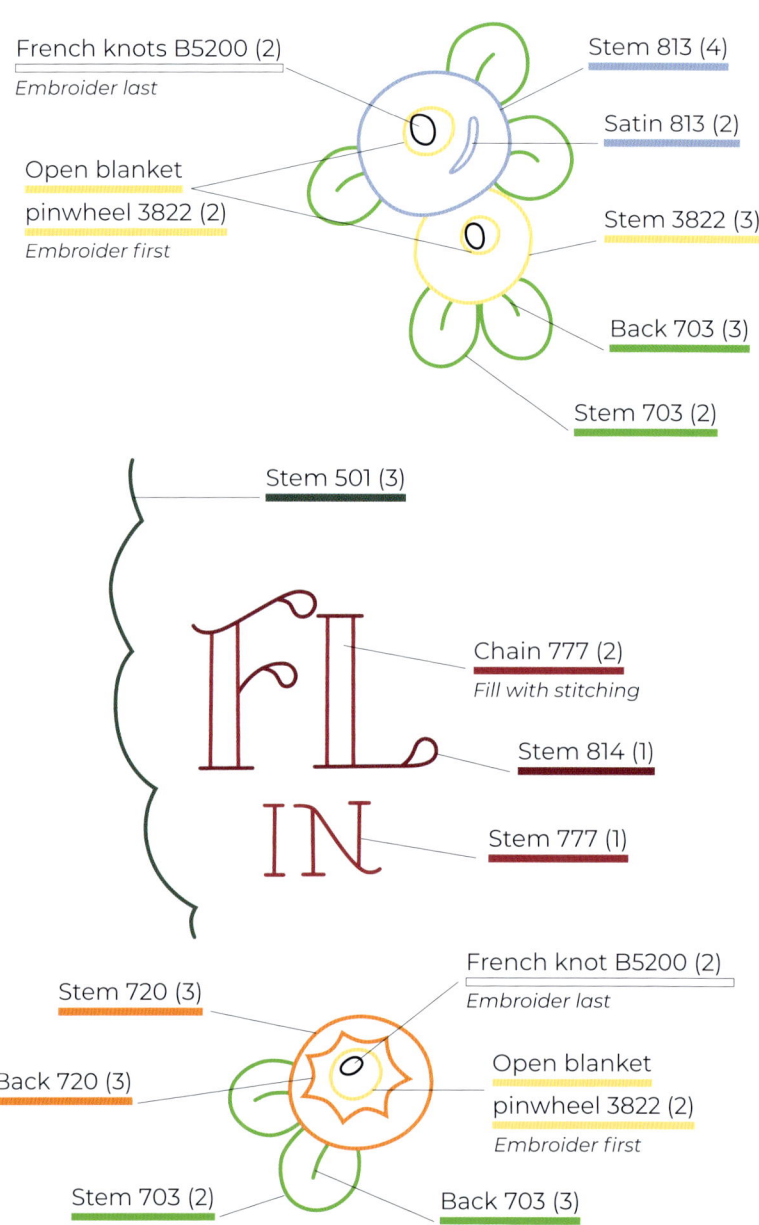

French knots B5200 (2)
*Embroider last*

Stem 813 (4)

Satin 813 (2)

Open blanket
pinwheel 3822 (2)
*Embroider first*

Stem 3822 (3)

Back 703 (3)

Stem 703 (2)

Stem 501 (3)

Chain 777 (2)
*Fill with stitching*

Stem 814 (1)

Stem 777 (1)

French knot B5200 (2)
*Embroider last*

Stem 720 (3)

Open blanket
pinwheel 3822 (2)
*Embroider first*

Back 720 (3)

Stem 703 (2)

Back 703 (3)

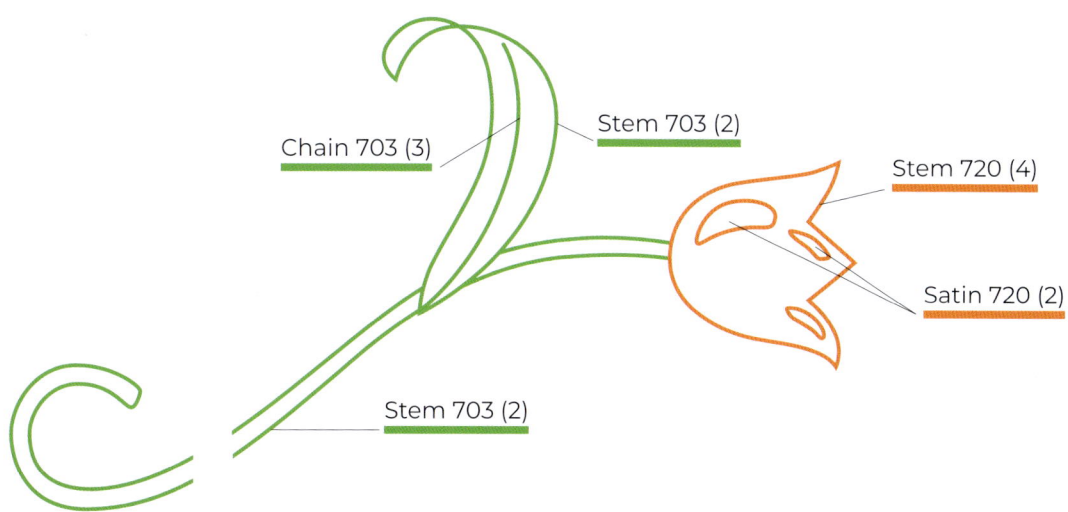

Chain 703 (3)

Stem 703 (2)

Stem 720 (4)

Satin 720 (2)

Stem 703 (2)

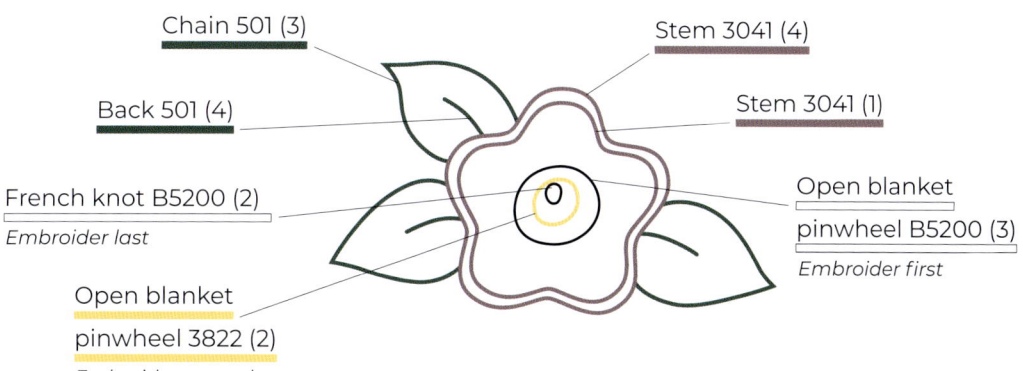

Chain 501 (3)

Stem 3041 (4)

Back 501 (4)

Stem 3041 (1)

French knot B5200 (2)
*Embroider last*

Open blanket
pinwheel B5200 (3)
*Embroider first*

Open blanket
pinwheel 3822 (2)
*Embroider second*

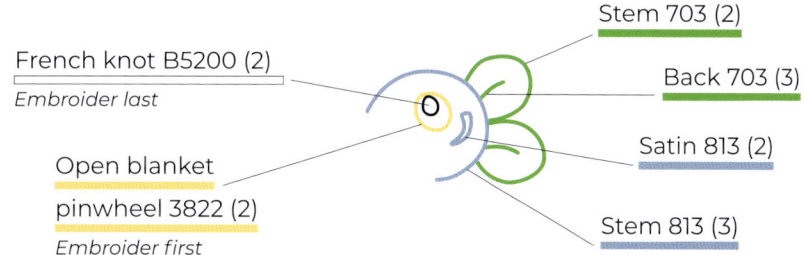

French knot B5200 (2)
*Embroider last*

Stem 703 (2)

Back 703 (3)

Satin 813 (2)

Open blanket
pinwheel 3822 (2)
*Embroider first*

Stem 813 (3)

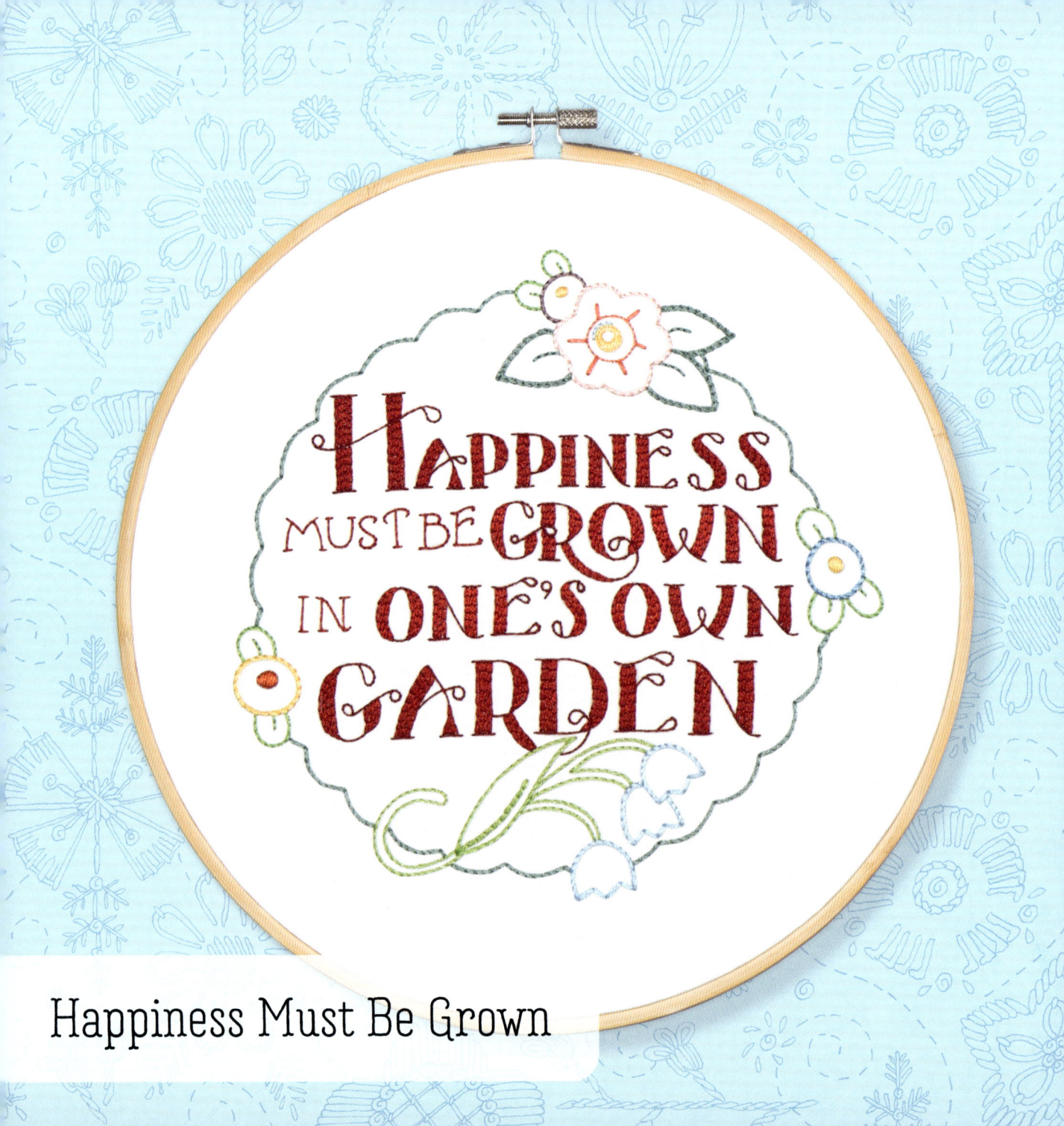

Happiness Must Be Grown

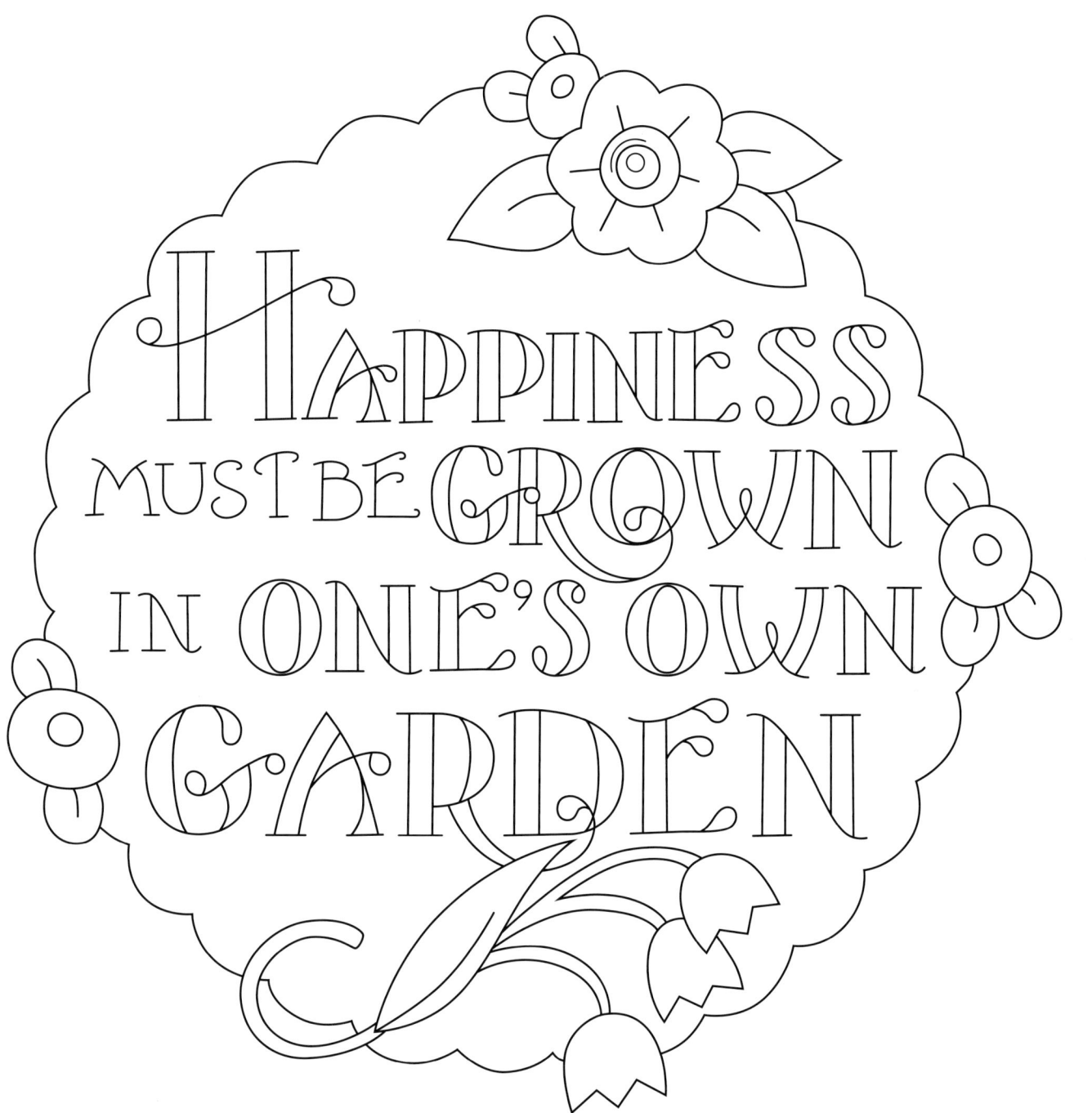

HAPPINESS MUST BE GROWN IN ONE'S OWN GARDEN

## SUPPLIES

### Fabric

12 x 12 inch (30x30cm)
ground fabric
12 x 12 inch (30x30cm)
backing fabric (optional)

### DMC six-stranded floss

| | | |
|---|---|---|
| ■ | 502 | Almond Leaf |
| ■ | 703 | Metallic Spring Green |
| ■ | 704 | Lime |
| ■ | 777 | Wine |
| ■ | 813 | Gallic Blue |
| ■ | 814 | Vin Rouge |
| ■ | 827 | Forget-Me-Knot |
| ■ | 3041 | Purple Slate |
| ■ | 3712 | Blush |
| ■ | 3713 | Rose Quartz |
| ■ | 3822 | Corn Husk |
| ■ | 3830 | Deep Blush |
| ☐ | B5200 | Pearlescent White Light |

### Needles

Embroidery: size 7 and 9
Milliner: size 9

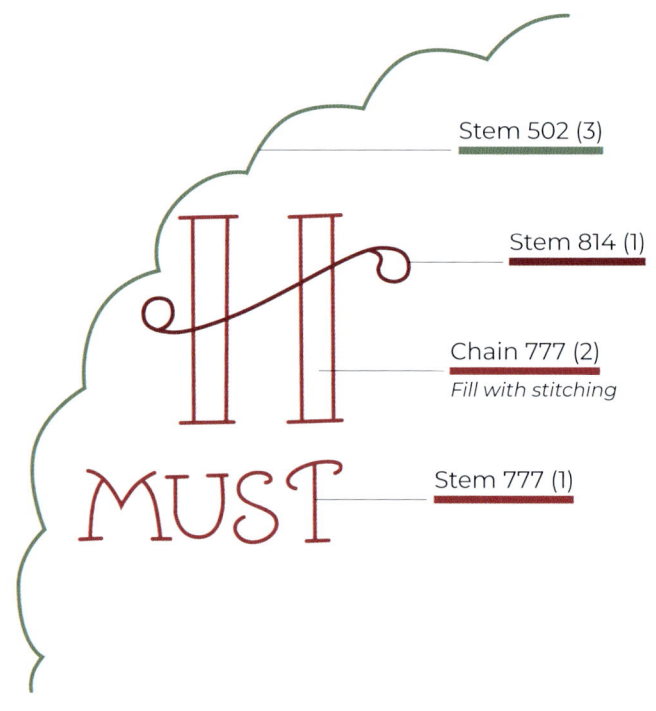

Stem 502 (3)

Stem 814 (1)

Chain 777 (2)
*Fill with stitching*

Stem 777 (1)

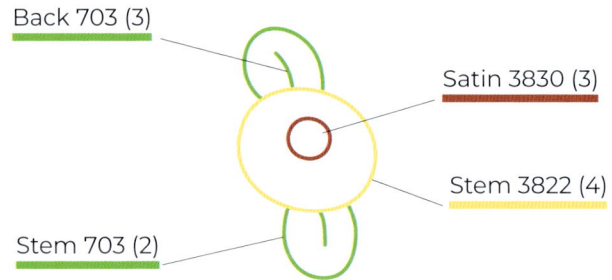

Back 703 (3)

Satin 3830 (3)

Stem 3822 (4)

Stem 703 (2)

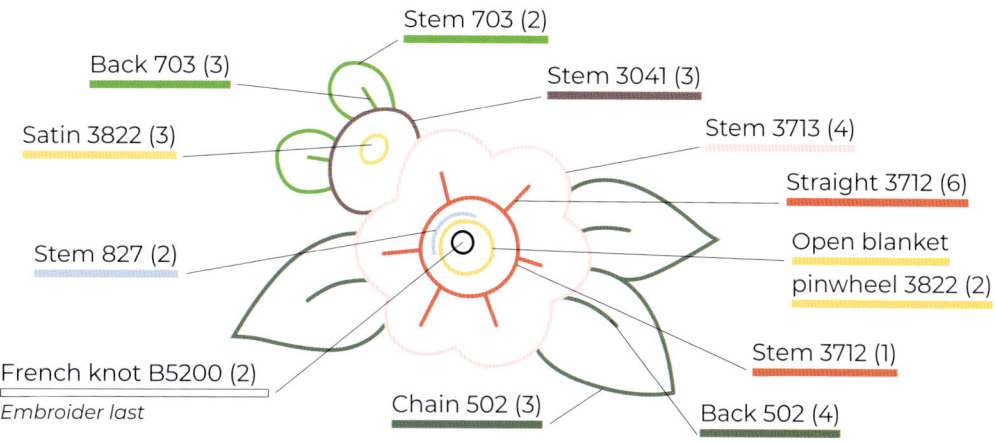

Stem 703 (2)

Back 703 (3)

Stem 3041 (3)

Satin 3822 (3)

Stem 3713 (4)

Straight 3712 (6)

Stem 827 (2)

Open blanket
pinwheel 3822 (2)

French knot B5200 (2)
*Embroider last*

Stem 3712 (1)

Chain 502 (3)

Back 502 (4)

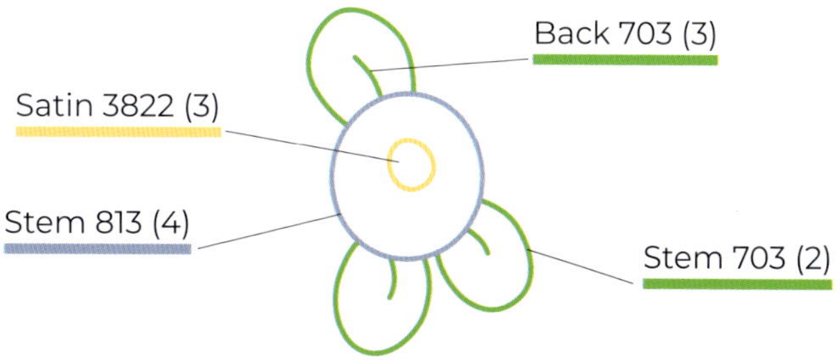

Satin 3822 (3)

Back 703 (3)

Stem 813 (4)

Stem 703 (2)

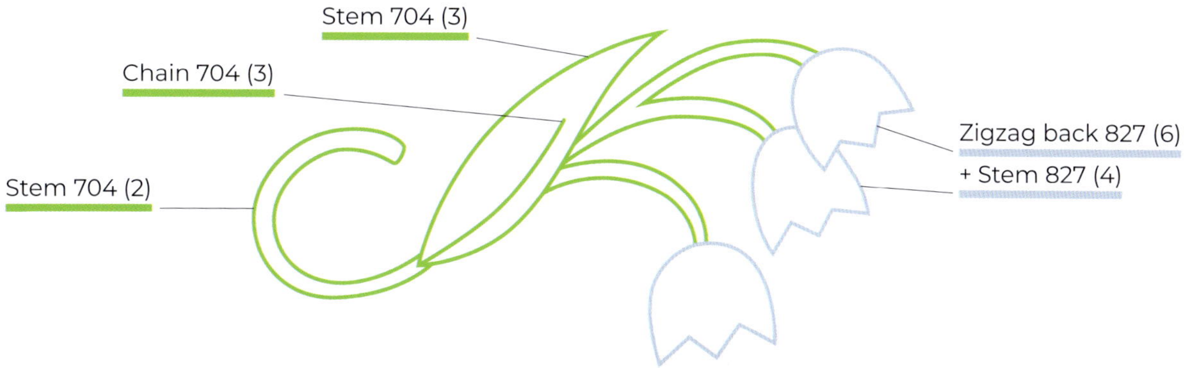

Stem 704 (3)

Chain 704 (3)

Zigzag back 827 (6)
+ Stem 827 (4)

Stem 704 (2)

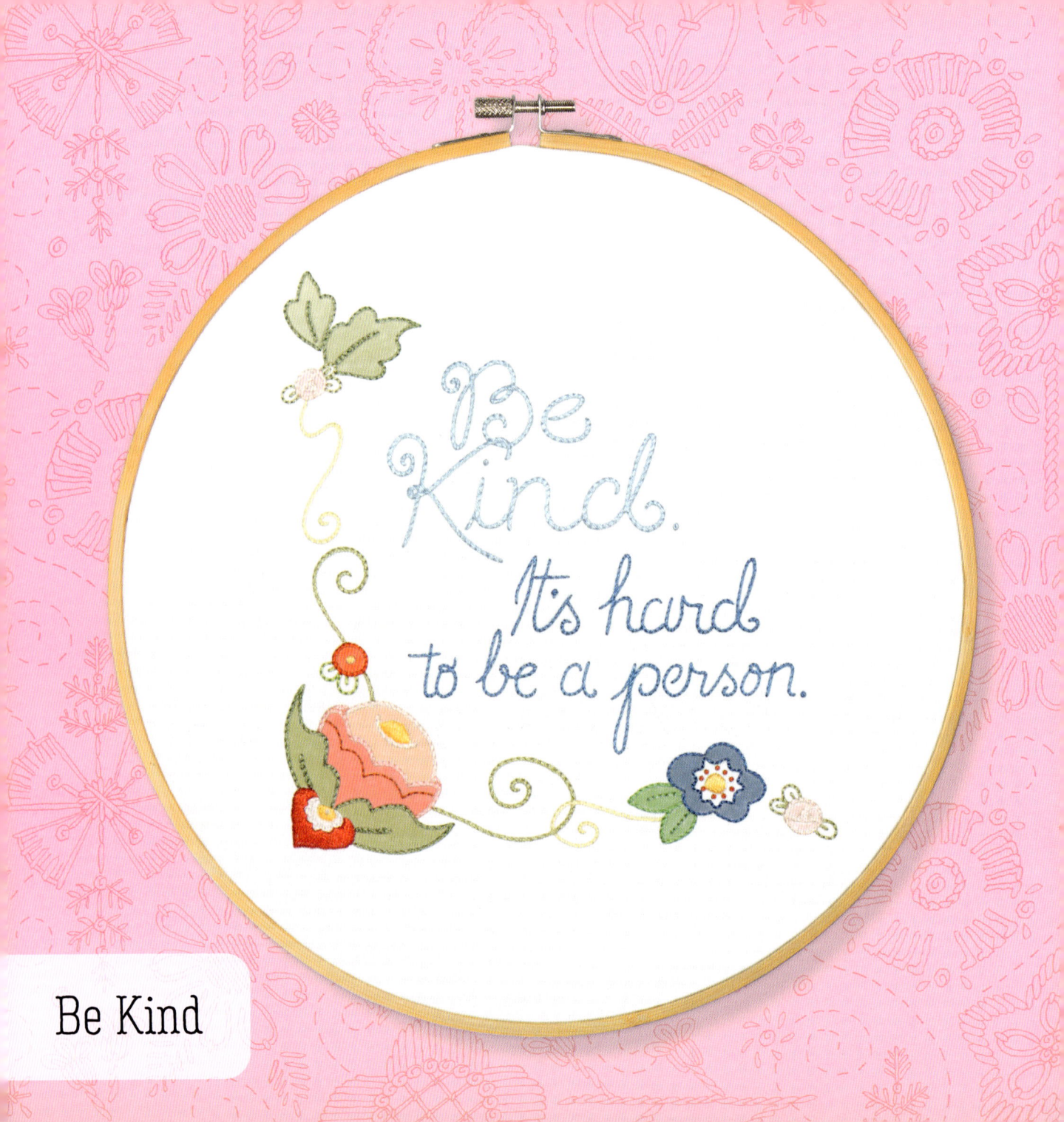

Be Kind.
It's hard to be a person.

Be Kind

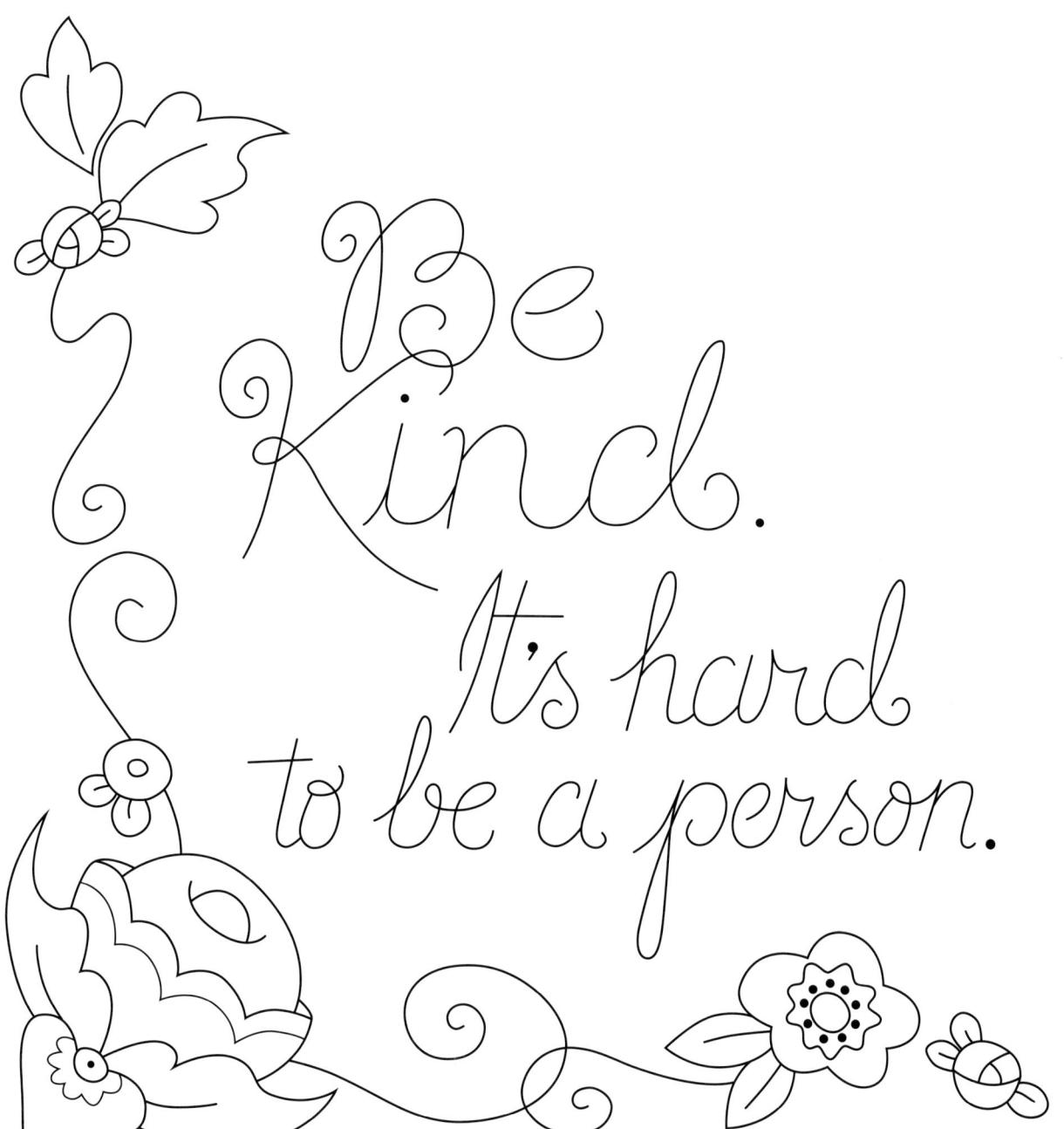

Be Kind. It's hard to be a person.

# SUPPLIES

## Fabric
12 x 12 inch (30x30cm)
ground fabric
12 x 12 inch (30x30cm)
backing fabric (optional)

## DMC six-stranded floss

| | | |
|---|---|---|
| | 11 | Lemon Drop |
| | 225 | Cherry Blossom |
| | 326 | Rhubarb |
| | 347 | Egyptian Red |
| | 702 | Spring Lawn |
| | 704 | Lime |
| | 743 | Banana |
| | 825 | Metallic Gentian Blue |
| | 826 | Tuareg Blue |
| | 827 | Forget-Me-Knot |
| | 3326 | Wild Rose |
| | 3363 | Bullfrog |
| | 3364 | Sage |
| | B5200 | Pearlescent White Light |

## Needles
Embroidery: size 7 and 9
Milliner: size 7 and 9

## Optional Fabric Marker Colors
Blue, Green, Red, Pink, and Light Pink
See page 140 for color placement.

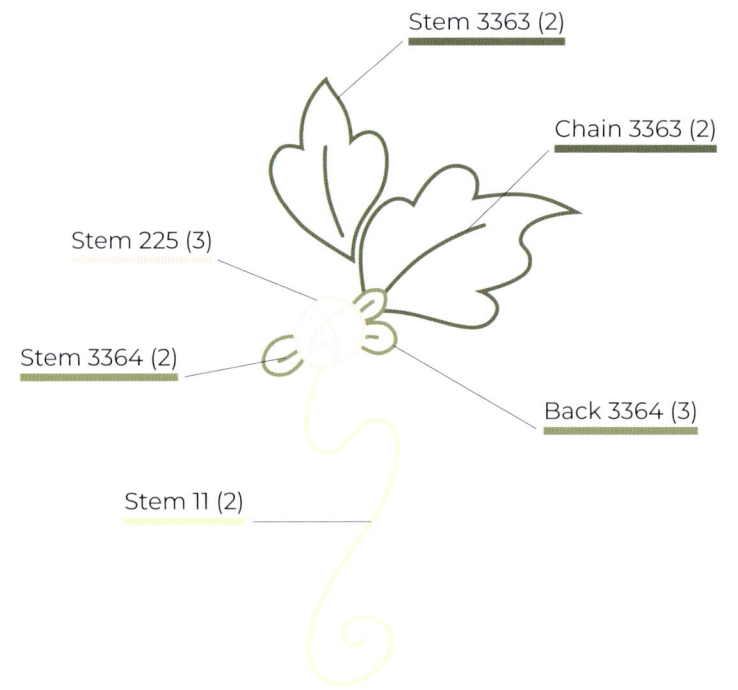

Stem 3363 (2)

Chain 3363 (2)

Stem 225 (3)

Stem 3364 (2)

Back 3364 (3)

Stem 11 (2)

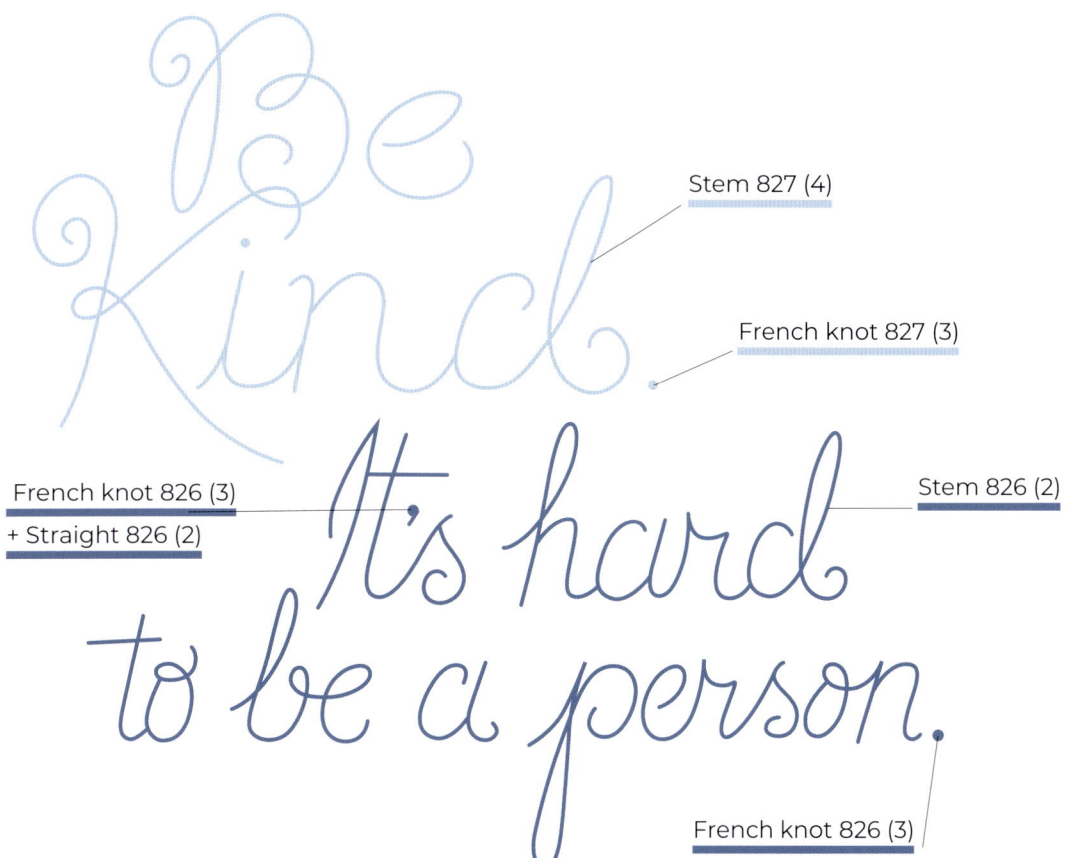

Be Kind

It's hard to be a person.

Stem 827 (4)

French knot 827 (3)

French knot 826 (3)
+ Straight 826 (2)

Stem 826 (2)

French knot 826 (3)

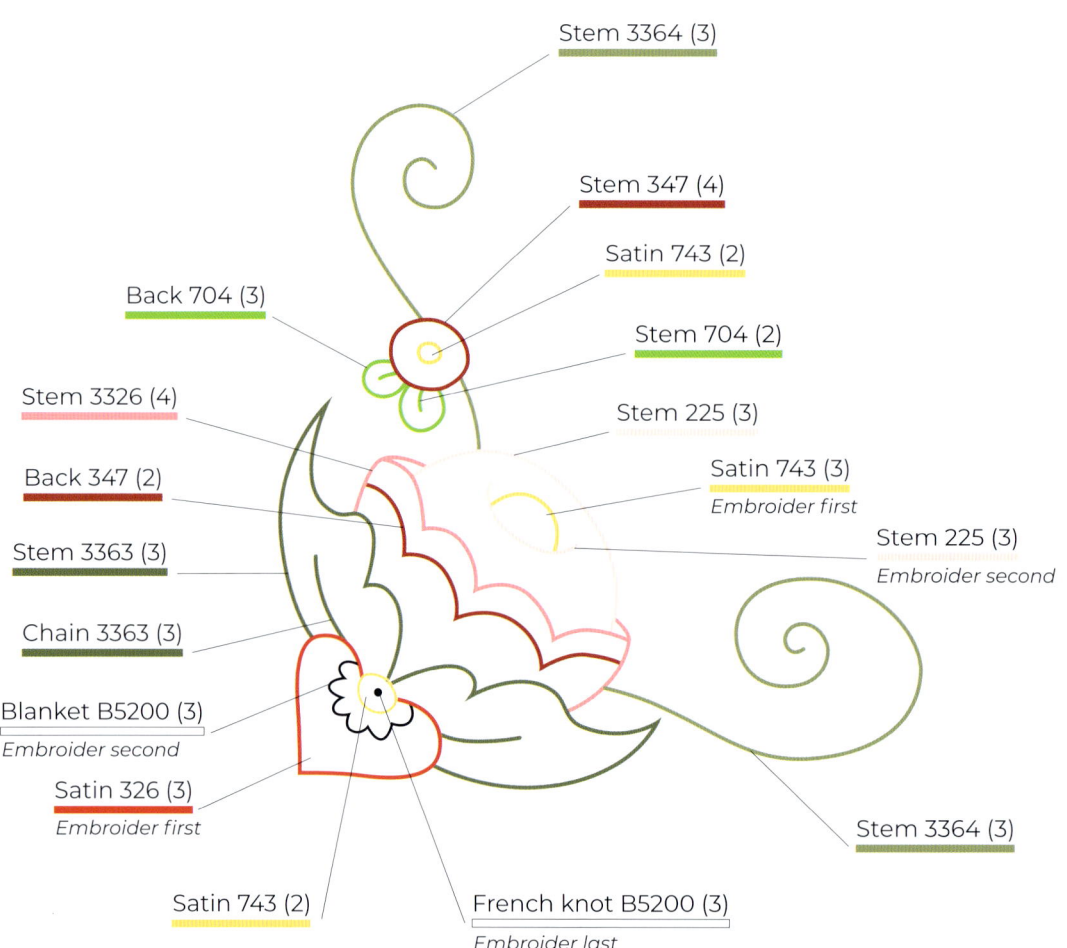

Stem 3364 (3)

Stem 347 (4)

Satin 743 (2)

Back 704 (3)

Stem 704 (2)

Stem 3326 (4)

Stem 225 (3)

Satin 743 (3)
*Embroider first*

Back 347 (2)

Stem 3363 (3)

Stem 225 (3)
*Embroider second*

Chain 3363 (3)

Blanket B5200 (3)
*Embroider second*

Satin 326 (3)
*Embroider first*

Stem 3364 (3)

Satin 743 (2)

French knot B5200 (3)
*Embroider last*

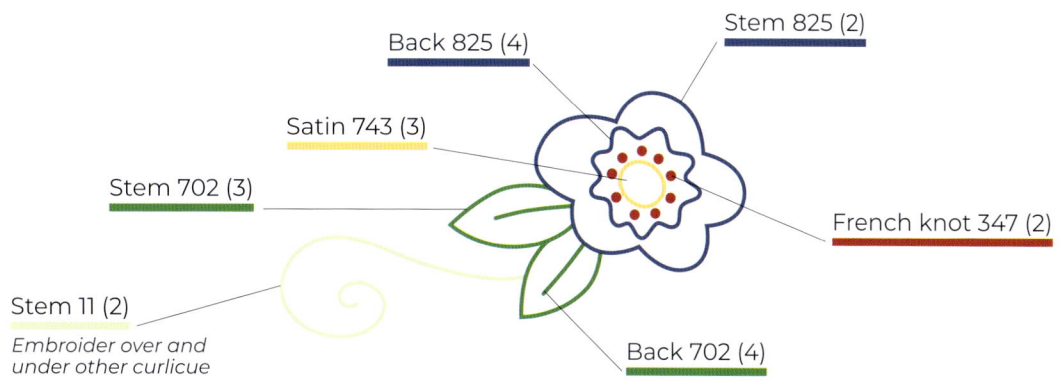

Back 825 (4)

Stem 825 (2)

Satin 743 (3)

Stem 702 (3)

French knot 347 (2)

Stem 11 (2)

*Embroider over and
under other curlicue*

Back 702 (4)

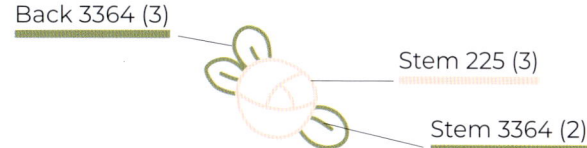

Back 3364 (3)

Stem 225 (3)

Stem 3364 (2)

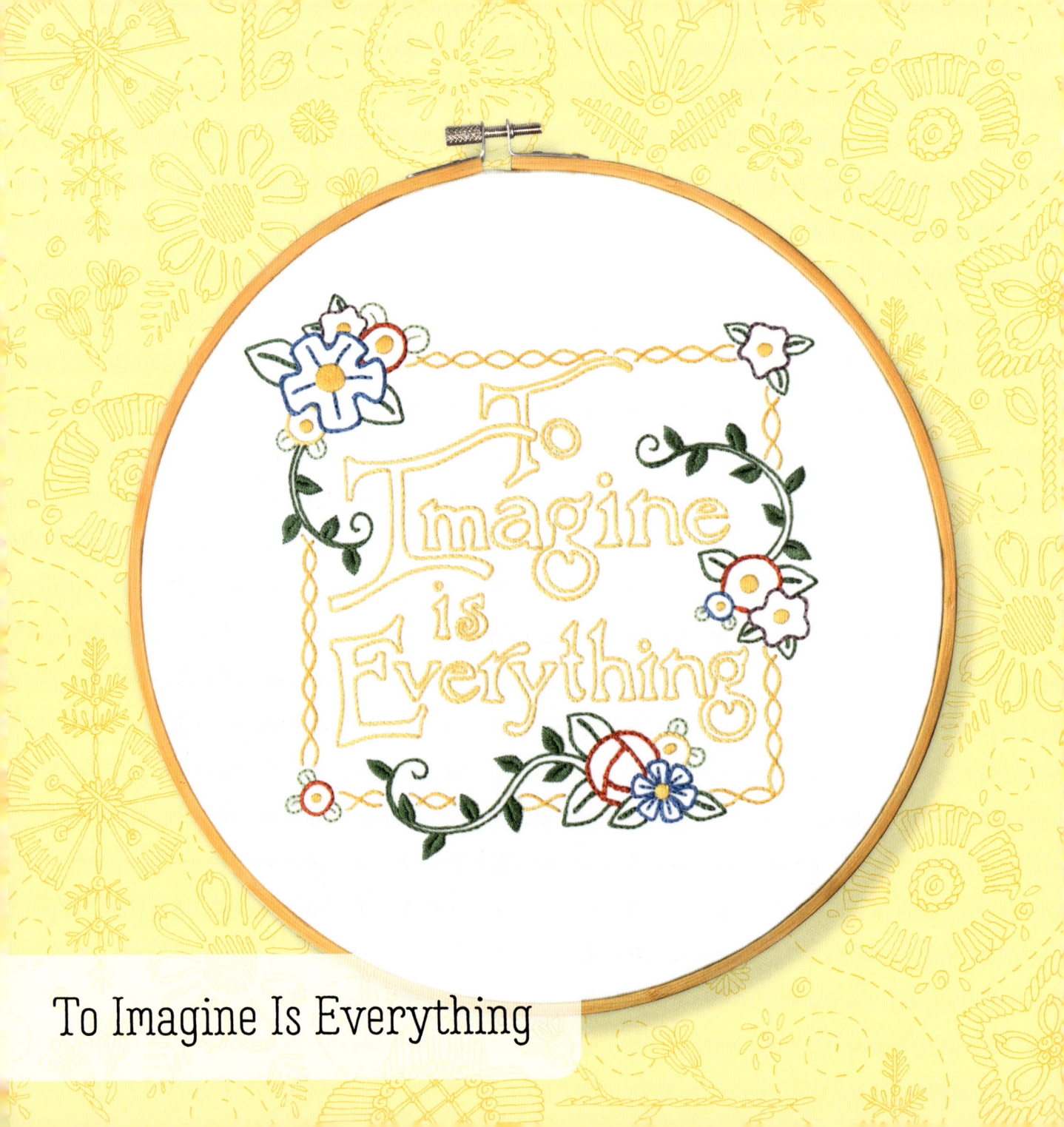

To Imagine Is Everything

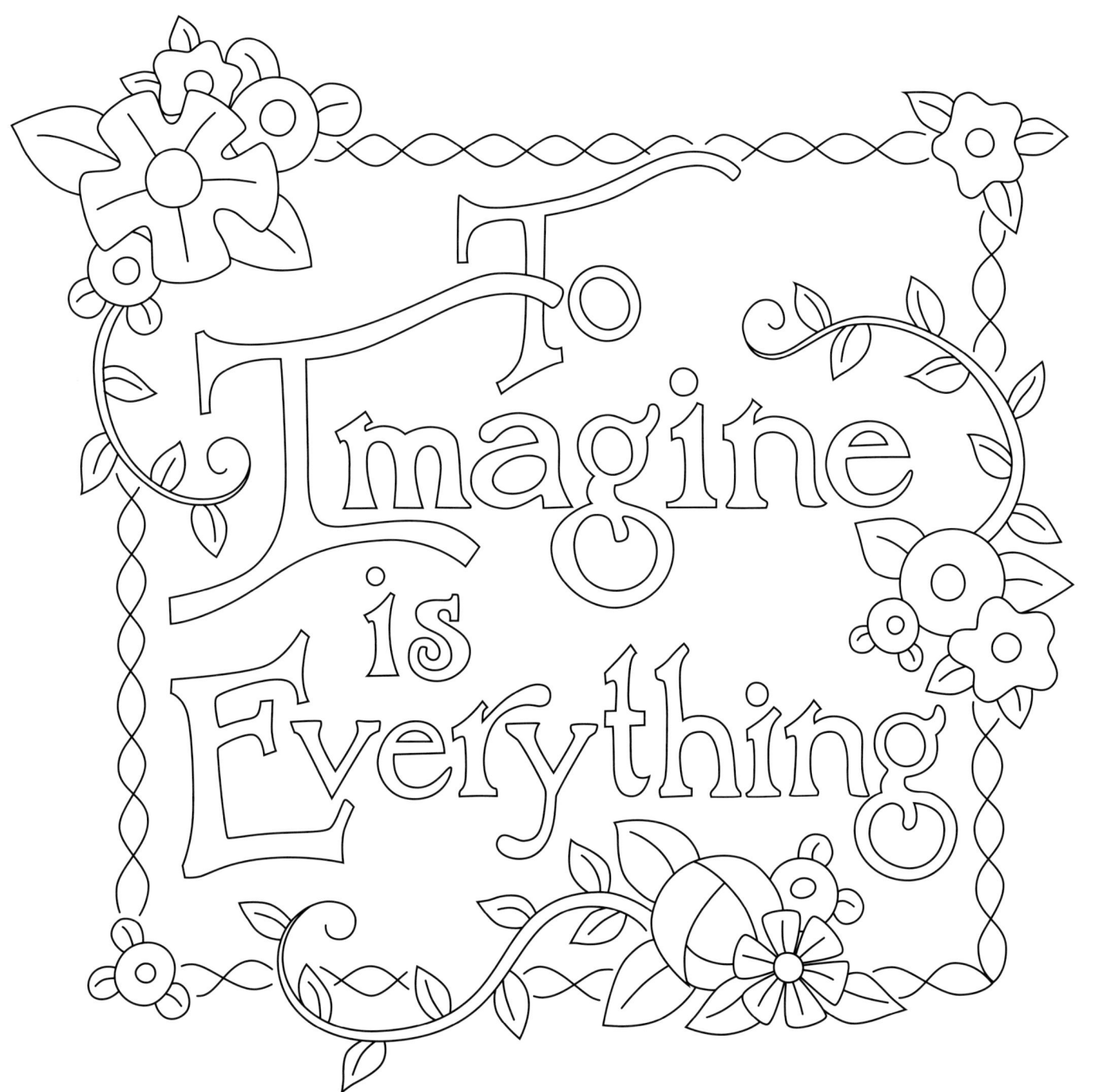

## SUPPLIES

### Fabric
12 x 12 inch (30x30cm)
ground fabric
12 x 12 inch (30x30cm)
backing fabric (optional)

### DMC six-stranded floss
| | | |
|---|---|---|
| ■ | 367 | Laurel |
| ■ | 368 | Eau de Nile |
| ■ | 826 | Tuareg Blue |
| ■ | 3831 | Wild Strawberry |
| ■ | 3041 | Purple Slate |
| ■ | 3820 | Sunshine |
| ■ | 3821 | Metallic Mango |
| ■ | 3822 | Corn Husk |

### Needles
Embroidery: size 7 and 9

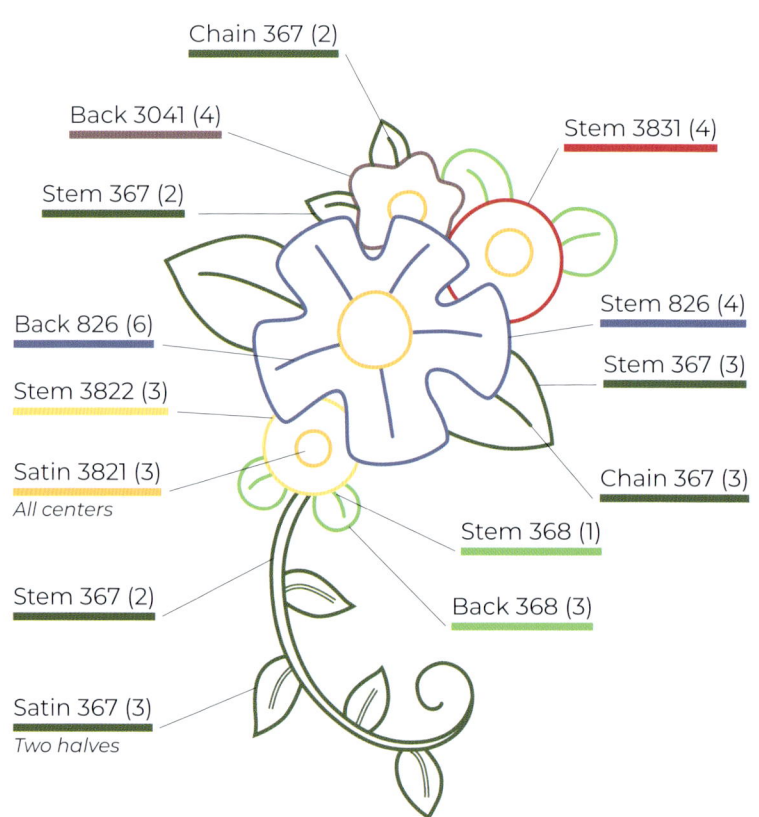

Chain 367 (2)

Back 3041 (4)

Stem 367 (2)

Stem 3831 (4)

Back 826 (6)

Stem 826 (4)

Stem 3822 (3)

Stem 367 (3)

Satin 3821 (3)
*All centers*

Chain 367 (3)

Stem 368 (1)

Stem 367 (2)

Back 368 (3)

Satin 367 (3)
*Two halves*

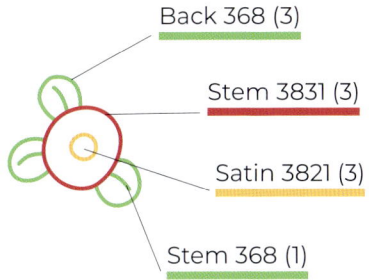

Back 368 (3)

Stem 3831 (3)

Satin 3821 (3)

Stem 368 (1)

Satin 367 (3)
*Two halves*

Stem 367 (2)

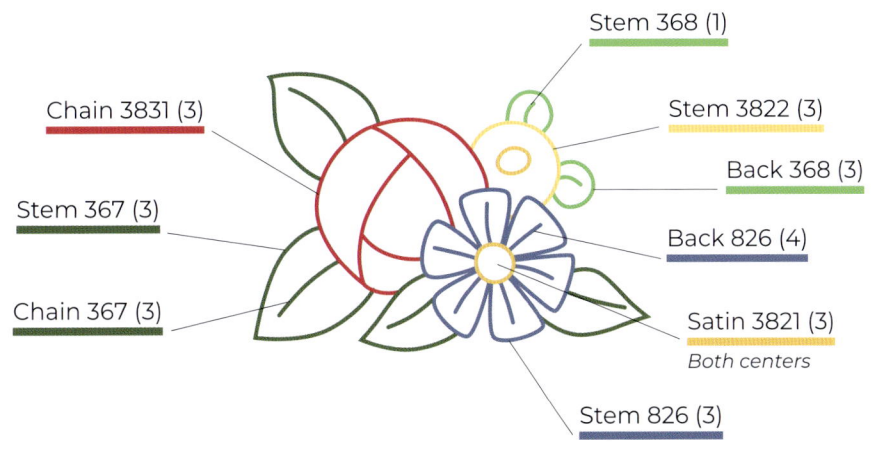

Stem 368 (1)

Chain 3831 (3)

Stem 3822 (3)

Back 368 (3)

Back 826 (4)

Stem 367 (3)

Chain 367 (3)

Satin 3821 (3)
*Both centers*

Stem 826 (3)

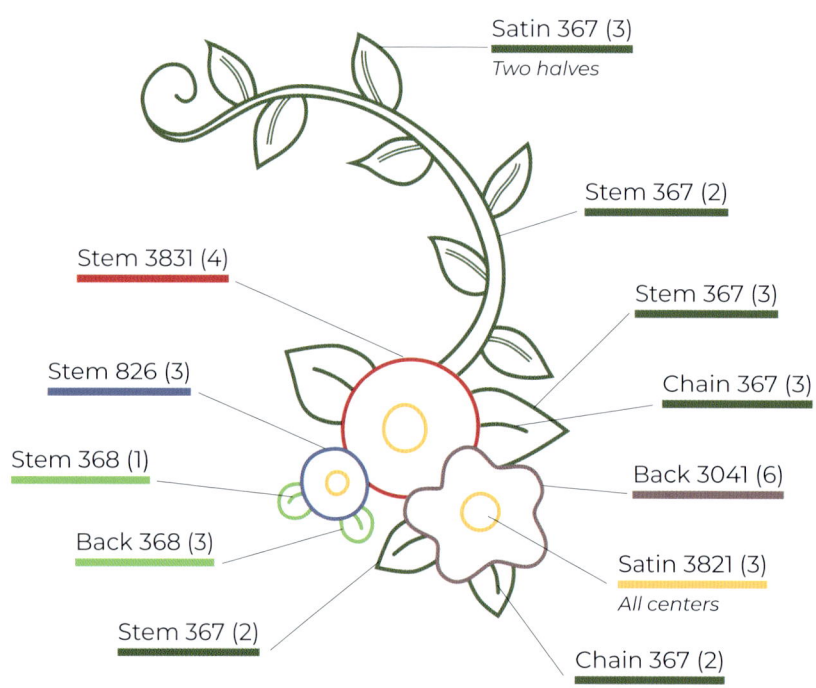

Satin 367 (3)
*Two halves*

Stem 367 (2)

Stem 3831 (4)

Stem 367 (3)

Chain 367 (3)

Stem 826 (3)

Back 3041 (6)

Stem 368 (1)

Satin 3821 (3)
*All centers*

Back 368 (3)

Stem 367 (2)

Chain 367 (2)

Satin 3821 (3)

Back 3041 (6)

Chain 367 (3)

Stem 367 (3)

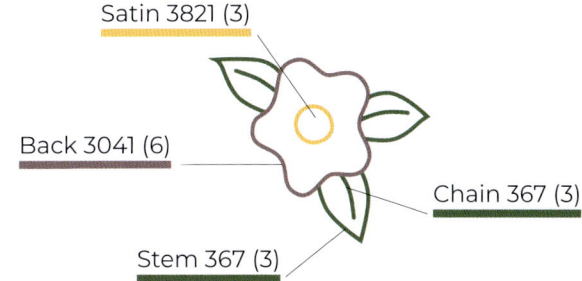

Stem 3821 (2)
+ Stem 3820 (2)

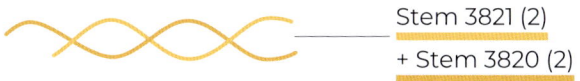

Stem 3822 (3)

Straight 3822 (3)
*Letterform tips*

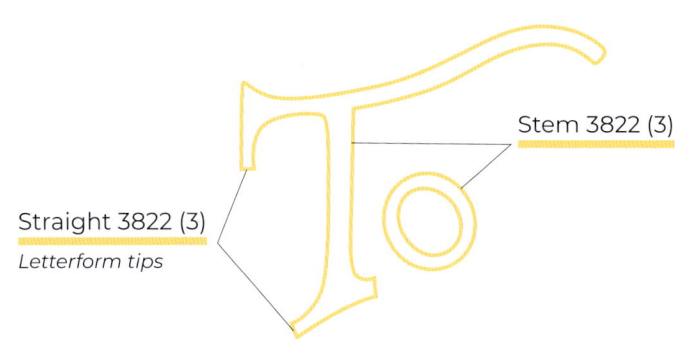

# The
# Stitches

## STRAIGHT STITCH

Bring your needle up through the fabric and take it down again a little ways away—depending on how much space you are trying to fill—to embroider a single straight stitch.

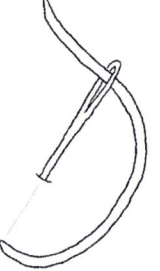 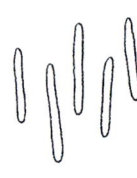

## SATIN STITCH

Start with a straight stitch across the center of your shape. Work outward to fill one side of the initial stitch first, then the other side. Place your stitches close together, so you get a solid area of stitching.

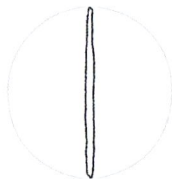 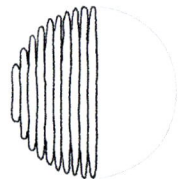 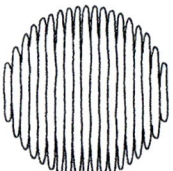

## BACK STITCH

Bring your needle up near the start of the row. Take a stitch from the start of the row to an equal length away from your emerging thread. Continue with this pattern, using the same holes in the fabric at the start and end of each stitch. Take your needle down at the end of the second-to-last back stitch to finish.

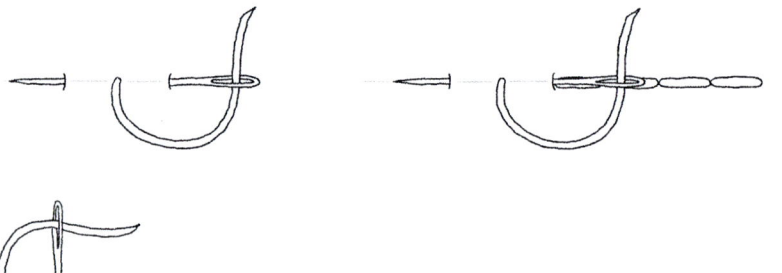

**TIP:** If you're left-handed, you'll want to flip the instructions. You can do this mentally or with a mirror. Or take a photo and use the flip function on your phone or tablet.

## ZIGZAG BACK STITCH

Bring your needle up at the first "peak" of the zigzag row. Take a stitch below this, from "valley" to valley, then another from peak to peak, using the same holes in the fabric each time. Continue to the end of the row. Take your needle down through the last peak to finish.

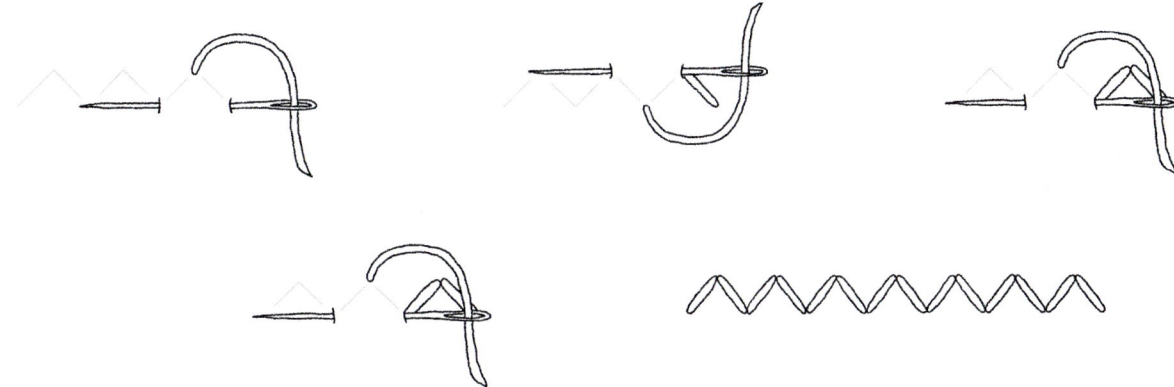

## STEM STITCH

Bring your needle up at the start of the row and complete a back stitch, coming up through the same hole as the emerging thread. Make another stitch, bringing your needle up at the end of the first stitch, and continue on. Keep your thread below your needle at all times, taking it down through the same hole at the end of the last stitch to finish.

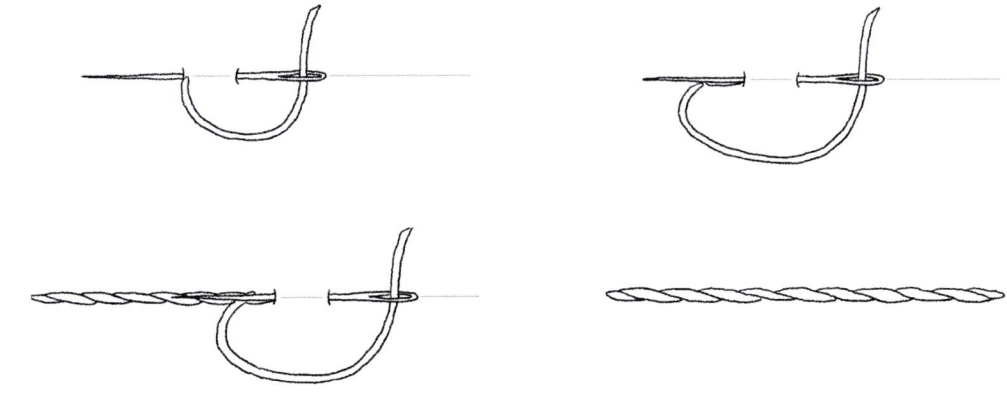

## CHAIN STITCH

Bring your needle to the front. Take it down through the same hole and up again a little ways away in front of the original hole, keeping your thread looped under the tip of the needle. Pull until a chain forms around the emerging thread. Insert your needle inside the first chain, through the same hole as the emerging thread, and bring it up again with the thread under the needle. Pull to form the second chain. And so on. Secure the last chain with a small straight stitch.

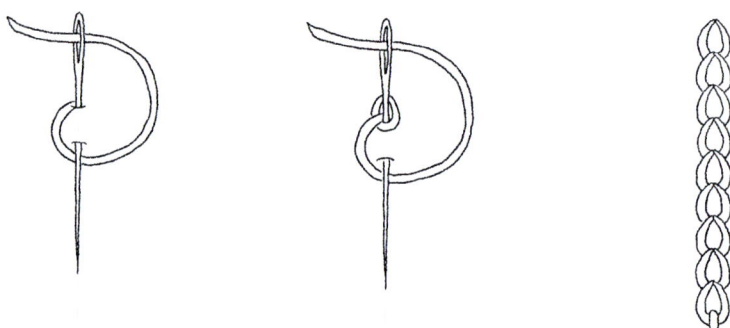

## DETACHED CHAIN STITCH

Embroider one chain stitch and secure it with a small straight stitch.

## WHIPPED CHAIN STITCH

Embroider a foundation row of chain stitches. Bring your needle up to the left of the first chain and slide it over the first chain and under the second chain, from right to left. Continue to the end of the row, taking care not to pierce the fabric. Take your needle down again to the right of the last chain to finish.

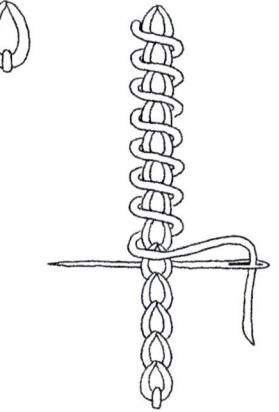

## FLY STITCH

Bring your thread up on the left and take an angled stitch from right to left. Keeping the thread under the tip, pull your needle through until the V-shaped loop lies snugly against the emerging thread. Take your thread down below the V to form a Y-shape and complete the first fly stitch. Repeat, bringing your needle up through the same hole in the fabric at the end of the previous securing stitch each time to create the V.

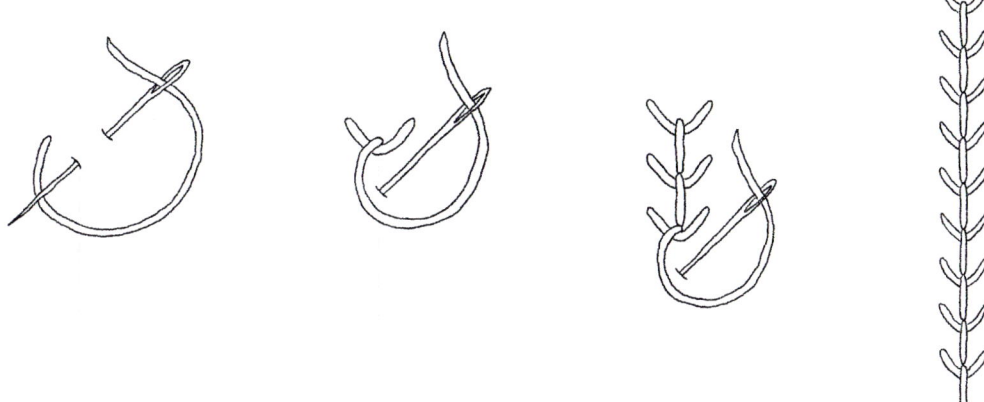

## FLY STITCH LEAF

Start with a straight stitch from the tip of the leaf. Embroider the first fly stitch below this, curving the V-shaped loop around the straight stitch and using a short securing stitch. Continue down the seam, adjusting the angle and length of the V-shaped loop each time to fill in the leaf.

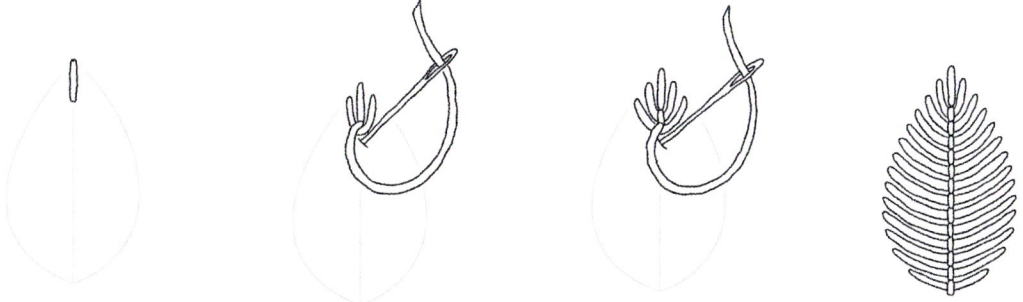

## FRENCH KNOT

Using a milliner needle, bring your thread up through the fabric. Hold your needle in one hand and with the other hand, wrap the thread around it twice. Stick your needle back into the fabric a tiny distance from the emerging thread. Pull your thread to tighten the knot and slide it down the needle so it rests on the surface of the fabric. Keeping the thread taut, pull the needle through the wraps of thread and to the back of the fabric.

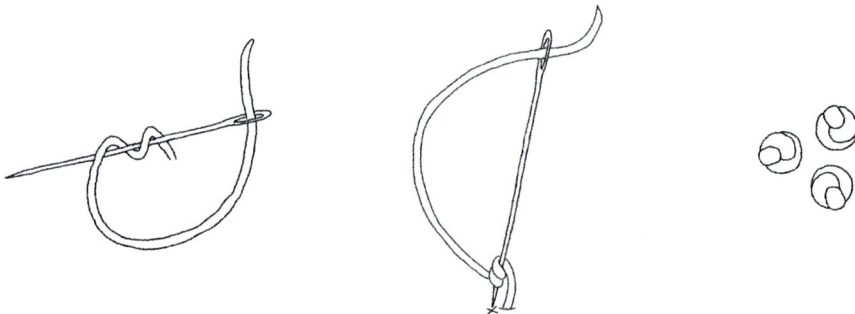

## BLANKET STITCH

Bring your thread up at the start of the line. Make a stitch perpendicular to the line with your thread under the tip of the needle and pull until your emerging thread is holding the blanket stitch in place. Repeat to the end of the row with evenly spaced stitches. Secure the last blanket stitch in the row with a small straight stitch.

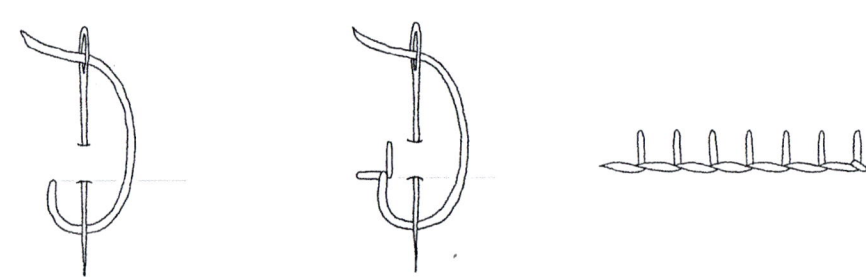

## CLOSED BLANKET STITCH PINWHEEL

Bring your thread up on the circle and take your first stitch from the center to the outer circle with your thread under the tip of the needle like for blanket stitch. Continue around the circle, using the same hole in the fabric at the center each time. Keep your needle perpendicular to the circle for each stitch. When your last blanket stitch overlaps the start of the first stitch, secure your thread with a straight stitch over the lower section of the first stitch.

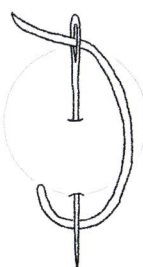 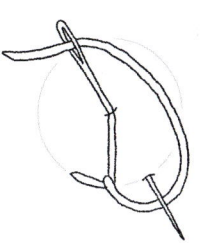 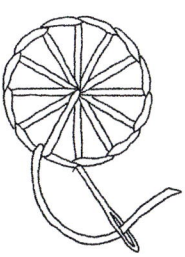 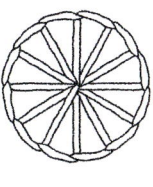

## OPEN BLANKET STITCH PINWHEEL

Bring your thread up on the outer circle and take your first blanket stitch from the inner circle to the outer. Work your way around, keeping your needle perpendicular to the circle lines for each stitch. End the same way as a closed pinwheel.

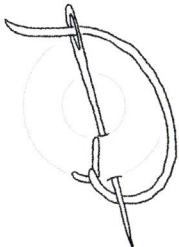 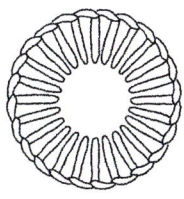

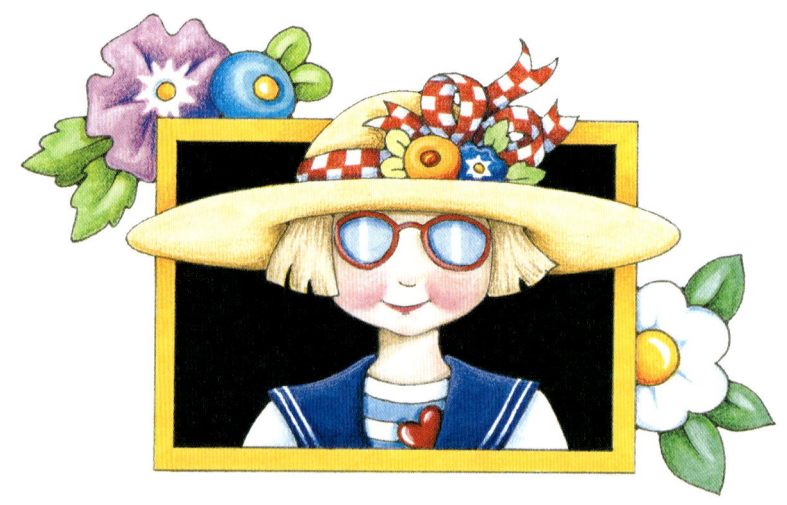

# WHO IS MARY ENGELBREIT?

For nearly 50 years, Mary Engelbreit has captivated audiences with her unique wit and undeniable style. Known for her illustrative calendars and greeting cards, timeless renditions of classic children's books, and an infinite array of home decorations for every season, Mary's legacy is a culture of cuteness, inspiring and touching the hearts of millions .